Conversations with Jesmyn Ward

Literary Conversations Series
Monika Gehlawat
General Editor

Conversations with Jesmyn Ward

Edited by Kemeshia Randle Swanson

University Press of Mississippi / Jackson

The University Press of Mississippi is the scholarly publishing agency of the Mississippi Institutions of Higher Learning: Alcorn State University, Delta State University, Jackson State University, Mississippi State University, Mississippi University for Women, Mississippi Valley State University, University of Mississippi, and University of Southern Mississippi.

www.upress.state.ms.us

The University Press of Mississippi is a member of the Association of University Presses.

Any discriminatory or derogatory language or hate speech regarding race, ethnicity, religion, sex, gender, class, national origin, age, or disability that has been retained or appears in elided form is in no way an endorsement of the use of such language outside a scholarly context.

Copyright © 2025 by University Press of Mississippi
All rights reserved
Manufactured in the United States of America
∞

Publisher: University Press of Mississippi, Jackson, USA
Authorised GPSR Safety Representative: Easy Access System Europe - Mustamäe tee 50, 10621 Tallinn, Estonia, *gpsr.requests@easproject.com*

Library of Congress Cataloging-in-Publication Data

Names: Swanson, Kemeshia Randle, editor.
Title: Conversations with Jesmyn Ward / Kemeshia Randle Swanson.
Other titles: Literary conversations series.
Description: Jackson : University Press of Mississippi, 2025. |
   Series: Literary conversations series | Includes bibliographical references and index.
Identifiers: LCCN 2025013237 (print) | LCCN 2025013238 (ebook) |
   ISBN 9781496856678 (hardback) | ISBN 9781496856685 (trade paperback) |
   ISBN 9781496856692 (epub) | ISBN 9781496856708 (epub) |
   ISBN 9781496856715 (pdf) | ISBN 9781496856722 (pdf)
Subjects: LCSH: Ward, Jesmyn—Interviews. | African American women authors—Interviews. |
   African American authors—Interviews. | Novelists, American—21st century—Interviews. |
   Authors, American—21st century—Interviews. | African Americans in literature. |
   Race relations in literature. | Mississippi—In literature. | Southern States—In literature.
Classification: LCC PS3623.A7323 Z46 2025 (print) | LCC PS3623.A7323 (ebook) |
   DDC 813/.6—dc23/eng/20250615
LC record available at https://lccn.loc.gov/2025013237
LC ebook record available at https://lccn.loc.gov/2025013238

British Library Cataloging-in-Publication Data available

Books by Jesmyn Ward

Novels

Where the Line Bleeds. Agate Bolden, 2008.
Salvage the Bones. Bloomsbury, 2011.
Sing, Unburied, Sing. Scribner, 2017.
Let Us Descend. Scribner, 2023.

Memoir

Men We Reaped. Bloomsbury, 2013.

Edited Collections

The Fire This Time. Scribner, 2016.
The Best American Short Stories. Mariner Books, 2021.

Contents

Introduction   xi

Chronology   xxv

Getting the South Right: An Interview with Jesmyn Ward   3
Nico Berry / 2009

Jesmyn Ward on *Salvage the Bones*   7
Elizabeth Hoover / 2011

In *Salvage the Bones,* Family's Story of Survival   10
Michel Martin / 2011

Jesmyn Ward by Rebecca Keith   14
Rebecca Keith / 2012

New Memoir Recounts Black Lives "Reaped" Too Young   19
Rachel Martin / 2013

Jesmyn Ward: *Men We Reaped*   23
Tobias Carroll / 2013

The Rumpus Interview with Jesmyn Ward   28
Kima Jones / 2013

An Interview with Jesmyn Ward   35
Roxane Gay / 2013

Jesmyn Ward on How Books Can Make Us Better People   39
Kiese Laymon / 2014

viii CONTENTS

Bookforum Talks with Jesmyn Ward   42
  Kyla Marshell / 2016

Literary Voice of the Dirty South:
An Interview with Jesmyn Ward   46
  Danille K. Taylor / 2016

Haunted by Ghosts: *The Millions* Interviews Jesmyn Ward   50
  Adam Vitcavage / 2017

Powell's Interview: Jesmyn Ward, Author of *Sing, Unburied, Sing*   57
  Rhianna Walton / 2017

Interview with Jesmyn Ward   66
  Jennifer Baker / 2017

Sing, Unburied, Sing: A Conversation with Jesmyn Ward   75
  Natalie Y. Moore / 2017

Ghosts of Our Past: An Interview with Jesmyn Ward   91
  Louise McCune / 2017

Ghosts of History: An Interview with Jesmyn Ward   97
  Louis Elliot / 2017

Jesmyn Ward: "So Much of Life
Is Pain and Sorrow and Willful Ignorance"   103
  Vanessa Thorpe / 2017

For Jesmyn Ward, Writing Means Telling the
"Truth About the Place That I Live In"   106
  Sam Briger / 2017

The Carnegie Shortlist Interviews: Jesmyn Ward   113
  Annie Bostrom / 2017

Jesmyn Ward   115
  Alma Mathijsen / 2018

CONTENTS **ix**

Jesmyn Ward on Writing Honest Novels with Good Titles,
Inhabiting Ghosts, and Learning to Love Faulkner   119
  Jennifer Acker / 2020

Two-Time National Book Award–Winning
Author Jesmyn Ward on Her Novel *Let Us Descend*   127
  Ayesha Rascoe / 2023

Poured Over: Jesmyn Ward on *Let Us Descend*   130
  Miwa Messer / 2023

Something Beautiful out of the Darkness   144
  Regina N. Bradley / 2023

"Writing is Restorative": A Conversation with Jesmyn Ward   150
  Kemeshia Randle Swanson / 2024

Additional Resources   167

Index   173

Introduction

I never have been in despair about the world. I've been enraged by it ... I can't afford despair. I can't tell my nephew, my niece. You can't tell the children there's no hope.
—James Baldwin

The above statement is author James Baldwin's response to broadcaster Mavis Nicholson's question, "Are you still in despair about the world?" in a 1987 interview on her afternoon show titled *Mavis on Four*. In this same interview, Baldwin discusses an array of crucial topics, including power and race relations, gender and sexuality, particularly his fear of sexuality as an adolescent and hiding from it in the pulpit, and he mesmerizes the audience when he deliberates over the idea of being what white America considered a "bad n----r," or nobody's n----r, practicing his freedom out loud and boldly, often in a way that impacted, and likewise offended, others. Baldwin died in December of that year, and while his controversial racial politics and sexual practices had previously forced him into a life of exile, having lived a good majority of his years outside of the United States, giving him time, as he states, "to vomit up a great deal of bitterness," he is remembered today as one of the greatest writers and activists of his generation.[1] His writing, similar to Jesmyn Ward's today, is like a "weird food" that may be difficult to digest but is even more difficult to put down.[2] Ultimately, Ward's personality and writing style, like Baldwin's, could be characterized as gentle, passionate, fastidious, queer, brutally honest, and highly tantalizing. Her soft-spoken voice and lyrical prose express a passion for the world so large and consuming that it often emanates as rage or grief but always leaves readers with a bit of hope.

Arguably one of today's most important authors, Jesmyn Ward's ire has mostly been aimed at her/my home state of Mississippi, where she frequently boasts of a love/hate relationship due to the state's pleasing, natural landscapes (which she describes beautifully in all her writings) and equally natural propensity to disregard and discard the needs of its minority residents. Her first three novels are set in the fictional Bois Sauvage, based off her hometown, DeLisle, Mississippi. Of course, with an imaginatively realistic

xii INTRODUCTION

setting such as this, Ward's works are often compared to Mississippi's favorite son, William Faulkner, though she admits that it took her quite a while to appreciate his body of work, and when she did, while it taught her that the socioeconomic status of her characters does not have to be a barrier to the language use and dialogue among them, his work also served as an example of what not to do when it comes to addressing the interior lives of African American characters. When asked how she contends with Faulkner's legacy, she tells Elizabeth Hoover, "The first time I read *As I Lay Dying*, I was so awed I wanted to give up. I thought, 'He's done it, perfectly. Why the hell am I trying?' But the failures of some of his Black characters—the lack of imaginative vision regarding them, the way they don't display the full range of human emotion, how they fail to live fully on the page—work against that awe and goad me to write." More poignantly, author and professor Regina N. Bradley insists in a social media post, "Jesmyn Ward is NOT WILLIAM FAULKNER'S HEIR. His racial politics is trash. Jesmyn Ward is the first Jesmyn Ward, and her throne's got subwoofers and tendrils of white sage and Black & Mild cigar smoke keeping her genius Black and ancestrally protected."[3] Indeed, Ward's works are "Black." They are steeped in Black culture, and critiques of race relations in Mississippi, and in the South, fly off every other page in such a poetic way. When speaking on why she centers her work on Mississippi and the South, she maintains in a *The Millions* interview that "we're so close to the past. So much of the past lives in the present. We live with the ramifications of the past that might not be as clear or feel as present in the rest of the country." But even more, she tells her friend and fellow Mississippi author Kiese Laymon, "Great trouble breeds great art."

Despite this, thus far, laser focus on the South, however, to avoid the possibility of her great art being pigeonholed as purely regional or one-dimensional, Ward has made a valiant effort to demonstrate that her works are universal, or cosmic rather, to invoke the sensibilities of one of my favorite authors, fellow Southerner and pioneer of authorial spunk, Zora Neale Hurston. In the same Elizabeth Hoover interview mentioned above, Ward defends the universality of her work and evokes a bit of rage akin to that of Baldwin, contending, "It infuriates me that the work of white American writers can be universal and lay claim to classic texts, while Black and female authors are ghetto-ized as 'other.' . . . The stories I write are particular to my community and my people, which means the details are particular to our circumstances, but the larger story of the survivor, the *savage*, is essentially a universal, human one." And certainly, readers find themselves bound to the gripping stories of the survivors, the savages, in each of her major works.

Since her introduction to the literary world just over a decade and a half ago, Ward has produced four novels, a memoir, two edited collections, and dozens of essays. Her riveting 2018 commencement address at Tulane University, about hard work and respect for oneself and others, was likewise adapted to book format, subsequently titled *Navigate Your Stars*. Still, Ward comes from very humble beginnings, admitting that after three years of constant submissions and rejections of her first novel, *Where the Line Bleeds*, she nearly resigned to giving up her dream of becoming a writer and was making plans to enroll in nursing school. Thankfully, Agate Publishing offered her a contract, published *Where the Line Bleeds* in 2008, and saved readers the dissatisfaction of having to imagine a literary world with no Jesmyn. In an article published in *The Evanston Roundtable* in 2022, Nancy McLaughlin shares Agate Publishing president Doug Seibold's excitement in celebrating twenty years as a small, yet successful, publishing company that found its niche by centering the voices of Black and Midwestern writers, authors whom Seibold suggests, are often overlooked by larger publishing houses and "getting the shortest end of the stick." About Ward, he states, "I knew that she was phenomenally talented, but you can't predict that someone is going to achieve that level of success."[4] Several awards later, including but not limited to the Library of Congress Prize for American Fiction, a MacArthur Fellowship, and the Strauss Living Award, she remains humble. Even after winning two National Book Awards for Fiction, first for *Salvage the Bones* in 2011 and again for *Sing, Unburied, Sing* in 2017, becoming the first African American and first woman to win twice, she still considers herself an underdog, and in an interview with Alma Mathijsen, even goes as far as to say, "I'm in no way a confident person, especially when it comes to my work. I feel inadequate." Her humbleness and lack of confidence are not synonymous with uncertainty, however, as Ward is sure of her purpose and very much unapologetic about it, countering in that same Mathijsen interview that "it's who I am. I can't change that. I feel so desperate to tell stories. The need to do so is bigger than my insecurity. That wins." Indeed, it does win, no pun intended, but again, she remains humble and laser-focused, telling Louis Elliot, "I give all the awards to my mom, and she keeps them at her house, because when I'm sitting down to really write, I can't think about nominations, or awards, or recognition. Then I'm too conscious of audience. I'm too aware of what people want. I can't work if I'm so aware of that."

On the contrary, what Ward is aware of, as indicated in her writings and speaking engagements, is society's lack of respect and empathy for human life, particularly the lives of African Americans, admitting to Kiese

xiv INTRODUCTION

Laymon that she has become obsessed with this "devaluation of Black life." Unfortunately, she has experienced lots of it firsthand in her personal life, but she uses it to fuel her writing. From experiences with death to natural disasters and racism, even racism during natural disasters, she writes realistic fiction and nonfiction that make the emotions of her characters feel real for her readers and help her manage her own grief. Her brother, Joshua Dedeaux, died in the year 2000 at the age of nineteen. He was killed by a drunk driver, and the state of Mississippi never made the driver pay justly for his crime. Ward insists that all her writing has a shadow of her brother in it, that writing about characters like him and other people from her community was the only way that she could take the grief that she had turned inward and use it positively. She dedicates her first two novels to him: "For Joshua Adam Dedeaux, who leads while I follow." Her memoir, *Men We Reaped*, exists because, as she tells Roxane Gay, "I have to. If I don't carry this [grief], then who will tell the story? Who will remember? I bear it because I must." Similarly, in a 2017 interview with Melissa Block, not collected in this volume, Ward reflects on her feelings after her brother's death and suggests, "I didn't have a choice anymore. . . . I couldn't run from that desire to tell stories, that desire to tell stories about us, and about the people I loved. . . . And it's not that I was confident that I could actually do it. . . . Confidence definitely did not get me here! More of like, desperation. And I thought, well, I can try. . . . And if I succeed, then I will have done something worthwhile with the time that I have been given."[5] Perhaps with more time, Ward will develop the confidence of her predecessors, authors such as Zora Neale Hurston, Margaret Walker, and Alice Walker, all of whom she suggests inspires her writing.

Nonetheless, the feeling of desperation reverberates through all of her works and characters, desperation for love, protection, safety, equality, empathy, etc. *Salvage the Bones* is where I, as a reader, initially felt that desperation most, and it intensifies tenfold in *Let Us Descend*. While discussing *Salvage* with Elizabeth Hoover and divulging her need to write about Hurricane Katrina, Ward shares her passion and rage, commenting, "I lived through it. It was terrifying, and I needed to write about that. I was also angry at the people who blamed survivors for staying and for choosing to return to the Mississippi Gulf Coast after the storm. Finally, I wrote about the storm because I was dissatisfied with the way it had receded from public consciousness." She reveals even more about this harrowing experience in an interview with Rebecca Keith months later, insisting:

INTRODUCTION **xv**

My family and I did encounter ruthlessness during and after the hurricane. Hell, during the hurricane, we were denied shelter by a White family who told us they didn't have enough room for us in their house to ride out the storm since we'd fled our house when it flooded. We suffered through most of Hurricane Katrina in our trucks in that family's field, terrified, watching the flood waters surge, the wind rip trees from the earth and break power lines in two. But then near the end of the storm, we left that field, and we were taken in by another White family who'd been rescuing people who lived closest to the DeLisle Bayou in a boat. After the storm, people banded together. My mother sent food down to our local park where a group of boys were living after Katrina destroyed their families' houses in Pass Christian. But then again, when I received my first jug of water a few days after the storm from volunteers at the local fire station, on my walk home, a rude man yelled at me, asking where I'd taken the water from, as if I'd stolen it. It was a difficult time. I know it's cliché, but that disaster definitely brought out the best and worst of humanity.

Seemingly, sharing her emotions about the disaster in book form brought out the best in Ward. While discussing the writing process, she suggests that she did not get a lot of notes for ideas, concepts, or plot points to revise in her draft of *Salvage the Bones*, unlike some of her other works that were more difficult to write, particularly *Sing, Unburied, Sing*, where she admits to having revised the novel fifteen times. Concerning *Salvage*, she states, "Two chapters took substantial revision: the dogfight chapter and the hurricane chapter. There were general problems of development and clarity there, so once I was done with the first draft, I had to do a substantial rewrite in those two places. The hurricane chapter was really hard to write because I felt as [if] I were reliving that awful storm, and I had to keep reminding myself that this was about the characters' experience of Katrina and not my own."

The toughest two chapters to write, the dogfight and hurricane chapters, were perhaps the most spectacular to read, and it goes without saying that the book won Ward her first National Book Award and began to garner her national and international recognition. In her acceptance speech, Ward acknowledges her brother's life and the role grief plays in her writing, then she lays out her purpose for a group of listeners/readers who may be encountering her writing for the first time by insisting that she creates stories and characters akin to her people, her community, "so that the culture that marginalized us for so long would see that our stories were as universal, our lives were as fraught and lovely and important as theirs." She ends with

xvi INTRODUCTION

a firm declaration: "This is a life's work, and I am only at the beginning."[6] Since this statement in 2011, indeed, Ward seems to be upholding her promise, but whether or not it is truly a life's work has been tested perhaps more intensely than she or anyone could ever be prepared for.

In January 2020, while she was working on *Let Us Descend*, Ward lost another one of her greatest loves and supporters, her partner, Brandon Miller. A seemingly healthy man otherwise, Brandon went to the hospital with respiratory issues and died fifteen hours later. When Ward is finally able to come up for a brief reprieve, she, yet again, shares her story of loss and hope with the world, pinning a disturbingly beautiful essay for *Vanity Fair* titled "On Witness and Respair: A Personal Tragedy Followed by Pandemic." In this essay, she explains how the entire family had been suffering from what they thought was a flu just days before she lost her "Beloved" and how just two months later, the world was under the strongholds of coronavirus, how our governments had failed us and racism still persisted even during a pandemic, how she grieved incessantly for her loss and the loss of so many others, how she almost gave up writing once again, and how the Black Lives Matter movement "broke something" in her and helped her to summon the strength to channel that grief, once again, into her writing.[7] She tells Ayesha Rascoe that her partner "would not want [her] grief to silence [her]" and that she "looked at it [*Let Us Descend*] as a physical representation of grief and also as a descent into a kind of hell." She states, "I also feel like it is a descent into an afterlife. In part, the book is about Annis finding her way through her grief to a different life than the one that she thought she might have and the one that she wanted. And in that, I very much identified with Annis, like, with her character because for me—like, that's one of the hardest things about grief—is that this life that you thought you had—once you lose that person, that life, that possible life—it doesn't exist anymore." Ward dedicated *Let Us Descend* to both her partner and her brother: "This book is for Brandon, who saw me and loved me, even when I could not see or love myself, and for Joshua, the first to show me that love is a living link to the dead." Once more, her grief and rage goad her to write and, paradoxically, the results are beautiful.

This beauty that comes out of darkness, a phrase Ward minted in an interview with Regina N. Bradley after the release of *Let Us Descend*, has become a trademark of Ward's writing. In a praise for *Salvage the Bones*, *School Library Journal* declares that Ward's second novel is a "beautiful yet disturbing book" that should find its way into the hands of all high school teachers and be discussed on a large scale.[8] They effectively convey one of

Ward's objectives, which is to write poetically engaging pieces that pierce readers in the gut, make them empathize with her characters, and, ultimately, understand that Southern Black stories are universal stories and that Black lives matter. Speaking on her poetic prose, she tells Elizabeth Hoover, "I'm a failed poet. Reading poetry helps me to see the world differently, and I try to infuse my prose with figurative language, which goes against the trend in fiction. While I admire writers who are able to write with a vitality based on order and action, I work in a different vein. I often feel that if I can get the language just right, the language hypnotizes the reader." When the hypnosis wears off, again, the hoped-for result is empathy. She divulges this purpose to Adam Vitcavage in response to his question "What is your hope of what people walk away with after they finish *Sing, Unburied, Sing*?" Ward insists, "I hope that the characters stay with them. . . . That next time readers encounter an older Black gentleman in the grocery store or the next time they unfortunately see a fourteen- or fifteen-year-old Black boy . . . dead from police violence, that maybe it's a bit more painful and a bit more prevalent for them because they've seen the humanity in the characters I've written. Maybe that makes it a little easier for them to see humanity and personhood." It's an interesting tactic, shocking and forcefully damaging readers with brutal truths in hopes that they, in the end, will become more empathetic, more loving. Though, it seems to work.

In a review of *Let Us Descend*, Scott Naugle pens somewhat of a petrified love letter to Ward titled "A Note to My Friend, Jesmyn Ward," in which he seems to acknowledge that Ward's previous hopes had been fulfilled, that Annis, this novel's protagonist, and her story, did indeed stay with him in a remarkably enlightening and noticeably uncomfortable way, proclaiming the following:

> What hangs over *Let Us Descend* as a shroud is the terror of inevitability, of knowing there is no plausible way out for Annis. I turned the pages as quickly as I could, knowing that you, a gentle soul, a loving mother of three, would somehow find a way to an inner peace of some measure for Annis, whom you created so perfectly and completely that I think of her as your fourth offspring, flesh, blood, breathing, grieving, crying, resisting. She's your daughter, so I know she's strong, determined, resourceful, kind—and a survivor. But my God, Jesmyn, what that poor girl must do to retain her dignity in a world of pure hatred.[9]

A world of pure hatred is often the overarching antagonist of Ward's novels; in this particular novel, the hatred materializes in the form of racism,

xviii INTRODUCTION

slavery, sexism, abuse, and neglect. Though, as is also her nature and along the lines of the Baldwin quote that opened this introduction, even after traveling to the pits of hell, as Annis metaphorically does, Ward always leaves readers with a bit of hope, some form of consolation for the mountains of grief. To this end, the closing line of her introduction to *The Fire This Time* aptly states, "I burn, and I hope."[10]

"Hope is at the heart of resistance" is what Ward tells Ayesha Rascoe, and along with her novels and memoir, one can regularly find Ward hoping, resisting, critiquing, and supporting, all the signs of an activist, on social media, in blog posts, and in essays where she serves as a guest contributor for publications such as *The New York Times*, Literary Hub, and *TIME*. Ward tells Danille K. Taylor, "I think that the advent of multiple social media platforms means that this generation has the kind of access to an audience that others haven't, and I think this is galvanizing my generation. That it is moving them to activism." Indeed, Ward accesses her audiences. In a Twitter post of January 17, 2019, under the username @jesmimi, she insists, "It's been nearly impossible for me to avoid posting expletive filled howls on Twitter lately. I need to meditate or something, because lately I just want to burn everything down." Likewise, on November 4, 2020, she exclaims, "They want to believe in this idealized, innocent, noble, and exceptional version of themselves & America so badly that they disavow the babies in cages, the over 200k dead, women and men of color dead in their beds and mid-jog and mid-walk, disavow it all, and vote for 45." A more recent post on Instagram, username @jesmynward, expresses hurt and agitation at Israeli attacks on innocent Palestinian civilians. An insurmountable number of her posts display rage and/or sadness caused by the actions or inactions of racist, inept Mississippi politicians. This is expected, as she tells Rebecca Keith, "Everyone knows that there's much that I hate about Mississippi, about the South. The only way that I can reconcile my hatred with my love is to fight; this is why I write my books" and presumably why she pens social media posts also. Though, of course, there is hope and light among it all as well, from thanking readers for their unwavering support, expressing shock at winning the National Book Award a second time, sharing her love for reading, supporting other authors, demonstrating a fondness for Prince and hip-hop music, and reminiscing on fun times with family. Just like in her novels, memoir, essays, and edited collections, what one can gather about Ward from her social media is that she is a complex, multifaceted, passionate master of words, and that her community, and the communities of other misunderstood and unfairly treated individuals, is always at the forefront of her mind. In a blog post created early on in her career, she shares that her interests are "swimming in rivers, walking pit bulls, sleeping, drinking with my family, eating my mama's gumbo, cranes, voodoo, swamps, global warming, Xena, live blues, country rap tunes, reading everything I can get my hands on."[11]

Ultimately, although Ward admits that she has grown fond of podcasts nowadays as she is "sliding into middle age" and allows her children to control the music choices in her car, she made it clear early on in her career that she does not subscribe to a particular way of being, that queerness is freeing, that neither information, education, nor activism have to be dressed in a particular kind of packaging. Specifically, she talks about the impact music has on her generation and those that follow, how it can serve as the soundtrack for one's life and convey messages more plainly and widely sometimes than books can, especially to marginalized groups who may see reading as a luxury. Ward tells Tobias Carroll, "I'm a consumer of popular culture, still: movies and music, particularly. I feel like these are the signposts of our lives" and likewise expresses to Nico Berry regarding hip-hop, "It was so good having someone talk about the realities of where we were from, and doing it in a way that lyrically, and sonically, resonated with us." As if it were not already clear that she is trying to speak for and to a particular group of people, or as youth would say today, "doing it for the culture," Ward opens her first three books, *Where the Line Bleeds*, *Salvage the Bones*, and *Men We Reaped*, with short epigraphs from the likes of Pastor Troy, OutKast, and Tupac Shakur. She tells Rebecca Keith, "I'm a big champion of rap music, and I'm not ashamed to say that I love the smutty, thumping Southern stuff as well as more conscious rap. But I like plenty of other music, too: old blues, indie rock, pop, opera, and classical. However, I choose to use quotes from rap in my books because I think people forget that rap is very much a lyrical art form, and there's power in those words." Speaking more firmly on the "smutty, thumping Southern stuff," in a 2016 interview, using a term popularized in Hip Hop culture and first introduced by Southern rap group Goodie Mob, Danille K. Taylor refers to Ward as a "literary voice of the Dirty South," and Ward relishes the moniker, suggesting:

I love the idea that my work is part of the Dirty South. My idea of the Dirty South is that there's a certain rawness to the art that comes out of it. A certain honesty. A willingness to bring secrets and despair and hope and all those other messy human emotions to life. To express what it means to be born and grow up into the cycle of poverty that has been bequeathed to so many of us. And finally, to reckon with how growing up in this place has affected us, and how we fight against it,

xx INTRODUCTION

sometimes foolishly, sometimes foolhardily, but always with a kind of courage born of desperation.

In line with this Dirty South attitude, while writing her second novel and reflecting on the first, she acknowledges that she loved her characters too much and protected them from traumas that the real world does not, so as a result, she developed narrative ruthlessness: "I realized that if I was going to assume the responsibility of writing about my home, I needed narrative ruthlessness. I couldn't dull the edges and fall in love with my characters and spare them. Life does not spare us." And each narrative thereafter has gotten conceivably more and more ruthless and more and more impactful.

This elevation of beauty and disturbance can be attributed to Ward's conscious and consistent efforts to grow as a writer. After gaining high esteem in such a short time, she could easily become complacent, but that has not been the case. She tells Natalie Y. Moore that she tries to "approach writing as part of [her] routine" and therefore writes "at least two hours a day, five days a week," more if time and responsibilities permit. Even more, in each new text, she challenges herself, sometimes in making familiar things new, and at others, in making unfamiliar things common, including pushing herself to write in a new style or genre and tirelessly researching related topics. For instance, when moving from *Where the Line Bleeds* to *Salvage the Bones* and choosing to adhere to the Bois Sauvage setting, she insists, "It's a challenge with every book to rewrite the Gulf Coast and make it a vivid, lived-in place where the reader is fully immersed. I have to consider that it's a place I've written about before, and I don't want to repeat things." Certainly, Bois Sauvage, and the lived experiences therein, as indicated by several reviews, is most vivid, and any existing repetitions are not detrimental; on the contrary, they make the setting feel familiar, and for some, like home. On the other hand, for Ward, *Men We Reaped* is too close to home, but in the same way that she makes readers uncomfortable in their understanding, she challenges herself in that way by writing a memoir. Ward confesses to Tobias Carroll, "I must say, after facing the emotional challenges of memoir, I'm really looking forward to thinking about character and plot rather than my own unhappy story." And indeed did she think about character and plot with *Sing, Unburied, Sing* following her memoir, from months of research about the Parchman Farm to incorporating magical realism to writing from the standpoint of two characters. To this end, she insists, "In some ways, writers are always growing, we're always maturing, we're always working to better ourselves and to better our work. And in some ways, writing a novel with alternating narrators was my way of challenging myself as a writer. I set the task for myself just to see if I could pull it off because it's difficult to write something like that." While the dual narrators and magical realism make *Sing* a little less like her previous two novels and perhaps more arduous of a read, it is indicative of an astute and continuously evolving author, quite possibly why it won her a second National Book Award. In fact, Ward seems to welcome difficult tasks as *Sing*'s follow-up novel brought about even more difficulty, and even more beauty and hope. In discussing *Let Us Descend* with Adam Vitcavage, Ward declares, "The novel is set in New Orleans at the height of the domestic slave trade during the early 1800s. It's unlike anything I've ever written before. It's definitely challenging me as a writer and as a human being because the main characters in this are people who were enslaved. It's really hard to sit with that. The subject matter is making it hard for me to write this novel."

Of course, when one's writing seems to blossom on the heels of struggle and they say things like "great trouble breeds great art," I am certain no one worried that Ward's difficulties with writing about the institution of slavery would make *Let Us Descend* any less enthralling. And in true fashion, her next novel is yet another challenge as she attempts to write a YA novel for the first time. Readers can only hope that it will be as difficult, painful, beautiful, and hopeful as all the rest.

Finally, what this edited collection displays to readers is that Jesmyn Ward is a master artist with a poetic command for words, that her voice is soft, but her words are firm; she critiques oppressive systems, and through her characters, humanizes and provides hope for Southern Black people. Ward tells Danille K. Taylor the following:

> I discovered that there are countless human dramas, countless stories worthy of being told right here [on the Gulf Coast]. Again, I keep circling back to representation. To what we see reflected back to us in our media, in literature, on film. There was such a dearth of stories about people like me that I encountered when I was growing up, so when I first began writing seriously and learning how to be a better writer, I thought no one would want to read anything I wrote, especially if it was about people like me. It took me a long time to unlearn that and to reach a point where I can confidently say that our lives are just as human and complicated and fascinating as anyone else's. I have so many questions. One of the most important is about how history bears in the present. How does the past bear fruit? And why are we often so blind to it? I find myself writing around that question again and again with different sets of characters.

xxii INTRODUCTION

Indeed, from 2008 to the present day, Ward's writing has been a mirror for many and a projector for others, providing representation for people who may have never seen themselves reflected in literature and media, certainly not in such an intimate, unapologetic, and loving way, while also forcing others to truly see and acknowledge the interior beauty and humanity of Black lives, to likewise see their struggles and to empathize, to be a part of the solution instead of the problem. Ward tells Louis Elliot, "I've always wanted to write Black characters who are multidimensional, who are complicated, who are sympathetic, who have soul." And undoubtedly, after those beautifully written characters and stories call upon all the joy and pain of their worlds and ring readers dry, they are sure, too, to deeply touch readers' souls, provide them with a modicum of hope, and, with any luck, leave them better than they came.

I would like to thank my editor, Mary Heath, for believing that I would do this work justice and being supportive along the way. I would also like to thank all the contributors and their representatives for granting me permission to reprint their remarkable interviews. Thanks to Jesmyn Ward for being an amazing subject to study and write about. Last but not least, thanks as always to my family and friends who support me and tell me that I am kind, I am smart, and I am important.

KRS

Notes

1. Charles Truehart, "Powerful 'Baldwin,'" *The Washington Post*, August 14, 1989. https://www.washingtonpost.com/archive/lifestyle/1989/08/14/powerful-baldwin/1d25516a-494b-4376-b090-d93838f75925/.

2. Hilton Als, "The Enemy Within: The Making and Unmaking of James Baldwin," The New Yorker, February 9, 1998. https://www.newyorker.com/magazine/1998/02/16/the-enemy-within-hilton-als.

3. Regina N. Bradley, "Jesmyn Ward is NOT WILLIAM FAULKNER'S HEIR," Facebook, June 9, 2021. https://www.facebook.com/share/p/TskYk2MQKTVuB2Xd/?.

4. Nancy McLaughlin, "Books: Ever Wonder How a Best-seller is Born?" *Evanston Roundtable*, September 26, 2022. https://evanstonroundtable.com/2022/09/26/books-ever-wonder-how-a-best-seller-is-born/.

5. Melissa Block, "Writing Mississippi: Jesmyn Ward Salvages Stories of the Silenced," NPR, August 31, 2017. https://www.npr.org/2017/08/31/547271081/writing-mississippi-jesmyn-ward-salvages-stories-of-the-silenced.

6. "Jesmyn Ward's 2011 National Book Award in Fiction Acceptance Speech." You-Tube.com, uploaded by National Book Foundation, November 16, 2011. www.youtube.com/watch?v=myVjJKeqNSs.

7. Jesmyn Ward, "On Witness and Respair: A Personal Tragedy Followed by a Pandemic," *Vanity Fair*, September 2020, 102–5. https://archive.vanityfair.com/article/2020/9/witness-and-respair.

8. *School Library Journal*, Cover Endorsement, *Salvage the Bones*, by Jesmyn Ward, Bloomsbury, 2011.

9. Scott Naugle, "A Note to My Friend, Jesmyn Ward: A Review of *Let Us Descend*," Leader's Edge, September 27, 2023. https://www.leadersedge.com/lifestyle/a-note-to-my-friend-jesmyn-ward.

10. Jesmyn Ward, Introduction to *The Fire This Time: A New Generation Speaks About Race*, Simon and Schuster, 2016.

11. Jesmyn Ward, "Jesmyn Ward, Writer." Blogger.com. www.blogger.com/profile/13585127393760030902.

Chronology

1977   Born in Oakland, California, on April 1.

1980   Moves to DeLisle, Mississippi, with family (where they were originally from).

1990   Attends Coast Episcopal School in Long Beach, Mississippi, graduates in 1995.

1999   Earns BA from Stanford University.

2000   Earns MA from Stanford University. Brother, Joshua Adam Dedeaux, dies in a car accident after being struck by a drunk driver. Brother becomes inspiration for most of Ward's writing.

2003   Enrolls in MFA Program at University of Michigan.

2005   Earns MFA from University of Michigan.

2006   Teaches at the University of New Orleans.

2008   Publishes first novel, *Where the Line Bleeds* (Agate). Wins Wallace Stegner Fellowship (Stanford University, 2008–10).

2009   Wins Black Caucus of the American Library Association (BCALA) Honor Award for *Where the Line Bleeds*.

2010   Serves as John and Renée Grisham Writer-in-Residence at the University of Mississippi in Oxford, Mississippi.

2011   Publishes second novel, *Salvage the Bones* (Bloomsbury). Wins National Book Award for Fiction for *Salvage the Bones*. Teaches at the University of South Alabama.

2012   Wins American Library Association Alex Award for *Salvage the Bones*. Daughter, Noemi, is born.

2013   Publishes memoir, *Men We Reaped* (Bloomsbury).

2014   Wins Heartland Prize for Nonfiction for *Men We Reaped*. Receives teaching appointment at Tulane University in New Orleans, Louisiana.

2016   Publishes *The Fire This Time* (Simon and Schuster), an edited collection of essays and poems. Wins Strauss Living Award. Son, Brando, is born.

xxvi CHRONOLOGY

2017   Publishes third novel, *Sing, Unburied, Sing* (Scribner). Wins Second National Book Award for Fiction for *Sing, Unburied, Sing*; becomes first woman and first Black American to win award twice. Wins MacArthur "Genius Grant" Fellowship. Portrait is added to Mississippi Literary Map.

2018   *Xavier Review* publishes special issue on Ward's work, first book-length publication. Ward gives the commencement speech at Tulane; it is later adapted to an illustrated book, *Navigate Your Stars* (Simon and Schuster). Recognized among *TIME* magazine's list of 100 Most Influential People. Honored with a marker to be displayed on the Mississippi Writers Trail.

2020   Partner, Brandon Miller (thirty-three), dies of acute respiratory distress syndrome. Ward writes about his death, along with the coronavirus pandemic and the resurgence of the Black Lives Matter movement, in a *Vanity Fair* article titled "On Witness and Respair: A Personal Tragedy Followed by Pandemic."

2022   At forty-five, becomes youngest person to win Library of Congress Prize for American Fiction. Second son is born.

2023   Publishes fourth novel, *Let Us Descend* (Scribner), selected by Oprah's Book Club.

2024   Wins the Mississippi Institute of Arts and Letters Award for Fiction for *Let Us Descend*.

Conversations with Jesmyn Ward

Getting the South Right: An Interview with Jesmyn Ward

Nico Berry / 2009

This interview was originally conducted by Nico Berry and published on *Fiction Writers Review* on August 19, 2009. Reprinted with permission.

Nico Berry: I was going to start with the two epigraphs that you have at the beginning of your novel—one from the Bible and one from [the rapper] Pastor Troy. Which had a bigger influence on your life—hip-hop or the Bible?[1]

Jesmyn Ward: When I was in high school, it was God. I went to a private Episcopalian high school, and I used to go on retreats, and I was really into it for a while. But my senior year, I was surrounded by people who were really close-minded about the Bible and Christianity. It turned me off, and I slowly stopped believing.

Hip-hop didn't really blow up for us in the South until after NWA, and then we started getting some people from the South like 8Ball and MJG and UGK, reinterpreting hip-hop in a Southern way. It was so good having someone talk about the realities of where we were from, and doing it in a way that lyrically, and sonically, resonated with us. That's when hip-hop became the big thing here. I think both hip-hop and the Bible have been really influential to me at different times in my life.

Berry: It seems interesting you used these two counterpoints to start the book.

Ward: Really I started with the Pastor Troy [lyrics]. I used to listen to the song over and over again when I was germinating the seed of the novel. I was doing a lot of driving at the time, from Michigan to Mississippi, sixteen hours each way. I would play that song on repeat. I decided to use this passage for a quote, and then, because of what it talks about, I wanted to pair it with something. The Pastor Troy [epigraph] came first—and then the quote from the Bible.

4 CONVERSATIONS WITH JESMYN WARD

Berry: Why did you feel like you had to pair it with something?

Ward: Because nobody respects Southern rappers—they're seen as just the latest trend that needs to end as soon as possible—or at least that's what it feels like. No one seems to respect Southern rappers lyrically, so I wanted to pair Pastor Troy with that quote from the Bible to add emphasis to the verse and add a certain legitimacy to it—to show that he's talking about real issues that should be taken seriously.

Berry: Do you worry that that attitude towards Southern rappers crosses over to how people treat Southern writers too?

Ward: Yeah, maybe. Before the book came out, I read an interview somewhere that said how Southern writers are pushed really strongly in the region, but not really outside the region. It's hard for a Southern writer to break through outside the region, which they thought was really odd considering that the South has this great history of amazing writers. Sometimes I wonder if this applies to Black writers also—if there's not space for anyone besides the heavyweights and big exceptions. There's a lot of room for hood writers, but it seems like it's hard to get into that other space—the one for Black literary writers.

Berry: What about being a woman writer? Do you think that makes it harder too?

Ward: Sometimes I wonder if because you're a woman someone's less likely to think you have great literary merit. If you look at the hot young writers, a lot of them are men—but I don't know. I've thought more about how being Black affects where my work is read—not as much about being a woman.

Berry: It's almost as if you've got three strikes against you as a writer—Black, Southern, and woman. Do you think that affects the way you write?

Ward: I think it makes me more motivated to write past all of that and create great literature. Maybe that's how it affects me.

Berry: I understand that some of the characters in your new novel you're working on right now have carried over from your first novel, *Where the Line Bleeds*.

Ward: In the first novel, there's a scene in Javon's house with the twins. There's a whole bunch of people gathered there, including a lot of peripheral characters—Christophe, who is watching the guys playing dice, Skeetah and Marquise, and I think the character Big Henry is there too. These are some of the main characters in the second novel [*Salvage the Bones*].

There was something about Skeetah's character that struck me. I knew that there was a pit bull that he was obsessed with. I wrote a short story about him, and then I kept coming back to him—these situations he was in with Big Henry. Skeetah's character was always there in the back of my head, and I wanted to live in that world he was living, explore that world, get to know who he was. I also had the idea of writing from a girl's perspective, this girl who lives in a world full of men. Basically I took both those ideas and smashed them together, and made Esch, who's the girl and the narrator, and Skeetah her brother. I created this family for her.

Berry: Was the Pastor Troy verse the seed for your first novel? Or was there a character who was the seed, the same way Skeetah was for the second?

Ward: The Pastor Troy verse was definitely one of the seeds for the first novel. I knew I wanted to create a fictional DeLisle, the town where I'm from, a fictional Southern small town. So I knew the setting. I just didn't know what it was going to be about. I did a lot of driving, and I listened to Pastor Troy a lot.

Berry: How much of Bois Sauvage [the setting of *Where the Line Bleeds*] is taken directly from DeLisle? Are any of the characters based on real people?

Ward: They're all imaginative amalgamations. I'm calling the place Bois Sauvage, but it's an idealized version of home. The Oaks in the book is modeled on the Pecan Grove in DeLisle, which is also a baseball park with a blues club right next to it. There's a park where a lot of stuff happens in both novels—and that's modeled on the county park we have here—as are all the swimming holes, and swimming at the river. But then there's a lot of things here that I haven't gotten into in my fiction, partly because I'm so homesick for that older version of home. That DeLisle I wrote about is different now because of the casinos, and Katrina also irrevocably changed it. Bois Sauvage in the book is still really rural and there's not a big police presence, which is how DeLisle used to be. Now there's definitely a large police presence in DeLisle. I know that I should write about the way things have changed, but I can't tackle it yet. I want to stay in that world for as long as possible.

Berry: Has anyone who lives there read and commented on the similarities?

Ward: I have this huge extended family, and I got really good press down here. A lot of people around here have read it. People have said to me, "I read it, and I couldn't put it down because I keep recognizing things." They're not talking about the characters, but the actual place itself. So far all the feedback I've gotten from everybody at home is that they love it. That was one thing that I was really nervous about. I wanted to get it right.

I've had people say to me, "You really representing." I think it feels new to them to see this place represented in another art form. There's a poet, her name is Natasha Trethewey. She's African American, and her family is from around here, and she's written poetry about the area. But there haven't been any African American fiction writers coming from this area. I think people think it's cool to see this place reflected back at them in fiction.

Berry: When you started writing, did you picture yourself as someone who would really represent for your area?

Ward: It wasn't until the very end of my senior year, when I was applying for college, that I wrote about DeLisle. That's when I realized that this place is my inspiration.

Berry: Do you think you could have ever written about it if you hadn't left?

Ward: I don't know—probably not. Throughout high school, I was thinking, *I just want to get away*. But when I realized I would be leaving, I looked back and saw the place differently. Both the good and the bad.

Berry: It's interesting because in the novel, neither of the brothers wants to leave. It doesn't seem to even really be an option for them.

Ward: I wanted to make it like that. For a lot of people here, that's how it is. Leaving's not an option.

Berry: But it's not a sad thing. The brothers are where they want to be. They're happy.

Ward: Yeah, I wanted it to be like that. Sometimes I used to wish that I had turned out like that.

Berry: You wish you were down at the docks.

Ward: Working offshore, making like 60,000 dollars slanging fried eggs to people.

Note

1. Epigraphs from *Where the Line Bleeds*:

1. "*And Isaac entreated the Lord for his wife, because she was barren; and the Lord was entreated of him, and Rebekah his wife conceived. And the children struggled together within her; and she said, If it be so, why am I thus? And she went to inquire of the Lord. And the Lord said unto her . . . two manner of people shall be separated from thy bowels. . . .*"
—Genesis 25

2. "Why Jesus equipped with angels and devils equipped with Pac?
For God so loved the world that he bless the thug with rock.
Won't stop until they feel me.
Protect me devil, I think the Lord is trying to kill me."
—Pastor Troy, "Vice Versa"

Jesmyn Ward on *Salvage the Bones*

Elizabeth Hoover / 2011

This interview was originally conducted by Elizabeth Hoover and published in *The Paris Review* on August 30, 2011. Reprinted with permission.

Elizabeth Hoover: Why did you want to write about Hurricane Katrina?

Jesmyn Ward: I lived through it. It was terrifying, and I needed to write about that. I was also angry at the people who blamed survivors for staying and for choosing to return to the Mississippi Gulf Coast after the storm. Finally, I wrote about the storm because I was dissatisfied with the way it had receded from public consciousness.

Hoover: You preface both your novels with epigraphs from Southern rappers and the Bible. How have these two disparate traditions informed your work?

Ward: Biblical myth is as integral to the spirit of the South as the heat and humidity. The epigraphs acknowledge that history. Hip-hop, which is my generation's blues, is important to the characters that I write about. They use hip-hop to understand the world through language.

Hoover: There is also an epigraph from the poet Gloria Fuertes. How important is poetry to you?

Ward: I'm a failed poet. Reading poetry helps me to see the world differently, and I try to infuse my prose with figurative language, which goes against the trend in fiction. While I admire writers who are able to write with a vitality based on order and action, I work in a different vein. I often feel that if I can get the language just right, the language hypnotizes the reader.

Hoover: As a writer from the South, you are fated to be compared with Faulkner. How do you contend with his legacy?

Ward: The first time I read *As I Lay Dying*, I was so awed I wanted to give up. I thought, "He's done it, perfectly. Why the hell am I trying?" But the failures of some of his Black characters—the lack of imaginative vision

8 CONVERSATIONS WITH JESMYN WARD

regarding them, the way they don't display the full range of human emotion, how they fail to live fully on the page—work against that awe and goad me to write.

Hoover: How did you come up with the title *Salvage the Bones*?

Ward: The word *salvage* is phonetically close to *savage*. At home, among the young, there is honor in that term. It says that come hell or high water, Katrina or oil spill, hunger or heat, you are strong, you are fierce, and you possess hope. When you stand on a beach after a hurricane, the asphalt ripped from the earth, gas stations and homes and grocery stores disappeared, oak trees uprooted, without any of the comforts of civilization—no electricity, no running water, no government safety net—and all you have are your hands, your feet, your head, and your resolve to fight, you do the only thing you can: you survive. You are a savage. *Bones* is meant to remind readers what this family, and people like this family, are left with after tragedy strikes.

Hoover: Your protagonist, Esch, obsesses over the myth of Medea, the Greek sorceress who slaughters her children to punish her husband for taking a new bride. Where do you see Medea in the book?

Ward: Medea is in China most directly. China is brutal and magical and loyal. Medea is in Hurricane Katrina because her power to unmake worlds, to manipulate the elements, closely aligns with the storm. And she's in Esch, too, because Esch understands her vulnerability, Medea's tender heart, and responds to it.

It infuriates me that the work of white American writers can be universal and lay claim to classic texts, while Black and female authors are ghetto-ized as "other." I wanted to align Esch with that classic text, with the universal figure of Medea, the antihero, to claim that tradition as part of my Western literary heritage. The stories I write are particular to my community and my people, which means the details are particular to our circumstances, but the larger story of the survivor, the *savage*, is essentially a universal, human one.

Hoover: We are at this weird moment with teen moms. They are vilified and yet made into reality stars.

Ward: We *are* at a weird moment. Their popularity as reality stars rests on an assumption of morality and repugnance by the viewer. These young women are still spectacle. It's interesting that few of the girls on *16 and Pregnant* and *Teen Mom* are Black. The figure of the Black teen mother continues to loom large in our public consciousness, and we're not willing to speak about the ethnic and class stereotypes associated with it because they're still too useful to some.

Hoover: Dogfighting has also been demonized, particularly in the wake of the Michael Vick scandal. At the heart of your book is this incredible relationship between Skeetah and China. Where did China come from?

Ward: My father owned pit bulls when I was young. He sometimes fought them. My brother and a lot of the men in my community owned pit bulls as well: sometimes they fought them for honor, never for money. My father's favorite and sole pit bull was so dear to us that sometimes it was my babysitter; I remember sitting in our dirt driveway as a six-year-old crying because I was alone while that dog licked me. But then I also remember the dogfighting, and being incredibly fierce. After my brother died, his pit bull was a living link to him.

Hoover: Do you think of your writing as political?

Ward: After I finished my first draft of *Salvage the Bones*, I felt that I wasn't political enough. I had to be more honest about the realities of the community I was writing about. After my brother died in the fall of 2000, four young Black men from my community died in the next four years— from suicide, drug overdose, murder, and auto accidents. My family and I survived Hurricane Katrina in 2005; we left my grandmother's flooding house, were refused shelter by a white family, and took refuge in trucks in an open field during a Category 5 hurricane. I saw an entire town demolished, people fighting over water, breaking open caskets searching for something that could help them survive. I realized that if I was going to assume the responsibility of writing about my home, I needed narrative ruthlessness. I couldn't dull the edges and fall in love with my characters and spare them. Life does not spare us.

In *Salvage the Bones*, Family's Story of Survival

Michel Martin / 2011

© 2011 National Public Radio Inc. News report that was originally broadcast on NPR's *Tell Me More* on December 5, 2011, and is used with the permission of NPR. Any unauthorized duplication is strictly prohibited.

Michel Martin: Sometimes, the stories of life's biggest triumphs and tragedies are best told not in the headlines or in a cable news crawl, but in literature. In her novel, *Salvage the Bones*, Jesmyn Ward tells the story of how one family on the Mississippi Gulf Coast endured Hurricane Katrina.

But it also tells the story of what they were enduring before the storm. Extreme poverty, sexual abuse, routine violence, and survival. It's all seen through the eyes of the fifteen-year-old narrator named Esch. *Salvage the Bones* recently won the National Book Award for fiction and Jesmyn Ward joins us now.

Welcome, and congratulations on this really significant honor.

Jesmyn Ward: Thank you very much.

Martin: What about the award? I'm told that you were very surprised. You were so surprised that you almost couldn't talk.

Ward: I was. You know, I just did not think that I was going to win. I'm very hesitant to assume that good things are going to come to me, so beforehand, I kept preparing myself for losing, you know, and I thought, well, I will prepare myself to be happy for whoever wins and clap.

Martin: But did you think that you were a—God, I hate the term "dark horse," but I'll use it just for now.

Ward: Underdog?

Martin: Underdog. Thank you. Because of the subject matter? Do you think that the subject matter, you thought, was just too gritty?

Ward: I thought that the subject matter was too gritty, and I thought that the people that I write about and the place that I write about, you know, where they come from. These aren't popular, I guess, with a lot of, you know, readers. Because of that, I just didn't expect to win and then, also, because I wasn't that well known and the book wasn't—it was out there, but it wasn't out there.

Martin: I hear what you're saying. But let's talk about the book. It is beautifully written, but it's also a tough read. I don't think that there's any question about that. It deals with subjects that, as you said, are often not dealt with in literature. One of them is dogfighting. It opens with a very graphic scene of a pit bull giving birth. Why did you start that way?

Ward: Well, I'd had Esch's character in my head for a while, and I knew that I wanted to write a novel about her, about a girl that grows up in a world full of men. I'd also had Skeetah, who's her brother. I'd had his character in my head for a while, but the relationship between Skeetah and his dog fascinated me so. It's like that's where a lot of the heat was for me and then . . . .

Martin: Let me stop you there. You know what's fascinating to me? I don't know if you mind my drawing this analogy. In a way, China, who is the dog, and Esch have parallel lives because they are both loved in their way, but they are used, each in their own way. And that's one of the things that I think many people might find puzzling.

I mean, Skeetah loves the dog, but he doesn't mind using her to fight. But Esch—one of the very disturbing aspects of the novel is that she is used sexually by many of the young men around her, and she describes this in this very detached way. Do you mind if I ask? Where did this come from? And I hope you don't mind if I ask whether this was part of your own experience.

Ward: No, it wasn't. But I think, when I was growing up, I knew girls like Esch, who approached sex in that way. When I thought about her character, in a way, it's almost like she's mirroring the attitudes of the young men around her in the way that she thinks about it. Right? And in the way that she sort of separates it from herself and it's something that she does and it's not connected to who she is, or she doesn't think that it is.

I saw it a lot when I was growing up. You know, sex was just something that you did and, from a very young age, you know, for Esch, something that you're sort of not that informed about, or not that sort of lucid throughout, I guess, which is, in a way, why I think that she—at the beginning of the book, she finds that she's pregnant because, you know, she is so detached from what's happening that I don't think she's thinking about, like, the ramifications, you know, of what could happen.

12 CONVERSATIONS WITH JESMYN WARD

Martin: If you're just joining us, you're listening to *Tell Me More* from NPR News. We're speaking with Jesmyn Ward. She is the winner of the 2011 National Book Award for fiction for her novel, *Salvage the Bones*. It describes one family's journey on the Mississippi coast and how they endured Hurricane Katrina. In fact, it describes the days leading up to Hurricane Katrina.

Do you mind if I ask you to read just a piece, a little passage so people can hear your beautiful words?

Ward: Okay. So I'll read a very short passage from the beginning of the twelfth chapter.

[*Reads*] The Twelfth Day: Alive. We sat in the open attic until the wind quieted from jet fighter planes to coughing puffs. We sat in the open attic until the sky brightened from a sick orange to a clean white-gray. We sat in the open attic until the water, which had milled like a boiling soup beneath us, receded inch by inch back into the woods. We sat in the open attic until the rain eased to drips. We sat in the open attic until we got cold and the light wind that blew chilled us. We huddled together in Mother Lizbeth's attic and tried to rub heat from each other, but couldn't. We were a pile of wet, cold branches, human debris in the middle of all the rest of it.

Martin: As I think anybody can hear, even just from that very brief excerpt, the writing is lovely. But I have to ask the question that artists are asked when they take on subjects like this and, in fact, you said in your remarks after winning the award. You said that you wanted to write about the poor Black rural people of the South who've so often been marginalized, who kind of live in this parallel universe nobody else knows anything about.

But now, people say, okay. That's on the one hand. On the other hand, could one argue that this is kind of some poverty porn? You know, it's like you're exposing people's lives in a way that perpetuates the stereotypes that people are just ignorant, passive observers in their own lives, you know, just living, really, in just a litany of sorrows. How do you react to that?

Ward: I get angry, because this is the truth. You know, like this is the reality for so many people where I come from, and it was the reality for me for a portion of my life. At one time, when I was eight years old, my mother and father, my brother and my sisters—we had to move back in with my grandmother, and there were thirteen of us living in one house. Like, some of the aspects of this, of the poverty that these characters experience, like, that's real. And I can't deny telling that truth.

I think, when I write, one of the things that I'm really attempting to do is I'm attempting to humanize my characters. I feel a lot of pressure when I'm writing because I know, you know, if they looked at a synopsis of the book, what they read could only confirm all the stereotypes that they have about us and about people like us.

But I want to make us so human and make our stories so powerful and so touching so that the reader will empathize with those characters. That larger story in *Salvage the Bones* is just about survival, and I think that, in the end, there are things about this novel and about these characters' experiences that make their stories universal stories.

Martin: Well, congratulations once again on . . .

Ward: Thank you.

Martin: . . . this great honor and recognition for this work. So what's next for you?

Ward: I just handed in a memoir about a very specific time in my life when five young Black men that I know died and the first was my brother, who was hit by a drunk driver.

Martin: I'm so sorry.

Ward: Well, thank you. Because I think that, when people hear about epidemics like that of young Black men dying, that they think about urban areas and they don't think about places like the place that I'm from, these small, you know, rural areas in the South.

And so, in the book, I'm writing about the five young men and I'm writing about their lives, right? And so I'm asking the question of, like, why an epidemic like that would happen.

Martin: Well, hopefully, you'll come back and tell us more about that one. I hope you will.

Ward: I'd love to.

Martin: Jesmyn Ward is the winner of the 2011 National Book Award for fiction. She won for her latest novel, *Salvage the Bones*. She joined us from member station WWNO in New Orleans. Jesmyn, thank you so much for speaking with us.

Ward: Thank you very much.

Jesmyn Ward by Rebecca Keith

Rebecca Keith / 2012

This interview, "Jesmyn Ward by Rebecca Keith," was commissioned by and first published in *BOMB Daily*, March 21, 2012. © *Bomb Magazine*, New Art Publications, and its contributors. All rights reserved. The BOMB Digital Archive can be viewed at www.bombmagazine.org.

Rebecca Keith: There are so many mother archetypes in the book [*Salvage the Bones*]: Medea, Esch's mom, Esch, China to her puppies and to Skeetah, even Skeetah to China, and Katrina, the killer mother who's compared to Medea (as is China). Esch's father is ineffectual and beaten down, not absent but nearly so. Were these roles of strong mother figure and weak father figure necessary? Were they the only options for these characters? Did you draw the father this way to make Esch's strength stand out more? On the other hand, Esch vacillates between strength and weakness, demonstrating the reality of teenage crushes, the power of a glance, or lack of a glance, to destroy a girl, the way one can focus all one's energy on staring at someone, clocking his every move, without actually looking at him.

Jesmyn Ward: I was nurturing the idea of writing a book about a girl who grows up in a world full of men for around two years before I began writing *Salvage the Bones*. Esch's character was the seed for the book, really, and in order for her to exist in that lonely place without women, her mother had to be dead. The fact that she was such a strong presence, in life as well as death, was actually a surprise for me. As was the father's weakness. I didn't set out to make him a weak character; he walked on the page, and he was one, mostly, until he began surprising me, in small ways, with his strength. I do think the lack of a strong paternal presence allows Esch some freedom to flounder and find her way that she would not have if her father were more together and authoritative.

RK: *Salvage the Bones* speaks to the metaphor of invisibility. Esch is unseen by Manny, both in his refusal to look at her and his not really seeing her when he does. She thinks, "I could be Eurydice walking through the underworld to dissolve, unseen." There's also the fetus growing unseen inside of her and her comparison of human "inside eggs" to searching for a hen's eggs hidden outside, and lastly, the people suffering from Katrina unseen, unacknowledged by the government. Can you talk about this a little?

JW: I think that Esch is very conscious of who she is and how that makes her invisible. She's Black, she's poor, and she's a girl growing into a woman, and she's intuitively aware of how these identities marginalize her. This is why she thinks about invisibility in other areas so much; she's trying to understand her place in the world, and this is where her thoughts lead her. When I decided to throw Katrina at the characters, part of the reason I did so was that I wanted people who are ignorant of the types of folks who didn't evacuate to see these people as human, as intelligent and resilient as the watchers, but operating from a different history, a different perspective. And I wanted that perspective to be so real for readers that it hurt to read.

RK: Esch's pregnancy naturally brings up the economic realities of choice and access to birth control and abortion. For a good portion of the book, she tries to ignore her swelling belly, much like the kids try to ignore the approaching storm. When she finally admits to herself she's pregnant, she thinks, "These are my options, and they narrow to none," having heard girls at school talk about nonmedical ways to get rid of a pregnancy. She seems pretty set on having the child by the end of the novel even though she finally stands up to Manny. Is it just pure economics? Or that she feels mother-hood is the role meant for her, like her mother, like Medea, like China the pit bull mother? Why does she make that choice?

JW: Esch doesn't really have a choice. It's damn near impossible to get access to an abortion in Mississippi. Jackson, the state capital, might have a clinic that offers them. Women who choose abortion on the Mississippi Coast have to travel to Mobile, AL, or New Orleans. It takes five hours to drive from the north of the state to the south of the state; this is a big state: imagine being fifteen, with no access to a car or the money to have an abortion. Your choices, like Esch's, narrow to one. You have the baby because choice doesn't exist for you. So given this, Esch does the only thing she can: she figures out what it means to be a mother.

RK: Other interview[er]s have asked you why you choose to stay in Mississippi. It's your home, so it seems like, of course you would stay there, no? Has much, or anything, changed in the area since Katrina?

JW: It is my home; that's why I stay. What's funny is that except for a two-year stint directly after Katrina, I've been living in other places since I was eighteen: California, New York, and Michigan. I've chosen to return now because I miss my people, and I miss the beauty of this place. I miss the feel of the air on my skin, that sense of familiarity, the weight of the humidity in the air. The smells. Everyone knows that there's much that I hate about Mississippi, about the South. The only way that I can reconcile my hatred with my love is to fight; this is why I write my books and rail against Haley Barbour and the backward politics of this state any time I get a chance to do so. The Gulf Coast has changed since Katrina. There's a lot of rebuilding, and people seem to be moving farther upcountry, trying to escape the water. It makes this place seem a little less wild, and that saddens me. But I do what I can with what I'm given. Sometimes I think that I might leave again, but today is not that day.

RK: Why does Esch's family choose to stay? It seems like they don't really weigh the costs of staying versus going; they just shore up the house to stay. Evacuation isn't even mentioned until the storm is well on its way and then only by the news. Is it their only option, to stay and try to defend the Pit, their home? Rather than attempting to fix his truck to escape, Esch's father hopes to use it for salvage after the storm.

JW: Something that I was trying to make clearer in the book is that many people down here never evacuate for any storms. Generations of families have never evacuated. In my extended family, which consists of over 100 people, nobody ever evacuates. Some of it has to do with tradition, and of course that tradition is influenced by economics. Who has the money to pack up everything we hope to save and all family members, transport them four hours away from the coast, and pay for hotel rooms? Few people realize that hurricane season is six months long, and that the Gulf Coast is menaced by storms all the time. Evacuating is a costly proposition. Most people stay upcountry with relatives when they can and depend on the preparations Esch details in chapter 10; this has enabled us to survive here for generations.

RK: Esch and her family, in the Pit, are their own little island through most of the novel, visited by her brother Skeetah's crew, but other than that, fairly isolated and doing their best to take care of themselves to survive. At the end, as Katrina is clearing, you see them walk to join the rest of the community, and their neighbors take them in, offering food and shelter. It's a moment that can break you. In your *Paris Review* interview, you said that you saw people fighting over water after Katrina, which is the kind of picture that was painted in the news, given the lack of resources. Did your family experience any of the banding together, community support that occurred in the novel, or did you write that scene as more wishful thinking? Was it more every man out for himself after the disaster?

JW: Every man wasn't out for himself in this disaster, but my family and I did encounter ruthlessness during and after the hurricane. Hell, during the hurricane, we were denied shelter by a white family who told us they didn't have enough room for us in their house to ride out the storm since we'd fled our house when it flooded. We suffered through most of Hurricane Katrina in our trucks in that family's field, terrified, watching the flood waters surge, the wind rip trees from the earth and break power lines in two. But then near the end of the storm, we left that field, and we were taken in by another white family who'd been rescuing people who lived closest to the DeLisle bayou in a boat. After the storm, people banded together. My mother sent food down to our local park where a group of boys were living after Katrina destroyed their families' houses in Pass Christian. But then again, when I received my first jug of water a few days after the storm from volunteers at the local fire station, on my walk home, a rude man yelled at me, asking where I'd taken the water from, as if I'd stolen it. It was a difficult time. I know it's cliché, but that disaster definitely brought out the best and worst of humanity.

RK: Given the novel's trajectory of the days leading up to Katrina, you probably didn't have all that many options for [the] sequencing of scenes. But how did you write the book? Did you go from A to B or jump around? Did you know how the storm scenes would play out from the beginning? Or did you write them first to take off the pressure of building up to them? Reading those last forty pages or so was so frantic and suspenseful—did a draft of that come out at once or did you have to labor over it?

JW: I had no idea what would happen. When I began the book, I knew who the characters were, and around halfway through chapter 1, I knew that these characters would face Hurricane Katrina at the end of the book, in chapter 11. But I had no idea what would happen in the middle. I find that I begin all of my fiction projects like that: I vaguely know the characters and the end, but I have no idea how they get there, and often it takes me a long time to find the entry point to the story, the beginning. But I wrote *Salvage the Bones* like I write everything: straight through, chapter by chapter. Two chapters took substantial revision: the dogfight chapter and the hurricane chapter. There were general problems of development and clarity there, so once I was done with the first draft, I had to do a substantial rewrite in those two places. The hurricane chapter was really hard to write because I felt as [if] I were reliving that awful storm, and I had to keep reminding myself that this was about the characters' experience of Katrina, and not my own.

RK: One of your epigraphs is from an OutKast song (yay). Do you write to music? If so, what?

JW: I love OutKast. Love them! Actually, I can't write to music. It muddles the rhythm of the prose for me, so I need quiet when I write. But I listen to a lot of music when I'm mulling over the germ of a novel. When I was developing the ideas for my first book, *Where the Line Bleeds*, I was listening to a lot of Pastor Troy (thus, the epigraph). I was listening to a lot of OutKast when I was feeling out *Salvage the Bones* (thus, the epigraph). I'm a big champion of rap music, and I'm not ashamed to say that I love the smutty, thumping Southern stuff as well as more conscious rap. But I like plenty of other music, too: old blues, indie rock, pop, opera, and classical. However, I choose to use quotes from rap in my books because I think people forget that rap is very much a lyrical art form, and there's power in those words.

RK: You've written a new novel, yes? What are you working on now, or are you giving yourself a break?

JW: Well, I haven't begun my next novel yet. I'm still mulling and listening to a lot of music while I do so. I'm planning to begin soon. I am currently revising my third book, which is a memoir about a very specific time in my life, from 2000 to 2004, when five young Black men from my community died. The first was my brother, who was hit by a drunk driver in October of 2000. The memoir is attempting to figure out why an epidemic like that would happen in a place like this: small, rural, working class, and Southern.

RK: On your blog when *Salvage the Bones* came out, you wrote, "I always imagined that I'd do an interview for the novel, and a special picture would accompany it: me, hair wild, wearing a tank top and cut-off jean shorts, barefoot, Mississippi green wild all around me, holding a leash while a dog, big and red, stands at my feet, mouth open, teeth white. Both of us, grinning. I'm getting generous reviews and given several good interviews, but this hasn't happened yet. I'm still hoping." If you have such a picture, I'm sure *BOMB* would be happy to run it next to this interview.

JW: It's actually been chilly and foggy and rainy here in Mississippi, which means I was not able to take this picture. This makes me very sad, since it seems that I'm missing my chance to have this daydream come true. But I plan to take this picture this summer, and then I'm sending you a copy.

New Memoir Recounts
Black Lives "Reaped" Too Young

Rachel Martin / 2013

© 2013 National Public Radio Inc. News report that was originally broadcast on NPR's *Weekend Edition Sunday* on September 15, 2013, and is used with the permission of NPR. Any unauthorized duplication is strictly prohibited.

Rachel Martin: This is *Weekend Edition* from NPR News. I'm Rachel Martin. It is a cliché of the writing world to write what you know, because that's meant to be truer, and also somehow easier. But there was nothing easy for Jesmyn Ward about writing her own story. The Mississippi native made a name for herself as a fiction writer, but when it came to writing her own story, well, that turned out to be unsettling, even painful. Ward's memoir is called *Men We Reaped*, and in it she tries to make sense of the deaths of five young men in her life, including her younger brother. Jesmyn Ward joins me now from Delisle, Mississippi. Thanks so much for being with us.

Jesmyn Ward: It's good to be here.

Martin: This book is, in many ways, you trying to make sense of the death of all these young people—friends and family members even. And, if you don't mind, I'll have you read a passage from your book that describes this a little bit. This is a scene—your reflections—right after your friend Demond has died. He was shot to death in front of his own house. I'll have you read that little, that passage there.

Ward: [*Reads*] On the day after Demond died, I sat on his concrete porch steps. When the sun set, the coven of bats that lived in Demond's roof burst from the vents and out into the night in a black, squeaking mass. Where we had parked and drank and gotten high on Demond's lawn, now there was yellow police tape draped from pine to pine circumventing the mimosa. It read: Caution. [Nerissa smoked, exhaling] cloud[s] into the cold air, the skin dry, [at] the sides of her mouth. And I wondered who had come out of the

20 CONVERSATIONS WITH JESMYN WARD

dark and killed Demond. Even as I knew the figure that had waited hidden for him in the shivering pockets of the trees was human, I wanted to turn to N[e]rissa and ask her: *[W]hat do you think it is? What?*

Martin: N[e]rissa is your younger sister. You're both trying to process what has just happened. And that question, *what is in there?* This is you trying to understand what's happening?

Ward: Yes. You know, I look at this epidemic and I see something greater than a collection of individual choices. I see history. I see racism. I see, you know, economic disempowerment. I see all of these things, you know, that come together, or that came together sort of in this perfect storm here in southern Mississippi, and I feel like that is what is bearing down on our lives.

Martin: You were given kind of exceptional opportunities. Your mom worked as a housekeeper for a wealthy white family. That family ended up helping pay for you to go to a private high school. And from there you went on to Stanford, which put you on kind of a different path than a lot of the other people that you grew up with. Was it hard walking back and forth between those two worlds?

Ward: It was harder for me to walk in the outside world than coming back here. You know, Stanford is a fantastic school, but then I was very much, you know, I was really scared when I went to Stanford. And I think that the entire time that I was there, that I was struggling with this feeling that I didn't belong there, maybe because I was so rooted in who I am here. And so therefore, when I was out in that world, I thought, I don't belong here, I'm not smart enough, I don't have the proper education to thrive here. And it, you know, subdued me in some ways. I wasn't able to, you know, I don't know, to really, like, grow into myself and express myself while I was there because I was so crippled by this sense of, like, self-doubt. And then, but it was also homesickness.

Martin: So, you would come home every chance you got, between school semesters, every kind of break. And you're back in this community. And there is a lot of drug use. You yourself talk about drinking an awful lot and that you and your friends are in a kind of cycle of self-medicating. Did you recognize it as such in the moment, that you were trying to anesthetize some kind of pain, or was it just a bunch of kids, friends, just having a good time?

Ward: I didn't. I mean, I, you know, of course, every day I woke up with that feeling of dread and that just overwhelming sensation of loss, and then of course that fear, right, like who's going to die next? And we talked about it, you know, we talked about it. So, we were aware of what we were going through, and we were aware that it felt like we were under siege, and so we just weren't smart about all the drinking and all the drugs and everything that we did. And I don't think that I was clear about the fact that I was self-medicating until I really sat down and began to write this book, really. I mean, because then that meant that I had to reckon with all these things.

Martin: I mean, we talked in the beginning about your friend Demond. I believe he's the only friend who died in an overtly violent act. Everyone else, even though they may have been wrapped up in some complicated drug dealings or made bad choices, sometimes it didn't have anything to do with how they died.

Ward: He was. He was the only one who was shot. And his murder hasn't been solved. You know, I think that readers, when they first pick up the book and they read the jacket, or they just hear, you know, about these young Black men dying in the South, will probably immediately draw conclusions about the ways that they died. And so I think that it's something of a surprise—maybe. I mean, there is a conversation in this country going on about young Black men dying from gun violence, right? But I think it's tricky because even some of the young people that I mention, right, in that last chapter who died in different ways—young women, too—you know, they're dying in surprising ways.

Martin: Which makes it harder to draw conclusions about it, I imagine.

Ward: Yes, it does. I have a lot of great friends who are writers who, you know, read my work, early drafts of my work, and I have a great editor. And so I don't think I could have come to the conclusions that I came to without having that first group of readers to really push me towards that painful material instead of letting me hold it at arm's length, which is what I was doing, because it was just too painful. Sitting with experience and then trying to find, you know, meaning in that painful experience, it was too much.

Martin: What did you want to say about these young men—your brother among them—that you couldn't convey in a work of fiction?

Ward: You know, I feel like, in the two novels that I've written before this memoir, the young men reflect my brother. He's there. And so I feel like I've always been writing towards him. But when I thought about what happened to him and then also what happened to my friends, I didn't think it would be successful as fiction because I didn't even think that people would believe it because it was so awful and large and horrendous. And I felt like their stories were powerful enough that I thought that they would be better served in creative nonfiction when I could just tell the truth about them.

Martin: Eventually, you felt the pull and moved back home. What is it like now? Do you still feel now as an adult that kind of specter looming over young people in particular?

Ward: Yes. I mean, it's different for them. You know, my nephew, he's seventeen, so there are more people in his generation now, in this community, who see college and some kind of, you know, life after college. They see that that's more of a possibility for them, I feel like. But, you know, in some ways I feel like the reality that was facing us and that faces him is merciless. There are some people in the world that will look at my nephew and see him as a thug, and think that whatever harm or violence befalls him, that he will have deserved it because he courted it. Regardless of the, you know, circumstances of his life or his behavior, just because of the way that he looks, and the fact that he's a young Black male, and that scares the—that really scares me. A lot.

Martin: Jesmyn Ward. She won the National Book Award for her novel *Salvage the Bones* in 2011. Her new memoir is called *Men We Reaped*. Thanks so much for talking with us, Jesmyn.

Ward: Thank you.

Jesmyn Ward: *Men We Reaped*

Tobias Carroll / 2013

This interview was originally conducted by Tobias Carroll and published on *B&N Reads*, a Barnes & Noble blog, on September 20, 2013. Reprinted with permission.

Readers of Jesmyn Ward's National Book Award–winning *Salvage the Bones* already know how harrowing the stories she tells can be. That novel followed a family living in the path of Hurricane Katrina, and before the arrival of the storm, numerous devastations have already befallen them. Her new book, *Men We Reaped*, turns away from fiction to draw more directly on the writer's own life, as well as the lives and deaths of five men, including her brother. The book that emerges may be hard to classify, but it's unquestionably powerful: Ward marshals the history, family, and community through the accumulation of small, potent details.

More than a memorial to lives tragically cut short and a portrait community dealing with their loss, *Men We Reaped* takes on broader societal concerns, exposing tears in the social fabric too easily overlooked. That blend of memoir, reportage, and political extrapolation has a long and storied history—George Orwell's *Down and Out in Paris and London* comes to mind—and Ward's book makes it clear why this form remains essential.

I talked with Ward via email to discuss the origins of her new book's title, the ways in which her personal geography has affected the settings of her fiction, and how myths and archetypes continue to inform her writing.

Tobias Carroll: The Harriet Tubman quote that gives *Men We Reaped* both its title and one of its epigraphs is immediately striking. I was wondering where you first encountered it, and when it was that you knew that it would apply to your memoir.

Jesmyn Ward: I first came upon this Harriet Tubman quote online, actually. When beginning a book, I'll often search for epigraphs in the hope that I can find a few that will serve as clues or hints of what will come in the

24 CONVERSATIONS WITH JESMYN WARD

rest of the book. "We saw the lightning and that was the guns; and then we heard the thunder and that was the big guns; and then we heard the rain falling and that was the blood falling; and when we came to get in the crops, it was dead men that we reaped." It's difficult not to be moved by this—that was my first reaction to it, and I love her use of metaphor. Also, I wanted to make the sad connection between that war, the Civil War, and the unspoken war against young Black people in the United States today. And to refer to the era of slavery, from whence all of our national issues of racism began, and from which my family and our problems grew.

Carroll: *Men We Reaped* features two parallel timelines, moving in chronological order through one series of events and in reverse order through the other. How did you arrive at the structure of your memoir?

Ward: Because this tells my story, my family's and community's story, and also the stories of five dead young men, it was not an easy book to structure. When I first started thinking about it, I knew it had to end with my brother. That was the hardest of the deaths for me, as he was the closest. Chronologically, however, his death was the first. So I decided to tell my family's story and my story moving forward through time, ending just before my brother died. I then revisited each of the five young men who died, moving backward in time, from the last death to the first, with the hope that when the two stories met with my brother, this most impactful moment in my life, I'd better understand why all of this happened.

Carroll: Beyond the story of your life and the lives of the five men at the book's heart, *Men We Reaped* has a sociopolitical aspect as well, particularly as with the statistics about race and poverty cited in the book's conclusion. At what point, as you wrote and edited it, did you realize that this additional dimension was needed?

Ward: In a way, the whole purpose of the book is to humanize the statistics we all read in the newspaper. Out of context, they're so easy to dismiss. That's why I wrote *Salvage the Bones*, at least in part, so people would understand why some families stayed put during Hurricane Katrina. That's why I wrote this memoir. I wanted to say, hey, we're not numbers. We're here, we're human beings. We have families and jobs and fun and sorrow, just like everyone else. The final chapter of the book, "We Are Here," is really my reckoning with all the loss and the reasons for it. And it's only here that I bring in the statistics, as a way of making the individual story more universal. As a way of also saying, we are many. Too many.

Carroll: In the section of the book focusing on Demond Cook, you talk about how, at the time, you told friends and relatives that you didn't write about "real-life stuff." You have since written realist fiction and nonfiction; what ultimately changed your mind?

Ward: For me, there's a distinction between "real-life stuff" and realistic fiction. My two novels were definitely drawn from my life and my community, but they were works of imagination. They were fiction, albeit of a realistic nature. The memoir is obviously something different, my version of the truth. At the time Demond was alive and we were joking about the potential or lack of potential in his life story as a subject for a book, I didn't imagine myself writing about him or any of the other young men in the book. In a way, all of the loss forced me to confront an actual truth rather than an imagined one. While I can play the benevolent god in a work of fiction, protect my characters—although I try not to—real life has not spared us.

Carroll: When you spoke with *The Paris Review* in 2011, you wrote about the influence of classical figures on *Salvage the Bones*. In *Men We Reaped*, you say about yourself growing up, "I wanted to be my own heroine." When writing nonfiction, how do you deal with classical archetypes?

Ward: There's a theme that runs through the memoir, beginning with the dedication to my brother that states, "For Joshua Adam Dedeaux, who leads while I follow." I'm the older sister, so the expectation was that I would lead. And I did, for many years. I took care of him. I left home first. He led at times, too. He had responsibilities and pressures at home that I never did. My brother and I used to take car rides together through the murmuring Southern Pines, under a hot, high sun, listening to rap music on the stereo. In this way we traveled together, and I loved those moments. Now that my brother has left us, now that he's died, I can't follow. I don't want to, not yet. But at times I think of him as the heroic traveler, an Odysseus in a dull blue '85 Cutlass. And me, I'm back at home, waiting—and living, too, and writing and enjoying my family—but still, waiting, to hear about his journeys and to ride with him again.

Carroll: As someone who also came of age in the late eighties and early nineties, the pop culture details definitely hit home for me. What did returning to that time period invoke in you, and how does writing from recalled memory differ from reporting on the lives of others?

Ward: On some level, it was really wonderful to revisit that period. Not only because my brother and his friends were still alive, but for the particulars: the books I was reading, the music my family and I listened to, the television programs, the movies we watched together. I'm a consumer of popular culture, still: movies and music, particularly. I feel like these are the signposts of our lives. When we share an era, we collectively share all of these memories, even if the particulars are individualized. So I'm glad to hear the details resonated with you. I've never really written reported nonfiction, and in writing *Men We Reaped*, I was very lucky to have my sisters, my mother, and several friends around to help me remember some of the details. The challenge for me was less in recalling the stories, more in drawing out the larger themes the stories illustrated.

Carroll: The "buffer" woods you wrote about in *Men We Reaped* reminded me of a similar location in *Salvage the Bones*. To what extent has the area in which you grew up had an effect on the geography featured in your novels?

Ward: The geography of my home is the geography of my novels. It will likely be the geography of my next novel, too. When I lived away from home, I longed for it and recreated it in my fiction. Even though I'm now living among those "buffer" woods again, I don't think I'll want my characters to inhabit any other landscape. Those woods, the bayous, the simple, squat houses—this place is part of who I am and part of what I want to explore as a writer. How does place form who we are?

Carroll: A number of the details in *Men We Reaped* abound with thematic implications. I'm thinking particularly of your discovery that a town graveyard could eventually supplant a playground. How did you go about learning this?

Ward: Yes, that is a sad fact I learned from Lucretia Lott, who is an older cousin. She's actually of my mother's generation, and she told me this fact while we were at the graveyard for the funeral of the young woman who was stabbed to death by her boyfriend. (I mention her death in the book.) In Lucretia's generation, they actually played baseball where my brother's grave is situated. Years later, our local park was the place where we hung out, away from our parents, out under the sky. We sat on the bleachers, talking; we shot goals on the basketball courts; we huddled in our cars, listening to music. This is where our lives happened. And that these same young people who lived and breathed and laughed in that park could occupy it in death, well, that's too great an irony to ignore.

Carroll: Have you written any fiction since completing *Men We Reaped*? Have you found that writing a work of nonfiction has changed the way you approach writing as a whole?

Ward: *Men We Reaped* was a tough book to write, on many levels. I struggled to get distance from the subject; I struggled emotionally. It's hard to be in those moments again. While I do get attached to my fictional characters, it's nothing like the cold reality of real-life loss. So getting back to fiction will be a relief. I'm in the early stages of writing my next novel, also set in Bois Sauvage. I must say, after facing the emotional challenges of memoir, I'm really looking forward to thinking about character and plot, rather than my own unhappy story.

The Rumpus Interview
with Jesmyn Ward

Kima Jones / 2013

This interview was originally conducted by Kima Jones and published on TheRumpus.net on October 10, 2013. Reprinted with permission.

Jesmyn Ward, National Book Award winner, returned this fall with her third book, a memoir titled *Men We Reaped*. It is the story of five young men in Jesmyn's life—her only brother, friends, a cousin—who all die violently, in the span of five years, in her hometown of DeLisle, Mississippi. The short lives of these young men are entombed between chapters of Jesmyn's childhood and adolescence, and in these chapters, she revisits the strained relationship of her parents and how their early choices, pronounced by poverty, shaped the people she and her siblings would become.

DeLisle, first named Wolf Town, a Gulf Coast community that survived both Hurricane Camille and Hurricane Katrina, is the specter of the memoir—the ravenous ghoul who eats its own children before maturation. Jesmyn articulates a violence specific to DeLisle and communities like it: a senseless, spastic, American violence, whose wounds never heal properly for being gnashed open repeatedly before mending. Jesmyn turns an eye to the conditions, the laws and frameworks that could allow for such miscarriages of justice again and again through the lens of the young men she knew and loved. Each chapter is a grave marker; the reader knows there is no possible happy ending in sight.

Jesmyn and I talked over the phone, and her daughter's cries peppered our conversation as I asked each question and waited for her soft-spoken answers delivered through an undeniable drawl. I found myself hesitant to say the names of her deceased loved ones. Instead of saying "Josh," I said, "Your brother." Rather than say "Demond," I would only say, "Your friend."

Each time I spoke the name of one of her dead loved ones, I felt myself trespassing on territory not my own in a space not privileged to me.

The fluidity with which my tongue said their names shocked me. I spoke of them as if I had always known them, as if I had laughed with them or drank with them or ridden through the streets of DeLisle with them, windows down, music blaring. In those moments, I wondered how strange it would be for me to hear the name of my brother coming from Jesmyn's mouth. How I would jump a little, startled. How I would probably tilt my head some, furrow my brow, squint in her direction intensely before asking my question. I would be respectful but assertive. I would read her body language and look her squarely in the eyes. *I'm sorry, Jesmyn, but my brother has never mentioned you before. What is your acquaintance? How do you know him?* And depending on her answer, I would harden or soften my gaze. Depending on her answer, I would decide whether or not to pounce.

The Rumpus: Were you ever a poet?

Jesmyn Ward: I was. I wrote poetry in middle school and high school and even through college. It was bad. I just don't think I'm very good at writing poetry. I mean, the distillation, I think, is hard for me, but I love poetry.

Rumpus: Your prose is so poetic, and I'm sure you hear that a lot.

Ward: I have and that makes me feel a little bit better.

Rumpus: The first line of Toni Morrison's *Beloved* is "124 was spiteful." In your opening chapter, your brother, Joshua, insists that your childhood home is haunted and that haunting extends to the town of DeLisle. As your memoir unfolds, we understand the real-life haunting is racism and poverty. Can you talk more about that?

Ward: I wanted that to come out, especially by the end of the book. When I decided to write about my brother and friends, I was attempting to answer the question *why*. Why did they all die like that? Why so many of them? Why so close together? Why were they all so young? Why, especially, in the kinds of places where we are from? Why would they all die back to back to back to back? I feel like I was writing my way towards an answer in the memoir. By the end of the book, I realized that it is the history of racism, the history of poverty, the history of economic inequality that bears really heavily on the present and lives in the present. By the end of the book, I wanted the reader to understand that.

Rumpus: I want to stay here a moment because when we visit Demond's home, you wonder if his dead grandparents haunt it. When you move to

30 CONVERSATIONS WITH JESMYN WARD

Gulfport, the memory of DeLisle haunts you and your siblings. In describing the trailer your mother bought, the way it sits on the ground on one side but supported by cement bricks on the other, I felt a fear for you and your family. As I read, I kept saying, "Oh God, please don't let one of the children get caught in that space. Please don't trap them in the house!"

Ward: You know, no one has pointed that out to me before. I've also never written about home in this way before. I guess a lot of it is subconscious, and I am intuitively making these decisions when I'm writing. I wanted to communicate in the book that on one hand, being at home—both in our homes and in DeLisle—gives us a sense of belonging and family and safety, but at the same time, being in those places makes us less safe.

Rumpus: There are several lines in the memoir that break me. One of which, on page fifty-eight, is: "They never touched each other in anger, but the small things in that house suffered." My mind keeps mapping the home you built for us in the narrative, and I am looking at the little things falling apart, the neglected and tired things. Can you talk about your choice to use the word "things" instead of "people"?

Ward: I wanted to encompass us as kids, but also my parents in relation to each other, and the house itself, and the things that they owned. When you have a family, even though you might move a lot, you collect all of these things. It's the detritus of your family, and they become the symbols of your family life, and your unit out in the world. In that moment, I wanted to allude to the fact that the way my parents' relationship was falling apart was impacting me and my brother, my parents, but also our symbols. I was thinking back to things that marked us as a family. We used to have this huge stereo. On Christmas, we played Jackson 5 Christmas albums and Motown Christmas albums. When I was thinking back on the memory, I was thinking of those things that marked us as a family. I was thinking of those albums being broken.

Rumpus: You write about your depression as an extension of your mother's. The ways in which she could not understand or express her sorrow foretold the ways you would come to handle grief. While you have writing, I am wondering if you have found other ways to speak.

Ward: I think so. Through the process of specifically writing this memoir, there was so much reckoning that I had to do. It was very difficult. It doesn't erase anything that happened, but I think that it was healthy for me to do it. The teenage self-loathing that I suffered from all of a sudden found itself turned into rapids with my grief after my brother died. I turned it inwards. In the same way that my mom processes her grief and her problems. This project, as a memoir, has helped me funnel it outwards.

Rumpus: Your father is a very easy-to-love, hard-to-hate, tragic hero. Even as you enumerate the transgressions against your mother, we love him. After your brother dies and your father is seated before those televisions, we love him. We want the freedom he wants for himself. How difficult was it to write your father?

Ward: It was difficult because when I was a child—and I hope it's reflected in the way I developed his character—I worshiped him. As I got older, I realized one of the reasons it was so easy for that to happen, besides his charm and humor and good looks, is because he did leave. He was able to swoop in and be the carefree, happy daddy. He could leave, but my mother was the responsible one who supported and provided for all of us because my dad didn't. It was interesting writing him because now that I have a daughter, I understand how my parents differed. Writing the memoir made me more aware of him and able to understand him and the things he yearned for because I yearn for them in my own life.

I was scared of writing my father because I didn't want him to become a flat character, a villain. The bare facts of what he did are really ugly. It would be really easy to dislike him, so it was important to complicate him as much as I could on the page. I had to be truthful about the bad but portray the good as well.

Rumpus: One of my criticisms of the memoir would have to be the idea that the absence of the Black father and Black husband is crippling the Black community. Can you talk a little bit about the fragile balance of writing accurately without perpetuating stereotypes and archetypes?

Ward: It worries me a lot, and it worries me in everything that I do. Speaking specifically about the memoir, I know that's a criticism that people can have about my work. When I look at the young men's lives, if they're reduced to the worst thing they've done, then it's easy for them to become a stereotype. I keep running into that with newspaper articles that are very short. They'll read, "Rog, a cocaine addict . . . ," "and so-and-so, who sold crack." It makes me angry. When I was writing the memoir, every page was a battle with myself because I knew I had to tell the truth. That's what the memoir form demands. I also had to figure out how much of the truth do I tell, how do I make the truth as balanced as I possibly can? How do I make these people as complicated and as human and as unique and as multifaceted as I possibly can? For me, that was the way I attempted to counteract some of that criticism.

32 CONVERSATIONS WITH JESMYN WARD

I knew it was going to come, but how do I not tell the truth about that? How do I not tell the truth about my father leaving and the ways I saw it cripple our family and affect my relationship with myself and others? The same things with my sisters and their relationships with others and men. My brother and the way he viewed masculinity, what it meant to be a man and provide. My dad's leaving affected all of those things, and it's not like I could leave it out. It's a risk I had to take.

Rumpus: Junot Díaz calls you a "beast" at writing male characters, and I concur. You offer your readers beautifully complicated renderings of Black men. Did writing *Salvage the Bones* prepare you in any way for the task of writing *Men We Reaped*?

Ward: I hadn't thought about that question before, but I think that it did. *Salvage* is told from Esch's point of view, and of course she is a young woman, but much of her gaze is on the young men in her life because she's surrounded by them. I already wrote a lot about young Black men living in difficult circumstances. The circumstances in *Men We Reaped* are even more difficult, so it was even more challenging for me to do so. I had to write about Ronald, for example, who was self-medicating with drugs and then also struggling with depression and suicidal thoughts. None of my characters and men in *Salvage* had to struggle with anything that dire and that difficult. The young men that I write about—my friends, my cousin, my brothers—their lives were even more difficult than the young men of *Salvage*.

Rumpus: You begin the title chapter of *Salvage the Bones*, chapter 5, with the line, "Bodies tell stories." The body of the widowed husband has become an empty glass; the family dog, China, a symbol of resistance; Big Henry, as graceful as he is large, is relief; Esch carries the child of loss, insecurity, and unrequited love. When you are shaping bodies and their histories and gestures, what do you have in mind for your characters, and how do you ask them to do things you wouldn't do yourself?

Ward: I want each character to be as unique as possible. I want them to reflect something of who they are in the way that they move and in how their bodies work. That was foremost in my head when I was writing *Salvage*: I wanted every gesture, every little movement, to really carry meaning and communicate meaning to the reader. I was very conscious of that when I was writing.

When I wrote the line, "Bodies tell stories," I was thinking of myself and my own scars that I've lived with since I was born. I had myself in mind but transferred those feelings to my characters and used that idea to inform their histories. For example, when Esch sees Skeetah's scars, I was thinking of myself.

Rumpus: *Salvage The Bones* is a novel about the savagery and salvation that is water. Esch's home, The Pit, is referred to as "empty as the fish tank dry of water and fish." Can you talk about writing and rewriting the Gulf Coast and Hurricane Katrina into your work? How do you renew this place for your reader with each new book?

Ward: It's a challenge with every book to rewrite the Gulf Coast and make it a vivid, lived-in place where the reader is fully immersed. I have to consider that it's a place I've written about before, and I don't want to repeat things. Part of what I was doing with *Salvage*, with Hurricane Katrina, was having the recurring imagery of water. I depended on that imagery and fleshed it out because I hadn't done it in my first novel or ever before.

Rumpus: And your next book is set in the Gulf Coast?

Ward: My next book is set in the Gulf Coast.

Rumpus: You live in Mississippi with your daughter and family. How important is it to you that your daughter grow[s] up there?

Ward: I've been all over the place—New York, Michigan, the Bay Area. There is the outside world and then home. I love the outside world and what it can offer. I love the diversity of opinion and experience and culture. I love having access to all of the things I have access to when I'm not in Mississippi, but I think I want my kid to grow up with a real sense of family and a real sense of community. This is the only place she'll be able to find that. And I mean blood family and blood community. That's home. That's the Gulf Coast. There are over two hundred of us, on my mother's side, and that means that family is not just a concept that encompasses the nuclear. Family is the nuclear, the extended, and the community as a whole, the generations that have been here. I think it's pretty special, and I want her to feel like she belongs to a place. I want her to have the experience of knowing home.

Rumpus: The funeral T-shirt, quite like the teddy bear and votive and altar candles, has become part of the assembly of the "gone too soon" memorial. You write about not wearing your funeral T-shirt for Josh until after Hurricane Katrina. Why then?

Ward: I could not wear it the day of his funeral because it was just too raw. It was just too raw, and I couldn't do it. I didn't even want to acknowledge that I had one. I couldn't face it. I didn't pull it out until after Katrina because a good enough amount of time had passed; I had about five years, at that point, to acknowledge his leaving and deal with the fact that, yes, he was gone and I had a memorial T-shirt for my brother.

34 CONVERSATIONS WITH JESMYN WARD

The second, more matter-of-fact reason, is that during Katrina, my grandmother's house, where we were staying, flooded. At one point, we had to swim up to higher ground. I was barefoot and wearing shorts and a skimpy T-shirt that I had slept in. The storm surge came up through the bayou, and the bayou itself is just disgusting. The storm surge is pushing God knows what all the way from the Gulf, up through the bayou and into DeLisle, so we were gross. We had to hike to my mom's house for clothes; you couldn't get up on the roads because there were trees and power lines down. We got to my mom's house, and the T-shirt was the first I pulled out of the drawer. I could have put it back away, but maybe I wanted to feel closer to Josh on that day. Maybe because the experience of the hurricane had been so harrowing. Maybe in that moment, the T-shirt was less of a curse and more of a comfort, because it reminded me of him.

Rumpus: In the acknowledgments you thank your sister, Nerissa, for saving your laptop during Hurricane Katrina. To wit, she was saving the lives of these five young men. For this little while, they are with you and your sisters again. Has this memoir brought any comfort?

Ward: It felt like an indulgence. Going back was painful, but, at the same time, it was nice to live with them again for a few pages. I got to live with my brother again for the entire book. Of course as I'm writing the book, I'm getting closer and closer to the end, and I know what that means. I knew exactly where I was heading. It was really difficult, but it was nice to make them come alive for those scenes. It was good.

An Interview with Jesmyn Ward

Roxane Gay / 2013

This interview was originally conducted by Roxane Gay and published on *The Toast* on November 19, 2013. Reprinted with permission.

Men We Reaped, by National Book Award–winner Jesmyn Ward, is a book about how place and home can shape lives indelibly. This memoir is a story of a grief so profound because those being grieved were cherished so keenly. It is a remembrance of five Black men who died too young and a chronicle of how a family grew together and fell away from one another but never came truly apart. *Men We Reaped* is a breathtaking book, one where both sorrow and song are palpable. The writing is as elegant as it is raw—a fierce declaration that Roger Eric Daniels III, Demond Cook, Charles Joseph Martin, Ronald Wayne Lizana, and Joshua Adam Dedeaux will not be forgotten.

Though she is busy on book tour, I had the chance to speak with Jesmyn Ward via e-mail about the expectations she faced after winning the National Book Award, the boundaries of writing truth, the savagery she and her family claim, and much more.

Roxane Gay: Did you feel a burden of expectations after winning the National Book Award for *Salvage the Bones*?

Jesmyn Ward: I didn't feel a burden of expectations immediately after because I had a first draft of *Men We Reaped* already completed. Writing memoir requires such a different set of muscles, both emotional and craft, and this is another reason that I didn't feel that burden. However, now that I'm returning to the novel, I'm definitely feeling the pressure of expectation. Nikky Finney told me to forget all of that and to remember why I came to writing initially, so I'm trying to follow her advice.

Gay: Home and family are such abiding themes in your work. How do you define home and family as a woman, as a writer?

Ward: Family is a mutable thing. Home is as well. Our nuclear families fracture and break, so we remake them throughout our lives. As I learned from Hurricane Katrina, homes can fracture and break as well, and these, too, will be remade. The home I grew up in will never exist again, and this is why I write so much about home, perhaps. Because I lost mine.

Gay: You write, "Most of the people here are kin. It is something that the 'Black' people will talk about among themselves, the way our families intertwine and feed one another, and it is something that 'White' people will speak about among themselves, but it is something that we rarely speak to each other about, even when those on both sides of the color divide share the same last name." Do you believe that these conversations will or should be had?

Ward: I don't know if these conversations will be had right now. I'm fairly pessimistic about the possibility of people in the current South having complicated conversations about race because we're so conditioned to respond quickly and emotionally, with all the vitriol that's been bred into us, when race arises. I don't think this is a conversation that we can avoid for long, however, because our past is our present and our future, in some respects. Love is ignoring color lines and prejudice even more frequently now, and the children of such unions and the culture of our time make avoiding that conversation moot.

Gay: As I read *Men We Reaped*, I enjoyed the sound of the sentences, which carried such musicality. Do you think about sound and sentence when you write?

Ward: I'm really conscious of sound and sentence when I write. I often read passages and sentences aloud in an effort to make them sound *right*. There has to be a rhythm to the language. I know when something is off because it sounds wrong, and then I'll read aloud and revise and read aloud again until, for some strange reason, it carries the rhythm it should. This is the reason I can't write to music.

Gay: What kind of boundaries do you create for yourself when writing memoir and truth?

Ward: Every page is a negotiation. Every page is a struggle. I know I must tell the truth, but I have to constantly wrestle with the material to figure out how much of the truth I'm willing to tell. So my boundaries are mutable. I know that some people in my family and community find some of the secrets I share about my life and my brother's and my friends' lives problematic: I decided that I wouldn't share anything that did not contribute to the greater conversation. In the end, I had to believe that the truth I told would make readers pay attention, would make them start asking questions and having conversations about why Black young people in the South self-medicate with drugs, why they suffer from mental illness in silence, why they believe they will die young, why they believe that selling crack at fourteen years of age is a viable choice.

Gay: The grief was palpable throughout *Men We Reaped*. Can you carry this grief for these men who have been lost without it breaking you?

Ward: I have to. If I don't carry this, then who will tell the story? Who will remember? I bear it because I must.

Gay: This memoir has a really elegant structure that reflected how, like family, the past and present are so intertwined in this story. You write about your family in one thread and remember the men you and your loved ones lost in the other. How did you come to this structure as the best way of telling all these stories?

Ward: It was an intuitive choice. I wrote an essay in 2005, which was the seed of *Men We Reaped*. The structure of that essay reflects the structure of the book. Regardless of form, I could only conceive of telling this story in one way. Before I began writing *Men We Reaped*, I tried to change the structure, to work against the structure I'd used in the essay, and I couldn't do it. It felt physically wrong to do so.

Gay: So much of this book focuses on young Black men, while the lives of young Black women in the South are just as fraught. Did you feel like, or, I suppose, do you worry that women were being absented from this narrative as you wrote it?

Ward: No, I wasn't worried that women were absented from the narrative. I saw the chapters about my life and my mother's and sisters' lives as addressing and telling the story of women in the South, fraught as our lives have been with teenage pregnancy and depression and racism and addiction and grief. And in the last chapter, I do try to point out that young Black women are dying in our community too, from accidents and domestic violence and poor health care. Unfortunately, I didn't feel comfortable including the young women I mention in the narrative in their own chapters because I wasn't as close to them as I was to the young men, and also because their deaths occurred between 2008 and 2011. I could only write the story that I'd actually lived: all of the young people who'd died during 2000 to 2004, the time when my grief was so raw and toxic, were men. In the end, I couldn't make the stories of the young women who died fit into the narrative organically as individual chapters.

Gay: Toward the end, you say that "[w]e survive; we are savages," and this line has stayed with me. Does survival beget savagery?

Ward: I think it does, but I feel that I've been remiss in explaining what I mean when I use the word "savage." At home, there's honor in proclaiming yourself a savage. Among the young, it means you're resourceful, smart, strong. That come hell or high water, hurricane or oil spill, or racism or loss, that you will stand. That you will find a way to survive. This is the kind of savagery we claim.

Gay: I was giving a reading recently and a young woman asked me how I feel about the label "Black woman writer." I told her, well that's what I am, but I knew she was asking about the responsibility and potential limitations that come with being identified as such. How do you feel about being labeled as a "Black woman writer"? Do you ever worry that your writing will be pigeonholed as such?

Ward: I worried that my writing would be pigeonholed when I began writing in my twenties. After years of writing and seeing my work either ignored or pigeonholed, I realized constant worry about how I was perceived would drive me crazy. I realized that I could only be who I am: Black and a woman and a writer, and that I could only do one thing: strive to write the best damn story I can. The rest is out of my control.

Gay: What do you like most about your writing?

Ward: One thing I've found about my writing is that it's always changing. It's always developing. My understanding of story, of how to write a good story, of how language can work, changes every time I write. It's a good thing to know that this part of me is always growing and maturing.

Jesmyn Ward on How Books Can Make Us Better People

Kiese Laymon / 2014

This interview was originally conducted by Kiese Laymon and published in *Esquire* on December 23, 2014. Reprinted with permission.

Jesmyn Ward, National Book Award–winning author of *Where the Line Bleeds, Salvage the Bones,* and *Men We Reaped,* is the greatest American storyteller of my generation. Of course, the greatest American storyteller of my generation is equally adept at literary fiction and nonfiction. And of course, she's from my Mississippi. Jesmyn's work taught me to practice. She taught me that it is necessary I write to home in every sentence I craft. More than anything, Jesmyn is the first writer of my generation whose work taught me to divest myself of the idea that everything I finish is good simply because I wrote it or because someone in New York likes it. In *Where the Line Bleeds,* Jesmyn—who, full disclosure, is also my friend—showed me that it was okay to write 3,000 dim words to find fifty that glow. In *Salvage the Bones,* she taught me that our revisions must be dirty, musty, and so so bright at the same time. In *Men We Reaped,* she begged me to write humbly into my family's fears with an awareness that we come from a lineage of wonderful practitioners whose practice eventually saved lives. Whenever people ask me, "Who do you write to?" I tell them the truth. I write to Jesmyn Ward because she writes to and from us. I sat down with Jesmyn for a short conversation about where we are and why literary work matters in this current political moment.

On writers who say they're indebted to her

It makes me feel really fucking weird. Awkward, ashamed, humbled weird. But good, too, because it means that I'm not alone in this battle, that I have other insightful, fierce writers with me, fighting the good fight. There's solace and camaraderie in hearing people tell me that. It means I must be doing something right.

On her first child

She's a shy, smart, opinionated two-year-old now. I know this is super-morbid, but I'm most afraid of her dying before me. I think about children dying before parents all the time, and I know that part of the reason I do is because of my mother's experience with my brother. And I know this anxiety has been heightened by the lives and deaths of Oscar Grant, Trayvon Martin, Mike Brown, and too many others. I want her to grow up into a confident, ambitious, loving, healthy adult, and I'm hoping I get many years to help her to grow into that person. I can't wait to read to her all the books that I loved as a child—I'm especially excited about that. So far, she likes books, so fingers crossed that she doesn't hate reading when she gets older. I think it's inevitable that she'll think I'm a hopeless nerd when she's a teenager and I'm trying to get her to read *The Handmaid's Tale* with me, but hopefully, she'll outgrow it.

On how the protests around Black deaths are impacting her writing life

I've heard some writers say that they are obsessed with certain ideas and that they find themselves writing around the same obsession again and again but [are] telling different stories to get at that same idea. I'm beginning to think that I suffer from this syndrome, too. I can't stop thinking about the devaluation of Black life, and I find it seeping into everything I write. Especially the novel that I'm working on now. At the same time, the protests make me hopeful. They make me commit to writing every day, and they make me believe in the power of speaking.

On how art and literature have impacted the fight for justice

I think art, especially literature, has the particular power to immerse the viewer or reader into another world. This is especially powerful in literature, when a reader lives the experience of the characters. So if the characters are human and real enough, then readers will feel empathy for them. A study published in *Scientific American* in 2013 confirmed this—that reading literary fiction increases a reader's empathy. How amazing is it that literature has the power to subvert preconceived notions about Black people, to change readers' perceptions of us, to induce empathy, to persuade them through feeling that Black lives matter?

On all the great literature to come out of Mississippi

Great trouble breeds great art, I think. Plus I think Mississippians grow up in a culture that prizes the art of storytelling and the art of using figurative language to understand the world. In every other sense, I have massive state shame. But in literature, I definitely have state superiority. Can't we have that one thing?

On how the movement to save Black lives changes the Black community

It's really important, I think, because it makes us more aware of how we treat each other, of how we value or devalue each other, and it makes us own it. It holds white supremacy accountable but also makes us accountable because it demands we see how we've internalized what white supremacy has taught us about our self-worth and how we act on each other in ways that reflect what we've been taught.

Bookforum Talks with Jesmyn Ward

Kyla Marshell / 2016

This interview was originally conducted by Kyla Marshell and published on *Bookforum* on August 24, 2016. Reprinted with permission.

August 2 would have been James Baldwin's ninety-second birthday. Across the internet, people celebrated by quoting his work, sometimes with just text, sometimes through memes, so much so that by early Tuesday morning, "James Baldwin" was trending on Twitter. But over the last few years, in our extended cultural moment of racism becoming tangible to more than those it affects, Baldwin—his ideas and forecast for this country—has resurfaced like a message in a bottle, the words he wrote always true, yet now eerily prescient.

His 1963 work, *The Fire Next Time*, with its forward-glancing title, was the call; *The Fire This Time*, a collection of essays and poems edited by Jesmyn Ward, is the response. Featuring the work of contemporary, mostly Black writers, it finds a way to touch on many subjects—the poet Honorée Fanonne Jeffers on researching Phillis Wheatley; Garnette Cadogan on "walking while Black"; Kiese Laymon on Outkast—that don't always come to mind when one thinks of "race in America," while pieces by Claudia Rankine, Carol Anderson, and Daniel José Older touch on more immediate issues, some recent enough to name Sandra Bland and the murders in Charleston, South Carolina.

Jesmyn Ward and I spoke by phone a day after the book's publication date—which, not by coincidence, was August 2.

Kyla Marshell: In your intro, you write, "The ephemera of Twitter, the way voices of the outraged public rose and sank so quickly, flitting from topic to topic, disappointed me." I was wondering what it was like for you, publishing *The Fire This Time* on James Baldwin's birthday, to see how popular his words and his ideas are via social media and on the internet as people are looking for a way to find meaning for what's going on in the world?

Jesmyn Ward: I really feel like there seems like a new generation of readers discovering him and his work. That's a great thing. I think back to when I was in undergrad or even when I was in graduate school, which was almost ten years ago—I feel like he wasn't that popular. There are people rediscovering him on their own now. He has been rediscovered by a larger group of people all at once.

Marshell: I've noticed that also. It's kind of hip now to know about James Baldwin or to be engaged with his work. Twitter and social media are such ephemeral ways for us to engage with those ideas, and this book is in one way a response to that, more of a lasting kind of conversation. How do you imagine continuing to respond to the transformations going on in our society, not having this book come out every twenty-four to forty-eight hours to mimic the news cycle?

Ward: Social media platforms are important because you still need to be able to respond to these things in a timely way, to be part of these needed conversations that are going on. There are kids out there who have access to social media and probably don't use it in the way that I use it, but there's still a need there for them to know that there's someone out there fighting along with them and fighting for them. It's hard to remain aware of that on social media because of how often the news cycle kicks over—people move on to different conversations and move on to different topics. The writers who've contributed to this book, their sentiments are lasting. I think they'll be just as relevant in a year, two years, three years as they are right now.

Marshell: Was the book intended as a love letter to some of those young people, young Black people, who might feel kind of at a loss?

Ward: I think so. The book's dedication, "To Trayvon Martin and the many other Black men, women, and children who have died and been denied justice for these last four hundred years," it's basically a dedication to the dead. We haven't forgotten that their loss is still very real. And I think that younger people may need that, to hear that now. It offers some form of comfort.

Marshell: Who were you intending to reach with this book? In the intro, you write, "Maybe someone who didn't perceive us as human will think differently after reading" these essays. Is that something you mean literally? Do you think the people most in need of it are perhaps trying to stay as far away as possible from literature like this?

Ward: Part of my intro was published on Lit Hub. Someone who follows Lit Hub who doesn't recognize Black people's humanity could come across that intro and read it and have their minds changed a little bit. People come across books in different ways and they might read things that they weren't expecting to read. Maybe they didn't search it out, but someone hands something to them. There's a possibility I can reach someone like that with a book like this. It was important to me that this book be able to speak to that audience even if that audience does not want to hear the message, but then also at the same time speak to Black Americans, or Americans of color, or queer Americans, people who may feel like their lives are valued less.

Marshell: Reading as a Black person who's already aware of these issues, I found myself thinking that Black people can take certain conversations for granted. Maybe we assume that we already know what microaggressions are, we already know what it's like to experience racism. But reading about it in such detail, as in Garnette Cadogan's essay on walking, "Black and Blue," was so visceral to me, even though I already know about stop-and-frisk. It felt like I was learning about it for the first time because I could see how deeply and intricately it affected him.

Ward: Nonfiction can be just as powerful as fiction in that it can make somebody else's experience very real, visceral, and immediate for the reader. The process of immersing yourself in someone else's experience can be transformative. Like you say, it can make you realize things that you hadn't thought about or understand concepts that you didn't have such an intimate understanding of. It can feel like somebody else's experience is your lived experience. That was definitely one of my hopes in soliciting the writers I did.

Marshell: And how did you go about choosing these writers and working with them on the subjects that they would write about?

Ward: [*Laughs*] I feel kind of guilty about this because I didn't really offer them much direction. I told them that I wanted to complete this collection of essays about race in America, and then just asked them to write about whatever struck their fancy. Whatever they were wrestling with, obsessing over, that had to do with race in America today. I chose writers who I admire for their boldness, for their fearlessness, their courage, for how insightful their work can be. I feel lucky that we received the caliber of work that we did.

Marshell: And there are a lot of poets, writing poetry as well as prose. What was the decision behind including poems in the book?

Ward: I love poetry. In some ways, I think of myself as a failed poet because I didn't pursue poetry. The subject matter is really raw around race in America, and around police brutality, and the worth of Black lives.

I kept encountering this great poetry, partly through Twitter. People would post links to these fantastic poems and I thought, *Wouldn't it be cool if we included poetry in this anthology? I mean, why not?* The poems are doing some of the same work as the essays. My editor also loves poetry, so it wasn't hard to convince her. I was happy about that.

Marshell: The other theme I got from the book was one of hope. Do you feel like something's changing right now in our society? Or do you think it's temporary, people's anger over the most recent cases of injustice?

Ward: I do think there's a shift happening—it seems like people are mobilizing more. I graduated from high school in the mid-1990s, and then I was in undergrad in the late nineties and then went back to school in the early 2000s. The people I knew who were having these types of conversations, about race and power and about the devaluation of different kinds of people, were marginalized when I was younger. It doesn't seem like that's the case now. There's a wider audience for those voices, and they've shifted to the center of the conversation, whereas before they were on the fringes of the conversation. There's cause for hope in that. At times I feel naive for feeling some hope because I know plenty of people who don't have it. But it's necessary to me. I feel that way in my personal life, and I feel that really strongly in the writing that I do too.

Marshell: In your piece in the book, you write about learning your genetic makeup, your ancestral breakdown, if you will. Did you feel any kind of nervousness about sharing that your ancestry was mostly not African?

Ward: It was a bit jarring for me when I got those results back. This part of my identity that was really important suddenly seemed challenged in a way, I guess, with those results, when I looked at the percentages. But then I looked at my life and the lives of the people around me, and thought about their experience, and I realized that the results I got back didn't change anything. We have lived for generations as Black people in the South, and when people look at me, they see a Black person. That will be the same for my children, and acknowledging that and claiming that is empowering.

I think about what other routes I could have taken or what other choices I could have made when I got those results back. Well now I'm going to explicitly state that I'm multiracial and everything, right? But that hasn't been my experience; that hasn't been part of the life that I've lived. When I move through my community, when I walk down the street in New Orleans, when I'm doing whatever I'm doing back home in Mississippi, that's just not how I'm perceived. The life that I've lived, and the lives of my family members over generations, we are Black Americans. I'm going to continue to live that.

Literary Voice of the Dirty South: An Interview with Jesmyn Ward

Danille K. Taylor / 2016

This interview was originally conducted by Danille K. Taylor and published in the *CLA Journal* vol. 60, no. 2, December 2016. Reprinted with permission.

Attendees of the seventy-sixth CLA convention in Houston were captivated by the powerful and moving speech given by author Jesmyn Ward. Author of two novels, *Where the Line Bleeds* (2008) and *Salvage the Bones* (2010), and a memoir, *Men We Reaped: A Memoir* (2014), Ward is a burgeoning contributor to the African American women's literary canon. Her work has received widespread recognition. *Salvage the Bones* won the 2011 National Book Award for Fiction and the American Library Association Alex Award. *Men We Reaped: A Memoir* won the Heartland Prize for Nonfiction and was a finalist for the Dayton Literary Peace Prize and the National Book Critics Circle for Autobiography. *Where the Line Bleeds* won the Virginia Commonwealth University Cabell First Novelist Award and was a finalist for the Hurston/Wright Legacy Award. The Mississippi Gulf Coast native received her BA from Stanford and MFA from the University of Michigan. She held a Stegner Fellowship at Stanford University and the Grisham Writer in Residence at the University of Mississippi. She currently teaches creative writing at Tulane University in New Orleans.

I was drawn to this award-winning author after reading *Salvage the Bones*—a depiction of Hurricane Katrina survivors in a small Mississippi town. I was working at Dillard University in New Orleans in the summer of 2005, and I vividly remember traveling through Mississippi along I-10 and stopping at the Waffle House near Biloxi. The cars were streaming east at a steady pace in the predawn hours, and my waitress commented on the heavy traffic, seemingly oblivious to the approaching storm. I was troubled and wondered what happened to her. After the storm, I drove several times from Atlanta to New

Orleans and once got off the interstate to witness the devastation in the coastal communities: they experienced a tsunami. Only steps told you where homes once stood. Who would tell this story? Jesmyn is the answer.

When I became chair of the seventy-sixth convention, I was eager to invite Jesmyn Ward to share her gifts with the body. What follows is our email interview, responses to the questions I sent her. Ward is the editor of *The Fire This Time: A New Generation Speaks About Race* (2016) anthology. Released on August 2, *The Fire This Time* features essays and poems from multicultural writers including Edwidge Danticat, Daniel José Older, Clint Smith, Claudia Rankine, and Isabel Wilkerson. I am grateful she was able to spare the time to respond to my questions.

Danille K. Taylor: You've been asked about the influence of William Faulkner on your work, but I'd like for you to discuss the influence of African American writers on your writing. Who did you read first that had an impact upon you? How do you see your writing in relationship to African American women writers like Zora Neale Hurston, Margaret Walker, or Alice Walker who are Southern, or does that matter?

Jesmyn Ward: Zora Neale Hurston and Alice Walker are two Black Southern writers who have been very influential to me. I first read Alice Walker's *The Color Purple* sometime in junior high or high school, and it was a revelation. It helped me to realize that African American Southern women writers existed, and not only that, they also wrote about Black Southern women. When I read that book, I realized that what I thought had been impossible was actually possible. And I also realized that characters like me existed in books. I'd been so starved for fictional representation, and it was such a relief to find it. I felt the same when I read *Their Eyes Were Watching God*: that affirmation that it was possible.

DT: Your writing is very grounded in the Gulf Coast with fluid movement from New Orleans to Mississippi communities. What have you discovered through the process of your writing about this region and its people? What is your question, and have you found the answer?

JW: I discovered that there are countless human dramas, countless stories worthy of being told right here. Again, I keep circling back to representation. To what we see reflected back to us in our media, in literature, on film. There was such a dearth of stories about people like me that I encountered when I was growing up, so when I first began writing seriously and learning how to be a better writer, I thought no one would want to read anything I wrote, especially if it was about people like me. It took me a long

48 CONVERSATIONS WITH JESMYN WARD

time to unlearn that and to reach a point where I can confidently say that our lives are just as human and complicated and fascinating as anyone else's. I have so many questions. One of the most important is about how history bears in the present. How does the past bear fruit? And why are we often so blind to it? I find myself writing around that question again and again with different sets of characters.

DT: What is your response to the idea I presented in my conference paper of you being part of the "Dirty South"? What does that term mean to you, and is it accurate? How do women artists fit into this cultural paradigm?

JW: I love the idea that my work is part of the Dirty South. My idea of the Dirty South is that there's a certain rawness to the art that comes out of it. A certain honesty. A willingness to bring secrets and despair and hope and all those other messy human emotions to life. To express what it means to be born and grow up into the cycle of poverty that has been bequeathed to so many of us. And finally, to reckon with how growing up in this place has affected us, and how we fight against it, sometimes foolishly, sometimes foolhardily, but always with a kind of courage born of desperation. I think that women can speak to those issues just as well as men. The hardships of this life don't discriminate by gender.

DT: Your books are filled with a variety of male characters who are brothers, sons, lovers, and friends who you have been asserting "lives matter." Have the rest of us just become conscious of the slaughter, and how is it impacting your generation?

JW: I don't think it's shocking or surprising for many. I meet so many people in my travels, at book events, readers who approach me and tell me their personal stories of loss. Who've lost brothers and fathers and sons and sisters and mothers. I've heard these stories in Boston and Houston and Atlanta and Los Angeles. I think that the advent of multiple social media platforms means that this generation has the kind of access to an audience that others haven't, and I think this is galvanizing my generation. That it is moving them to activism. That they are realizing the power of voice. It's one of the things I wanted to tap into with *The Fire This Time*, this multitude of voices speaking the truth. Calling for justice. Reckoning. Recognition that we are human beings.

DT: And finally what frames your writing; do you write from a visual or tactile sense? Is there a rhythm or sound that you hear that culturally frames your work: hip-hop, blues?

JW: I actually can't write to music. It muddles my sentences and confuses the rhythm of my paragraphs. I have to write in silence. But I am aware that

I'm trying to tap into that same fountain of emotion and feeling that comes when people listen to music that speaks to them, when people listen to hip-hop and blues and soulful R&B, when I write.

DT: Tell us whatever you'd like about *The Fire This Time.*

JW: It's a great book that I'm so honored to be a part of. There are so many fantastic writers in this collection, and I'm so grateful that their essays and poems are so thoughtful and so full of courage. None of them shied away from material that was painful for them or that made them vulnerable. It's such a dynamic collection of ideas, of statements. Again, I'm just so happy I was able to help usher it into the world.

Haunted by Ghosts:
The Millions Interviews Jesmyn Ward

Adam Vitcavage / 2017

This interview was originally conducted by Adam Vitcavage and published on *The Millions* on September 11, 2017. Reprinted with permission.

Jesmyn Ward hadn't realized it's been more than half a decade since her National Book Award–winning *Salvage the Bones* made her a literary star. That's because she has been extremely busy, both professionally and personally.

Since her Hurricane Katrina–centric novel, the author wrote the raw and emotional *Men We Reaped*, a memoir about losing five family members and friends to drugs, suicide, and accidents that can only happen to young, poor Black men. She also edited *The Fire This Time*, an essay and poetry collection about race and identity written by this generation's brightest talents. She also moved with her husband and children back to DeLisle, Mississippi, the small, poverty-stricken town where she grew up. She lived there and survived Hurricane Katrina [after] going to Stanford and the University of Michigan to pursue higher education.

Even though Ward was busy producing nonfiction, readers anxiously awaited her fiction follow up to *Salvage the Bones*. Ward's third novel, *Sing, Unburied, Sing*, returns to similar settings and themes as her previous works but is wholly original. Set in modern Mississippi, the novel follows Jojo, a thirteen-year-old of mixed race, and his drug addict mother as they drive to pick up his father from state prison. The mix of harsh reality and magical realism creates a sense of wonderment that makes readers question what they know about identity.

Ward and I spoke via phone about racial tensions, why history is so important, how hurricanes affect those who survive them, as well as what she hopes readers will remember about her novels.

The Millions: I wanted to start our conversation with *Salvage the Bones*. It came out in 2011 and won the National Book Award. It's been a little more than half a decade, and I was curious about how your relationship with the book or the characters has changed since the book's release.

Jesmyn Ward: I didn't realize it had been so long. That's so crazy. My characters remain with me in one way or another even after I'm done. I don't know if I'll ever return to those characters in a sequel, but I definitely still think about them. Especially now with Hurricane Harvey and Houston or whenever we encounter another hurricane and we witness the kind of devastation we are witnessing right now. I think about them lately because I wonder if people who read the book and read about this family who couldn't leave see what is happening currently and think about *Salvage the Bones* and those characters.

Those characters still live with me. I still think about Skeet, Esch, and Big Henry. I actually roped them into the end of *Sing, Unburied, Sing*, and it was nice to see them again. Part of the reason it's been a surprise to me that it's been so long since *Salvage* was published is because whenever I think about those characters, I can only age them by a couple of years. It's hard for me to think of where they'd be now, eleven years later after Hurricane Katrina.

That showed up in *Sing* because when I was writing that moment when Esch showed up, I felt she was two years older than she was at the end of *Salvage* and my editor, of course, caught it. She pointed out that the character would need to be ten years older now. She hadn't aged at all in my head. Maybe that's a deficiency on my part because I can't age them. They live with me, though, as they existed in their books.

TM: Were you working on *Sing, Unburied, Sing* during the entire time since *Salvage*?

JW: No, not really. After I finished the rough draft of *Salvage the Bones*, which was in 2009, I began working on *Sing, Unburied, Sing*, but it was a very different book then. When I say I was working on it, I meant I was working on unsuccessful first chapter after unsuccessful first chapter. Jojo's character was the only character that was present and real to me at that time. I didn't know anything about his mom, his dad, or the rest of his family. In the beginning, his mom was white [as opposed to Black in the final version]. My understanding of who the members of his family are changed a lot. I couldn't write a good first chapter when I didn't have a clear understanding of who the other characters were. I spent a good four or five months writing bad first chapter after bad first chapter.

52 CONVERSATIONS WITH JESMYN WARD

Then I decided I should work on what would become the memoir *Men We Reaped*. I just put those bad first chapters away. I set Jojo aside and worked on the memoir. Following that, I edited the collection *The Fire This Time*. While I was working on *The Fire This Time* was when I started working on this novel again. I did take a substantial break, but I came back to it again.

It was very hard with me for *Sing* to find a successful entryway into the story. I think part of the reason it was difficult was because I couldn't figure out who the people around Jojo should be and who they were. That's where I start: I need a vague understanding of who the most important characters are and what their motivations are. That was very hard for me to pin down with this book. It took me a long time.

After I finished *Men We Reaped* was when I returned to Jojo. I threw out everything I had before, and I just started again. Once I figured out who Leonie, Pop, and Mam were, I gained some traction. I used the momentum to move into the second chapter. Then I was able to move through that first rough draft.

TM: This novel has a very serious, realistic undertone, but it also has this notion of ghosts and magical realism thrown in. When did that come into play with the story?

JW: From the very beginning, I knew that Leonie was seeing a phantom. In the very beginning, she was seeing a phantom of Michael. For the first four chapters of the rough draft, she was seeing a phantom of Michael, and it just wasn't working. I figured out it wasn't working because his presence didn't add to the understanding of who she was. Leonie was a very difficult character for me to write because I couldn't figure out what was motivating her to be such a horrible parent and sometimes a horrible person. All that told me about her was that she was in love with this man and perhaps she was hallucinating because of the drugs she was using. It didn't tell me anything that I already didn't know about her and who she loved and valued. It felt like something was wrong.

Then I began rethinking that phantom of someone she actually lost; not just a man she loved who was in prison. What if it was a family member she lost? That's when I stumbled upon the fact that she would have lost a brother and that it was his ghost she was seeing.

Instead of going back and correcting that in the first four chapters I had already written, I wrote going forward with that idea that the phantom was her brother. I wrote with that assumption and suddenly she began to work for me as a character. She took on new life. I understand her motivation. I understood the pain in her heart that she carried with her. By her not dealing with that pain, it feeds into how selfish and egotistical she is. It makes her a worse parent because she's so wrapped up in this pain that she isn't able to resolve. That's when I knew there was one ghost: the ghost of her dead brother. At the same time I was working on the beginning of this, I read about Parchman Prison. I came across this bit that there were Black boys as young as twelve that were charged with petty crimes and spent time in Parchman. I read that, and I knew how brutal the prison was, and that fact was heartbreaking.

I wanted a child to be part of my novel and be present in the moment. I figured the only way I can make that happen was to make him a ghost. I wanted him to exist in the present moment and not just exist in a flashback. I wanted him to be able to interact with Jojo.

TM: When I was reading *Sing*, I thought a lot about *The Turner House* and *Swamplandia!* Is this idea of ghosts, ghost stories, and the past a part of everyday life in Southern or Black culture?

JW: I think that ghosts are embodiments of the past. Especially here in the South because we're so close to the past. So much of the past lives in the present. We live with the ramifications of the past that might not be as clear or feel as present in the rest of the country.

I sit and think of the furor we live with regarding Confederate monuments and the endless debates about whether or not to take them down. I think about all of the advocacy and opposition. We're still dealing with monuments from a war that happened 150, 160 years ago. The violence that surrounds that history is still very present.

In the South, we may not talk about it or it may not be a part of public conversation around these issues, but the underlying understanding is that the history of this region bears very heavily on the present and informs our actions. I think the ghost story form is a great way to explore and express that.

TM: You've been very outspoken about racial tension in America. I know the media is discussing this more, but I think there is still a disconnect where most of the country doesn't really understand what it's like to be in these situations. Do you think about this when you're writing?

JW: I do. It influences my work because my awareness of history and the legacy of racist violence in this country bears heavily on my thinking when I'm casting about for ideas for my novels. I'm always thinking about race, violence, the history of the South, and how that history bears on the present.

I saw Ann Patchett speak ten or fifteen years ago, and one thing she mentioned in her speech was how she thought writers write the same book over and over again because they're obsessed with the same ideas. Those ideas

54 CONVERSATIONS WITH JESMYN WARD

always surface in each story they write. As I've written more fiction and creative nonfiction, I've found that is true in my case. I'm always thinking about how Black people survive. How people are marginalized in the South and the way they still survive that oppression.

I do have to say that when I'm writing and I've immersed myself in that world with those characters, then I am just thinking about the characters in the story and who they are and how they are evolving. I'm trying to find the important moments in their lives—moments beyond which nothing is the same. That's what I'm thinking about when I'm writing. I'm not thinking about themes or symbolism. When I'm actually writing, I'm just thinking about the people.

I think about the issues and big ideas when I'm thinking about novel ideas, but once I begin writing, I throw that all out the window because the work is able to come alive, and these people are able to live when you immerse yourself in the world.

TM: Earlier you mentioned how devastating Hurricane Harvey is to the people of Texas. I know you were still living in the Mississippi Gulf Coast when Hurricane Katrina hit. If you don't mind, I was just curious what life was like for residents after the media and most of the country move on from these tragic events? What do families go through? What is it like having to restart?

JW: It's really difficult. Donations do make a difference because they help people who are attempting to rebuild their lives. Habitat for Humanity did a lot of work here after Hurricane Katrina. They rebuilt a lot of homes. It's a hard question to answer because a lot of people had house insurance and made house insurance claims, but that didn't work for everyone. Some claims were denied on technicalities. A lot of the rebuilding that people had to do down here was out of their own pockets. It was a slow process. They rebuilt as they were able to slowly save the money that they needed to rebuild.

That's one of the reasons a hurricane appears out in the Gulf—and I don't want anyone to go through the pain we went through—but I'm always grateful when the hurricanes don't come for us. I still feel like a decade after Katrina, we're not ready. There was just extreme flooding in New Orleans two or three weeks ago from just a bad rainstorm. The streets were flooding, and homes were damaged. It's a hard question for me to answer because it's still a continuous process.

TM: Your memoir came out between *Salvage* and *Sing*. Do you ever think about more memoirs on different topics?

JW: Right now, no. I really don't want to write another memoir. There are many reasons for that. *Men We Reaped* was the hardest book I've ever written. It required that I make myself vulnerable. It required that I make the members of my family vulnerable. I had to tell the truth and reveal all of these secrets about our lives, and that was very hard to do. I don't know if I can do that again.

It was important to me because I had to write that book to tell my brother's story. I had to tell the story about my friends and my cousin. *Men We Reaped* came out before Black Lives Matter was a movement. I almost feel like at that time I was trying to express the sum of the opinions that Black Lives Matter has expressed, but I didn't have the vocabulary to do so. That book was difficult to write because I didn't have that vocabulary to write about these people that I loved and lost.

Fiction is easier than creative nonfiction for me. Creative nonfiction is hard for me in general, whether it's essays or a book-length memoir because I tend to shy away from the pain of what I'm writing about. It makes me write around my subject instead of focusing. Creative nonfiction is a lot of work for me and my editors because they have to make me focus on whatever I'm trying to avoid in the piece I'm working on.

So, no, I don't want to tackle another nonfiction book, but who knows in twenty years?

TM: Is it going to be another half decade before your next work of fiction comes out?

JW: I have something percolating, but it's probably going to take me some time to finish. It might be another four or five years before it comes out. I'm writing the first chapter of the rough draft. I'm at the very beginning of the process.

The novel is set in New Orleans at the height of the domestic slave trade during the early 1800s. It's unlike anything I've ever written before. It's definitely challenging me as a writer and as a human being because the main characters in this are people who were enslaved. It's really hard to sit with that. The subject matter is making it hard for me to write this novel. Hopefully it will be done in four or five years. That's including the rough first draft and multiple revisions of that.

TM: What is your hope of what people walk away with after they finish *Sing, Unburied, Sing*?

JW: I hope that the characters stay with them. That Jojo, Leonie, Kayla, Ritchie, and Pop stay with them. That next time readers encounter an older Black gentleman in the grocery story or the next time they unfortunately see a fourteen- or fifteen-year-old Black boy like Jojo dead from police violence that maybe it's a bit more painful and a bit more prevalent for them because they've seen the humanity in the characters I've written. Maybe that makes it a little easier for them to see humanity and personhood.

Powell's Interview: Jesmyn Ward, Author of *Sing, Unburied, Sing*

Rhianna Walton / 2017

This interview was originally conducted by Rhianna Walton on August 8, 2017, and published on the Powell's Books Blog on August 29, 2017. Reprinted with permission of Powell's Books.

Jesmyn Ward's new novel, *Sing, Unburied, Sing*, is a taut triumph, rich with the poetry and political nuance for which her award-winning fiction is known. Set in the rural woods of Bois Sauvage, a bayou town in the Mississippi Gulf, the novel follows thirteen-year-old Jojo and his family as they deal with a maelstrom of terminal illness, poverty, drug addiction, child abuse, incarceration, and racism. The characters' struggles are by turns eased and complicated by the ghosts who haunt the forests and fields of Mississippi and by their connections to the flora and fauna of the Gulf. Inspired by both the present-day realities of African American life in the rural South and the spiritual and folk traditions of voodoo and hoodoo, *Sing, Unburied, Sing* tells a story that is both specific and universal, about how the lives we lead are influenced by the natural world and the open wounds of our shared, often brutal, national history. Vivid, sharp, and instantly engaging, *Sing, Unburied, Sing* is a powerful work by one of America's foremost novelists. We're excited to present it as volume 69 of *Indiespensable*.

Rhianna Walton: The promotional copy for *Sing, Unburied, Sing* markets it as "the archetypal road novel," but that label feels inaccurate to me. While the family's trip to Parchman takes up a significant portion of the novel, the main object of a typical journey—to get from Point A to Point B and back again—relies on linear notions of space and time that are inconsistent with your novel's focus on the simultaneity of the past, present, and future. Additionally, in a standard road novel, the protagonists encounter characters and situations that change them, so that the people they were when the journey began are not the same people who return home. But in *Sing, Unburied, Sing*, it seems like it's their experiences at home that alter the characters. What's your take on reading *Sing, Unburied, Sing* as a road novel?

Jesmyn Ward: That's an interesting question because when I began writing the rough draft of the novel, I thought it would be a novel about a journey or a road trip novel. Then I realized I had to do research for the novel because I knew nothing about Parchman prison. Once I began reading about the history of Parchman Farm in Mississippi and discovered that there actually were twelve- and thirteen-year-old Black boys sent to Parchman in the late 1930s through [the] '50s, that fact was so horrible and striking to me that I realized that one of those kids had to be a character in my book. That character had to exist in the present and not just in memory because I really wanted to give him the opportunity to live in the present and to speak.

Once I discovered that, early on in the first draft, I realized that there would be ghosts in my novel. I didn't really know what [Richie] wanted when I introduced him. As I wrote more and got deeper into the manuscript and the story took on a life of its own, I began to figure out what he wanted.

My understanding of what the novel was about changed as I wrote it. I would agree with you that it's not just a story about a journey, that it has become something more. Much of what is important to the characters happens at home once they've returned.

Walton: Regarding the importance of home, I kept thinking about the notion of "terroir" while I was reading *Sing, Unburied, Sing*. The ways in which Jojo and his family are tied to the land and water of the Gulf—and then the way the land and water are peopled by the ghosts of history—made it feel as though the characters and certain events in the novel could only occur in Bois Sauvage. that there is a very specific quality to the soil, air, and sea there, born of both natural and historical conditions. Could you speak to the importance of place in *Sing, Unburied, Sing*?

Ward: When I first began writing the book, I didn't really realize that one of the things that most of the characters are searching for is home. They all have different understandings of what home is and of what it can be and what it means, but in some way that's what they're all searching for.

It's true that those definitions of home are very particular to this place and to the Gulf Coast—not only to the Gulf Coast, but also to the history of Mississippi. I do think that this is a story that could only happen here.

I hope, though, that although readers see that this is a story that can only happen here, they can also identify with the search for home, as well—that they understand that it's universal. It's funny, because like I said, I didn't understand that that's what Richie was searching for from the very beginning. Even though he said, "I'm going home," when I first introduced his character, I didn't understand what home was for him.

Walton: I'm not sure he totally understands that. As the reader, I thought, *he's confused*. His idea of home changes.

Ward: I actually had to do a couple of revisions of the book before I began to tease out what home meant for the other characters as well. It was pretty clear for me from the beginning what home meant for Leonie, but my understanding of what home meant for Jojo changed throughout the book. As my understanding of what home meant for them changed, I think that they grew as characters. They took on new life. They became more complicated. Their inner lives were richer because they were more complicated.

Walton: One of the things I really appreciate about your writing is that every character is complex.

You mentioned—and you've said this in prior interviews, too—that you hope your stories are read as universal. I think *Sing, Unburied, Sing* does that, because although the novel felt very place-specific to me, it also deals with issues that are endemic to rural areas across the country, like poverty, child abuse, addiction, racism, violence, and incarceration.

I was wondering how incorporating the prosaic and spiritual elements of Black life on the Gulf Coast helps you process and explore Black life in America more generally, or if that's something you're even trying to do.

Ward: It's interesting, because I think that part of the reason that I wanted to incorporate spirituality into the book—so, voodoo and hoodoo—and that I wanted the characters to be able to access the supernatural world is because this is part of my characters' legacy. At the same time that they've inherited the simple facts that they live in poverty, that they are struggling against entrenched, systemic racism, they also have a different legacy. This spiritual legacy allows them not to transcend their reality, but to access a different understanding of their reality.

In some ways, it makes their reality richer because they're able to connect with those who have gone before. You know what I'm saying? I think that that allows them some joy, and some love and connection. I think that's important to their survival.

I think that because, at times, the story is very dark and the characters are living through some pretty difficult things, having that spiritual element

60 CONVERSATIONS WITH JESMYN WARD

allows them some light. I think that's important, especially if you are trying to figure out how people survive. They need some light, and that was my way of giving the characters that.

Walton: The poetic nature of your prose is something that gets brought up in a lot of reviews of your work, and a criticism that I've seen repeated is that the poetry can weigh down the narrative. I disagree! [*Laughs*] Not just because I enjoy your writing, but because the critique suggests that figurative language is somehow too decorous or fantastical for the rural characters and settings you choose for your novels. One of the things I think your lyricism does is it reminds the reader of the uniqueness and complexity of individual experience.

I was wondering if you would talk to that a little bit—if lyricism is just a part of how you write, or if you cultivate a poetic style to give your characters greater dimensionality.

Ward: I think it's a combination of the two, because I've been in lots of writing workshops and I've done a lot of reading of contemporary literature, and I know from both that the way that I write is not in vogue. People don't read me and say, "Oh, it's so clean and elegant." [*Laughs*] I understand that. I could stifle my voice, or strip it. I know that I could, because we can do anything we put our minds to.

I know that I could, but it feels very unnatural for me to strip my prose like that, in part because place is so important to me. I feel like in the reading I did when I was growing up, and also in the way that people talk and tell stories here in the South, they use a lot of figurative language. The stories that I heard when I was growing up and the stories that I read taught me to use the kind of language that I do. It's hard for me to work against that when I am writing.

I agree with you. I think that part of the pushback that I get is from people who see the kind of characters that I write about, who are mostly uneducated, poor, working class, Black. They're not voracious readers, most of the time, and because I write from a first-person point of view, people feel that the way the characters use language is too poetic.

I always think about Faulkner, and I would argue that there can be a difference between the way that characters express themselves internally and externally. I think that their interior life can be very rich and poetic, have such texture, and that their vision can be very complicated, while the way that they express themselves in their speech can be very different. You know what I'm saying? Their verbal speech can reflect more of their circumstances, but people are complicated. I don't think that the way that my characters see and experience the world should be limited by their circumstances. Faulkner taught me that.

Also, I was just thinking today about Carson McCullers. Especially with her writing, there's such a big difference between the way that characters experience the world and the richness of their interior lives and the ways that they speak to others.

Maybe this is an argument that Southern writers have had to make in their fiction for decades. I'm just one in a line of writers who are doing the same thing.

Walton: The other thing I was thinking about is that in *Sing, Unburied, Sing,* figurative language allows you to tell a very complex story in which everyday aspects of life in the rural South—poverty, addiction, etc.—are both connected to and subjected to a larger order made up of history, nature, and the supernatural. I don't know if you could do that without poetry.

Ward: Yeah, I think so. Like you're saying, the characters that I'm writing about are living through very difficult situations. They have to process them. They have to attempt to understand them. I feel like the language communicates how complicated that process is for them, how layered; they're wrestling with multiple legacies at the same time as they're attempting to understand and deal with what they're living through.

Walton: I had a hard time sympathizing with Leonie. Maybe it's because I'm a mother myself, but her selfishness and neglect of Jojo and Kayla really upset me. I wanted to feel for her for a lot of reasons: her grief over Given's death, her strong, tender relationships with Michael and Mam, her moments of self-knowledge—but in the end, I couldn't forgive her for being a drug addict and an abusive parent. That said, there's this beautiful moment at the end of the novel that feels redemptive to me. It's when Kayla soothes the tree of ghosts and mimics the way Leonie used to rub her children's backs "when we were frightened of the world." In the same scene, Jojo tells us that Kayla "says *shhh* like she remembers the sound of the water in Leonie's womb . . . and now she sings it." It's almost as if Leonie's abuse is at least partly nullified by the intrinsic goodness of mothering. I know that you're a mother, too, and I was wondering how you feel about Leonie and why it felt important to give her character a voice.

Ward: She was a really difficult character for me to write. I think, initially, because I was very aware of the fact that she was abusive to her kids and did neglect her kids. I just couldn't understand . . . I just didn't like her, and I usually love most of the major characters that I write. I always feel a deep sympathy for them. It was really hard, in the beginning, for me to

62 CONVERSATIONS WITH JESMYN WARD

access that sympathy for her. When I began to figure out who she was and I wrote the first chapter for her that really stuck, then it felt like I could progress through the novel with this character.

From the beginning, she was who she was. She was an addict. She was neglectful. She was really self-centered. One of the things that I had to do in order to avoid failing her character was to figure out what drove her, what motivated her. You've already touched on some of those, but the way that I was able to do that was by figuring out where her pain comes from. There are multiple pains that she's lived with in her young life—the loss of her brother and the fact that she feels like a disappointment to her mother and father and to her children. Once I figured all those things out, I think it was easier for me to write her, to understand and to feel some sympathy for her. Because I realized that she was wounded in ways that had never healed, that she's carrying these wounds around with her, and that that's what is motivating much of her behavior.

Then, of course, I began to understand, too, that she was who she was from the beginning. She's self-centered throughout. It's really hard for her to see beyond her own pain and mess and to be a mom—to focus on her children, and meet her children, and provide for them, to care for them, and to show that she cares for them, because of who she is, because of her personality.

By the end of the novel, that earlier distaste that I had felt for her was gone. It was really important for me to have her speak and to tell nearly half of the story from her point of view. Because she's like Esch [from *Salvage the Bones*] to me; if you just look at who she is on the surface, many readers would say, *This person doesn't deserve any sympathy.* I mean, Esch was a fifteen-year-old, poor, Black, pregnant teenager. Those kids never get to speak. They never get to be complicated and textured. They never get to tell their truth. I initially felt the same way about Leonie.

Here's this younger mother who's struggling with addiction and who, in many ways, is abusive towards her kids. This is the kind of woman we hear about on the news or whom we read inflammatory posts about on Facebook, who neglected her kid, you know, really harmed or actually killed her kid.

Those are the people that we read about and immediately feel distaste and horror for. I wanted to break that, I think. I wanted to give this character a voice so that she becomes as human as I can make her on the page. Maybe because the next time people encounter a woman like her, they'll think about her differently.

Walton: Richie's another character that I spent a lot of time thinking about. You touched on him a bit earlier. He's a lost soul, a dead boy tethered to earth by a giant hunger for love. He seems to illustrate something profound about motherhood, home, and the history of violence in the world of *Sing, Unburied, Sing*, which is that the ghosts who haunt the characters and terrain of the book haven't just died violent deaths—they also lack a mother figure to usher them "home," in the spiritual sense.

Ward: While I was writing the book, I did think about mothers and motherhood. I feel like that's something that I write about often. I guess it's one of those ideas that I return to again and again in my work.

Richie was interesting for me because he'd been failed in multiple ways, too, while he was alive. His mother wasn't a good mother to her children. There's that line toward the end where Pop is saying that when he went and found Richie's mom and told her what happened, she just shut the door in his face. There's no outpouring of grief—her response is, in some ways, very cold. Part of the reason why I gave him a mother like that is because I felt like he had to have a reason to still exist here on this plane and to search.

If he'd had a better mother who really gave him a home, I think, and who was his home, then perhaps he would have stuck around, despite his death being so horrible and the crimes done to him when he was sent to Parchman. Maybe he would have returned to her and that place and found some peace. Because she isn't that type of mother and because she doesn't provide him with that idea of home, he goes elsewhere. He can't rest. He can't return to her and to the place where he was with his siblings. For Richie, the person who came the closest to providing him with that feeling of home, of being safe, cared for, and loved, was River, and that's who he's searching for.

That's why he is drawn to Jojo. That's why he gets in the car. That's why he goes south with them. He's still a child, even though he's existing in an afterlife, and so when he realizes that he can't interact with River and he can't get home by interacting with River, that's when he turns his attention to Mam.

It was heartbreaking for me when I discovered that she couldn't provide that for him, either.

Walton: There's a long, problematic history, going back to Petrarch, of literary authors conflating Blackness with darkness, and *Sing, Unburied, Sing* seems to be confronting and exploring this history. In the novel, as in America, Blackness is one half of a terrible racial dichotomy, which leads to many of the story's most horrifying moments, but it's also intimately tied to the novel's evocations of the earth, death, and the experience of want. Richie's character in particular is subject to shifts in light and darkness, but there are many other compelling uses of the white/black trope, like the white snake that becomes a black vulture. The novel's exploration of light and dark complicates

64 CONVERSATIONS WITH JESMYN WARD

Blackness so that it becomes a concept of cosmic proportion and significance, as well as something inseparable from soil and life, rather than simply a racial or political category. There's a lot of artistic value in this representation, but I was wondering if you intended for it to be read politically, as well?

Ward: I'd been thinking about the interplay of light and darkness while I was writing the novel. I think that it began because I was doing research about Voodoo, Hoodoo, and spirituality.

That research forced me to be aware of the way that, while darkness can be associated with death, and sorrow, and awful things, at the same time, it can also be pregnant with possibility, with life. Conversely, we're conditioned to see whiteness as light, and as pure and good. I know people have already had this conversation, but I thought it was really interesting that the symbol of the white snake is the one that's associated with the afterlife in Voodoo. From the beginning, I began to see the symbols within that spiritual tradition that are in opposition to how I'd been programmed to think about light and dark as I grew up.

I wanted to open up those ideas and play with the audience's expectations of them, maybe jar the audience a bit, because I think, at least in this culture, that most readers associate light and dark with good and evil. I thought that I could challenge those ideas in the text, in certain ways. That's what I was attempting to do.

Walton: There's a devastating scene late in the novel that recalls Sethe's actions in Toni Morrison's *Beloved* and maybe also Medea's, although it lacks the latter's spite. Then, a page later, the character adds, "I washed my hands every day, Jojo. That damn blood ain't never come out," which is a reference to Lady Macbeth.

I know you sometimes incorporate classical texts into your fiction, and was wondering if you could talk a little bit about how and why you selected these particular texts for *Sing, Unburied, Sing.*

Ward: When I wrote that line, I was sort of thinking about Lady Macbeth. Because I wrote so much about the Medea myth while I was writing *Salvage the Bones*, I was also thinking about Greek mythology, the Medea myth in particular, and maybe even about the Bible in some ways—the idea of sacrificing human beings for whatever reason.

The reason that I like to use classical myths as models is because African American writers and African American stories are usually understood as occurring in some kind of vacuum—because of slavery.

I think about slavery and entire cultures, people from those cultures, being robbed of their cultural traditions. Yet, something that is so great about

African American art is that we incorporate aspects of our lost African heritage with aspects of the various people in this country whom we've mixed with and encountered. I think that, in part, is what I am trying to argue in my work. Not overtly, but that's part of the reason I love to incorporate stories from various world cultures into my work—because that's what African American art does. It would be nice if that was more widely recognized.

Maybe part of it, too, is that by using easily recognized tropes, common stories, it will be easier for the reader to understand the characters and what they're going through in my work. I want to jostle the reader to make them realize that these are universal human issues.

Interview with Jesmyn Ward

Jennifer Baker / 2017

This interview was originally conducted by Jennifer Baker and published on the *Minorities in Publishing Podcast* on September 28, 2017. Reprinted with permission.

Jennifer Baker: Hello and welcome to the latest episode of the *Minorities in Publishing* podcast. This is Jenn, and for new and returning listeners, you may know you can find the podcast on Twitter @minoritiesinpub or on Tumblr at minoritiesinpublishing.tumblr.com. You can also find the podcast on iTunes, Google Play, and TuneIn. As always, I am excited, and I love all my guests equally, and I do use the word "excited" even more enthusiastically this episode. I know after three years you're probably thinking "find a new verb," "check your thesaurus," something—but this week's episode is Jesmyn Ward, National Book Award winner and longlisted for the National Book Award again this year for her new book, *Sing, Unburied, Sing*, which if you haven't gotten it, please go out and get it. It is amazing. Jesmyn took time out of her super busy schedule to talk to me on the phone while she's on the road and so this will be a shorter episode. And like I said, because it was on the phone, you may notice some audio variation, which I've edited as best as I could. Thank you so much Jesmyn, again, for your time and to your publicists at Scribner, Kate and Rosie, for their time in helping get this all together. Thank you and hope you enjoy this episode.

So, thank you so much Jesmyn for taking time from your super busy schedule to talk to me about your latest, *Sing, Unburied, Sing*. It's a novel I have a lot of feelings about.

Jesmyn Ward: Thank you for having me, yeah.

Baker: I think you've probably been having this conversation a lot with many people. "I have a lot of feelings about your current book." But I wanted to talk, eventually about that, but I also wanted to start off talking about— you're on sabbatical at the moment and you actually are, you're a professor of, is it English and Creative Writing?

Ward: No, just Creative Writing.

Baker: In terms of that kind of environment that you introduce to your students, because your work is so lush, it's so specific, it always invokes emotion, and I wonder if you kind of go over that in terms of, not necessarily your process, but trying to help your students find their process in terms of being new to writing, maybe they've been writing for a while but being new to the game, as someone who's been doing this for a bit.

Ward: Well, you know, when I teach I attempt to, I think, expose them to as many of young contemporary—they don't necessarily all need to be young, but as many contemporary writers as I can, because I think that often they come to me and they're well-versed in the classics but not really, you know, in like contemporary lit, so I try to switch up my syllabus every semester and just try to like introduce them to new voices so they can see what people, what other writers who would be their contemporaries, what they're writing, what they're working on, what they're thinking about. And then you know, of course my hope is that they read the work and then they find something in it that maybe that they like, that they find impressive, that maybe they want to emulate in their own work. One of the most important things that I think that I teach them early on is that, you know, that writing requires revision and that writing is a process. I teach undergrads, and so I think often undergrads don't realize that. They think when you're a writer, especially a creative writer, that you write something and it's perfect and you hit send and it goes out to the world and you know, they don't, really don't understand what a process it is and how there's an entire group of people sort of working together to revise your work, to refine your work, before it ever reaches an audience. And so, yes, I think that's one of the most important things that I attempt to teach them, right, you know, that writing requires revision, that it requires you sharing your work with a group of first readers and then, and then taking their feedback into account, right, when you're revising. I don't know, that's just, I guess, some of what I try to teach them, because I know that reading is very important to my process and also revision is very important to my process.

Baker: And do you ever broach the subject of the business or do you kind of concentrate on the craft itself? Because I know when I was an undergrad, we didn't really talk about the business of writing. We were talking about trying to figure out what the topics were. I think in terms of those discussions we saw a lot of trauma brought up in the creative writing workshop because people wanted to get those immediate reactions to work, and we didn't discuss so much about what that can mean in terms of marketing and publicity, but really what are you doing and why did you choose to have trauma be the introductory way of seeing these characters, or why were five people all writing about sexual assault? It was very interesting what we saw. There were these consistent themes that came up in the workshop, and I wonder, like, do you ever broach the business side or really try to help them ease in? Because it sounds like you're talking mostly about craft, but I wondered if business ever came into it, too.

Ward: I mean, we mostly talk about craft in my courses, but I do always on the last day of class or the next to last day of class, I just normally set that day aside just for any questions that they might have about the business of being a writer and the business of publishing and, you know, and then they can ask me anything and so, you know, on that day. So we at least devote, at least one class period to talking about the business of writing, talking about what it's like to find an agent, what it's like to work with an agent, what it's like to, you know, work with a publishing company and, yeah. Yeah, so I try to do some of that, but the majority of what we do is all about learning about craft.

Baker: In terms of your own craft and your own schedule being, again you're on sabbatical right now, but when you do teach, how do you balance that? Or is balance kind of a wrong word that people use when they kind of think everything is doable, but how do you find that balance of writing, working, also being a mom, traveling when you do have books out? Do you have specific schedules? Do you have like these niche times you always carve out for yourself, or is it kind of like Jason Reynolds, he does it whenever he gets a chance to?

Ward: When I'm traveling, I just do it whenever I get a chance to. Hypothetically I guess I could be better about it, but I know that Nikky Finney, when she's traveling, she's writing. She writes every day—wakes up super early in the morning and she does it, but I can't. I don't. I just, my brain is not working at five a.m. It's just not. I can't produce anything that early in the morning so, you know, I write whenever I can when I'm traveling. When I'm home and when I'm teaching—when I return to teaching in fall of 2018, both of my kids will be in—well, one will be in kindergarten and the other will be in preschool, so that will be really helpful because I will have time during the day to work, and so, you know, once I drop my kids off, I bring them to school, then I can spend at least two hours a day, sometimes more than that, sometimes three or four working in the morning, from eight until noon. And when they're not in school, then I try to—my kids sleep late, which is good, because then I'll wake up early in the morning before they get up and I'll get at least an hour, sometimes two hours' worth of writing in, and so that's also helpful. You know, teaching is something that I have to work really hard at. Teaching doesn't come easily to me, so I do put in the work. Sometimes in the daytime hours, I might cut my writing session a little short because planning, lesson planning or lecture planning, or something to do. I tend to prioritize writing, you know, so I will always devote more time to that, but I try to treat my writing as a job in some respect. As in this is something that I have to do for so many hours every day, in the same way that I also have to do prep work for teaching, but I try to carve out more space for writing.

Baker: Tying back into mothers and motherhood, I feel—and I don't know if you agree or disagree—and I was thinking a lot about the discussion you had with Lisa Lucas when you were at the Schomberg of motherhood. You know, the reality of Black bodies, and I write a lot about that, but also Black motherhood and those kinds of stereotypes we have. You know, like the Mammy character that is so indelible into what we see even at the supermarket and that kind of automatic assumption of caregiver in terms of Black women and Black mothers specifically, and you have this juxtaposition in *Sing, Unburied, Sing* I felt, and Leonie is a very raw character and she was a very well-drawn character, and obviously she's someone we feel a lot of things for, she invokes a lot of reactions from us, because I had my own specific reactions, and I'm sure everyone has been telling you that as well, and that speaks to the powerfulness of the prose. And I wanted to ask you, as a mother writing a character like Leonie and also writing Jojo and Pop and Mam, how do you kind of converge upon getting them all on the page in such a way that you feel like you can step away and effectively say, that's what I was going for? Or do you even recognize that's what you were going for?

Ward: I don't know. I think that it is an organic process. I mean, I think that as I write, especially through the first draft, you know, like the rough draft, that I'm discovering who the characters are, that they're just taking on some kind of life on the page and off the page as I'm writing my way into the story.

Because the process of writing about them complicates them, and they do things that surprise me as a writer, and so yes, I think that when I commit to writing a story that, you know, part of what I'm really focused on, a part of what I'm committed to doing, when I am interested in telling a story, is to bring all the characters to life in one respect or another and make them complicated and as human as I can on the page. You know, and so they take on shape, but they continue to take on shape even after I'm done with the rough draft, so when I'm going back into a draft and then revising and revising, I mean, they're still, I'm still adding more dimensions. I'm still complicating

70 CONVERSATIONS WITH JESMYN WARD

them again and again and again, so it's a continuous thing, right? It's a continuous task to complicate my characters and to, you know, make them more human, more believable, more, more surprising, I think. So like human beings are surprising in that you never fully know, you never fully know a human being so, you know, that's why I think for *Sing, Unburied, Sing,* that's why I think that a thirteen-year-old boy, Jojo, that he can be at the same time that he's like, learning how to be a man. And that part of learning how to be a man is to suppress his emotion and stand up straight and to walk a certain way and to act a certain way in violent situations, but at the same time, he can also care for his little sister and nurture his little sister and be very maternal in a lot of ways. And I think that that happened over, you know, multiple drafts of the work, as I revisited him again and again and again, and, you know, my understanding of the story became more complicated.

Baker: I remember that awareness of what is "expected" or the stereotypes or these assumptions made, especially about Black life; [are they] ever in your mind when you're writing, or are you able to block that out? Because I find that I'm often thinking about how not to do things, and that can actually inhibit the process. I wonder, do you ever think about that, or just let it pretty much flow and then think about that later on when you're talking with people about the book where you're getting reactions from editors and agents about the book?

Ward: That's an interesting question. I don't think about what not to do. I think, you know, like I really focus on the situation that the characters find themselves in, and I focus on the place where they're from, and I take all of that with me to the text as I'm trying to understand who the characters are, right, because those things, place and the circumstance, right, of course that influences them, that determines certain aspects of their personality. So yes, I think that's what I really focus on. That's what I think about. I try to always think in, I don't know, terms of positives instead of negatives. I try to think in terms of like, dimensions and adding dimensions and I want to add this, I want to do this, I want this person to look at the world and understand it in this prism, and that just works for me in my process. Thinking about audience and about, perhaps, what they expect to see in my characters or what they understand of them, like, I can't, I can't do that. I have to forget all that, because it makes me so anxious, right, like being aware of audience and what they might hypothetically want. If I'm aware of that, then I feel like I lose my focus a bit, you know, and I'm not focusing on rendering these characters on the page, rendering the story on the page because I'm too worried about reception, so I tend to avoid thinking about that.

Baker: Something else I noticed is, I don't want to say it's a theme, but I feel like this is so true of Black life or at least maybe working-class Black life or how one might want to word it, is the need for the younger characters to grow up quickly. And I wonder if that's kind of indicative of being a Black child in America and that was referenced in some of the essays in *The Fire This Time* as well as we're not seen as children. We're seen as threats and that was such a big part of, especially in your introduction, *The Fire This Time*, and that really struck me in *Salvage the Bones*, but also here with Jojo of that road trip they took, of the consistency of him having to be the adult when he is surrounded, theoretically, by adults.

Ward: By adults, yeah. No, I mean, I think that's true. Yes, I think that's true. I think that Black children in America are not seen as, they're not afforded the gifts of childhood, you know. They're not seen as children, like you said, like they're seen as threats. They're seen as adults. That assumption there that they can handle whatever burdens. There's a thoughtlessness to it, right? I mean, especially when I think about like Leonie and the way that she treats her children, there's a thoughtlessness to it. Childhood for her is not some sort of sacred space. She believes the world is a harsh place and so therefore Jojo should be, you know, aware of that fact and treated accordingly, you know, from the time that he's eight, nine years old, and I think that that assumption on her part, that that's telling, and that's like symptomatic of like the larger, of our larger culture. I mean, not just like Black families and Black parents and, you know, Black parental figures, but also the culture as a whole. And I think that, you know, I think that some more thoughtful Black parents, that's a struggle that they have, you know, that's something that they have to actively push back, you know, they have to actively attempt to create this space where their children are just allowed to be children. But, you know, when Tamir Rice is being murdered in a park by police for playing with a toy gun, and he's, what, twelve years old, I mean, that's harsh. You know, how do you protect your children's childhood when the world is doing everything it can to rob them of that childhood? It's tough.

Baker: I think that's also what makes this a tough but really necessary read because of the fact that we're getting it from Jojo's perspective, and I think it's very—I don't know if it's combatting, really, in terms of having Leonie and Jojo but it's seeing those moments in different eyes is so eye-opening, in a way, and also seeing how Michael treats Kayla and that is how children are doing this to be mean. You're reacting to her because she didn't want to eat and just, you know, she should've listened to me, and that automatic reaction of frustration and wondering where that comes from. Does

72 CONVERSATIONS WITH JESMYN WARD

that feel, is that a misogynist thing as well as a racial thing, as well as, I, you know, just a pent-up anger, anger management thing, and how much does that deal with the issues of seeing those children not as children but as adults or people who just need to adhere to expectations?

Ward: That is a great question. I actually never thought about it before, but I think that that is true, right, so maybe that is at the heart of the way that, you know, that Michael treats his children, that Leonie treats her children. I mean, it seems that, you know, that this idea that the larger culture has that Black children aren't really children, that that's part of we're conforming, you know, their reasoning, you know, and their treatment of their children. Yeah, I mean I think that's at the root of it all, and it reveals just how ingrained it is, you know, these characters, I don't even think they're aware—I don't think that they're consciously aware of it, but—

Baker: Yeah, they didn't seem it at all.

Ward: No, but I think that it's, because it's something that they've seen their entire lives that they accept it, you know, and they propagate it, because, because I think subconsciously part of them believes it, yeah. I mean, it's a great point.

Baker: And my last question to you is actually going back to *The Fire This Time* and I was curious about how that—I mean, your introduction was very thorough in terms of why you wanted to create this, and it's something I go back to over and over again, and as someone who is also editing an anthology and knowing how stressful that is, deadlines are movable, constantly, but how was that process for you? Especially reading the concept that you're reading and that's something I discuss a lot and I say, the strength of *The Fire This Time*, it doesn't exist to exemplify Black pain. It really expands on Black humanity because every essay isn't specifically about police brutality. It's about our humanity, it's about where we came from, it's about our experiences, and having that range is what I think makes it one of the best tomes that I've read in the past year and one I consistently teach and discuss and talk about with people.

Ward: Well, thank you. I mean, that was one of the joys of that project because I did get such a wide range of responses from the writers that I worked with, and I think that one of the reasons that I did was because, you know, when I solicited work from them just, I was very vague. You know, I just said, would you like to contribute something about race in America? I mean, you can't get any more vague than that. And so people were given really like free rein, you know, to write about whatever, you know, like whatever was troubling them or whatever they were obsessed with or whatever they were passionate about. One of those things I'm very proud of about that project is that, you know, you have essays as disparate as Kevin Young's, which is like, hilarious, and all about imposters, right, and you know about race, anyways, and then you have something like the various poems, like Jericho's poems or Kima's poem, and they're all—

Baker: Claudia Rankine. And Clint's poem *whoooo*.

Ward: Exactly. And they're all totally different things.

Yeah, I don't know, I tend to agree that, I think because I wasn't directing the writers that they just naturally gravitated towards whatever they were obsessed with. And the final product you get this like wide array of experiences and opinions and just different stories that I do, I think that book does explore Black humanity, it explores Black life, Black joy that exists at the same time as pain, struggle, and triumph. I am not a natural editor, you know, it reminded me a little bit of teaching. But I felt like I had such a great group of writers that I didn't have to do much. I was sort of a coeditor because I worked with my editor on the book, you know, she was helping me and that's what she does, so she was doing a lot of training. She's training me in a way. Yeah, it wasn't an easy process, but I feel lucky because there's such a great group of folks, and they create such solid, important work that I feel like my job wasn't that hard.

Baker: Oh, that's a good thing. That's a really good thing for the editor. Yeah, 'cause that's a really, really hard part—not to say writing isn't, but editing and, yeah, emotions, yeah.

Ward: Yeah, it can be really difficult, yeah.

Baker: Yeah, especially with nonfiction, I imagine, when it's different. I mean, it's different but it's still people's words, so yeah, yeah. I'm glad I got to finally tell you how much I loved that anthology and loved what you did with it. I just adore it so much. So I'm very happy that it exists in this world.

Ward: Yeah, me too.

Baker: So, congratulations on the nomination for *Sing, Unburied, Sing*.

Ward: Yeah, that's crazy. Thank you, I'm really happy about it. Happy and also, you know, stressed-out, but also really happy.

Baker: I hope not. I just hope you get sleep. Because I'm like, writers are no good if we're not sleeping. I really hope you're getting some sleep or you will get some sleep in the next day.

Ward: Yes, yes, I don't know. I think I might be a week away. I think I'm a week out from good sleep.

Baker: I'm holding hope.

Ward: Next Friday, next Friday I think I will finally be able to rest.

Baker: Just hibernate. Jesmyn's hibernating. You can't talk to her [*laughs*].
Ward: Jesmyn's not here.

Baker: Thanks again, Jesmyn, for being on, and you can find her on Twitter @jesmimi, find her, Google her, get the book *Sing, Unburied, Sing*, get her whole catalog because it's fantastic. And I do hope you enjoyed this episode, which you can also find portions of on Electric Literature and that's at electricliterature.com. So once again, you can find the podcast on Twitter @ minoritiesinpub, on Tumblr at minoritiesinpublishing.tumblr.com, as well as iTunes, Google Play, and TuneIn. And feel free to rate the podcast as well. We'll be back. I have a slew of many new episodes to come for the remainder of the year with amazing women of color artists. And thanks so much for listening as we enter the fourth year. Take care.

Sing, Unburied, Sing:
A Conversation with Jesmyn Ward

Natalie Y. Moore / 2017

This interview was originally conducted by Natalie Y. Moore and published on Family Action Network (FAN) on October 7, 2017. The transcript below was transcribed (by the editor of this series) from a video recording and may omit filler phrases for clarity and conciseness. Printed with permission of Lonnie Stonitsch, executive director of Family Action Network.

Natalie Y. Moore: So Jesmyn's going to start off with a reading and then we'll jump into some questions; she might do another reading while we talk, but we'll have plenty of time for her Q&A.

Jesmyn Ward: First of all, I'd like to say thank you all for coming; thank y'all for being here. (I have to angle myself this way so you can hear me on the mic.) I thought that I'd read two small sections from the beginning, right, so from the first chapter, which is JoJo's chapter. Jojo is one of the main protagonists of the novel; he's a thirteen-year-old mixed-race boy growing up on the Mississippi Gulf Coast. His mom is named Leonie; she's somewhat absent, so because she's absent (she's also a drug addict), he's being raised by his mother's father and his mother's mother, so his maternal grandparents, Pop and Mam. Jojo has a two-year-old little sister; her name is Michaela, but they call her Kayla for short, who he takes care of often. So, the first bit that I'm going to read is from his chapter; the second bit that I read is from Leonie, his mother's chapter, and much of it concerns her brother, Given; he was her older brother, and he died when they were teenagers. (I think that's all I need to tell you.) Oh, this book has a bit of magic in it, magical realism. Jojo can hear things, right, so when he's around animals, he can understand them. He feels like he can understand what they are saying to him, so that's like one of a couple of different magical elements in the book.

So, first, this is Jojo.

75

76 CONVERSATIONS WITH JESMYN WARD

[*Ward reads*]: Usually, the singing is my favorite part of my birthday, because the candles make everything look gold, and they shine in Mam's and Pop's faces and make them look young as Leonie and Michael. Whenever they sing to me, they smile. I think it's Kayla's favorite part, too, because she sings stutteringly along. Kayla's making me hold her, because she cried and pushed at Leonie's collarbone and reached for me until Leonie frowned and held her out to me, said "Here." But this year, the song is not my favorite part of my birthday because instead of being in the kitchen, we're all crowded into Mam's room, and Leonie's holding the cake like she held Kayla earlier, out and away from her chest, like she going to drop it. Mam's awake but doesn't really look awake, her eyes half open, unfocused, looking past me and Leonie and Kayla and Pop. Even though Mam's sweating, her skin looks pale and dry, like a muddy puddle dried to nothing after weeks of no rain in the summer. And there's a mosquito buzzing around my head, dipping into my ear, veering out, teasing to bite.

When the happy birthday song starts, it's only Leonie. She has a pretty voice, the kind of voice that sounds good singing low but sort of cracks on the high notes. Pop is not singing; he never sings. When I was younger, I didn't know because I'd have a whole family singing to me: Mam, Leonie, and Michael. But this year, when Mam can't sing because she's sick and Kayla makes up words to the melody and Michael's gone, I know Pop isn't singing because he's just moving his lips, lip-syncing, and there's no noise coming out. Leonie's voice cracks on *dear Joseph*, and the light from the thirteen candles is orange. No one but Kayla looks young. Pop is standing too far out of the light. Mam's eyes have closed to slits in her chalky face, and Leonie's teeth look black at the seams. There's no happiness here.

"Happy birthday, Jojo," Pop says, but he's not looking at me when he says it. He's looking at Mam, at her hands loose and open at her sides. Palms up like something dead. I lean forward to blow out my candles, but the phone rings, and Leonie jumps, so the cake jumps with her. The flames waver and feel hotter under my chin. Pearls of wax drip onto the baby shoes. Leonie turns away from me with the cake, looking to the kitchen, to the phone on the counter.

"You going to let the boy blow out his candles, Leonie?" Pop asks.

"Might be Michael," Leonie says, and then there is no cake because Leonie's taken it with her to the kitchen, set it on the counter next to the black-corded phone. The flames are eating the wax. Kayla shrieks and throws her head back. So I follow Leonie into the kitchen, to my cake, and Kayla smiles. She's reaching for the fire. The mosquito that was in Mam's room has followed us, and he's buzzing around my head, talking about me like I'm a candle or a cake. *So warm and delicious.* I swat him away.

"Hello?" Leonie says.

I grab Kayla's arm and lean into the flames. She struggles, transfixed.

"Yes" [Leonie says].

I blow.

"Baby" [Leonie says].

Half the candles gutter out.

"This week?" [Leonie says].

The other half eating wax to the nub.

"You sure?" [Leonie says].

I blow again, and the cake goes dark. The mosquito lands on my head. *So scrumptious,* he says, and bites. I swat him, and my palm comes away smeared with blood. Kayla reaches.

"We'll be there" [Leonie says].

Kayla has a handful of frosting, and her nose is running. Her blond afro curls high. She sticks her fingers in her mouth, and I wipe.

"Easy, baby, easy."

Michael is an animal on the other end of the telephone behind a fortress of concrete and bars, his voice traveling over miles of wire and listing, sun-bleached power poles. I know what he is saying, like the birds I hear honking and flying south in the winter, like any other animal. *I'm coming home* [*Sing, Unburied, Sing,* 27–30].

So this next section is written from Leonie's point of view, and it starts the night before JoJo's birthday. She's sort of telling the story of what she did the night before Jojo turned thirteen.

[*Ward reads*] Last night, he smiled at me, this Given-not-Given, this Given that's been dead fifteen years now, this Given that came to me every time I snorted a line, every time I popped a pill. He sat in one of the two empty chairs at the table with us, and leaned forward and rested his elbows on the table. He was watching me, like always. He had Mama's face.

"That much, huh?" Misty sucks snot up her nose.

"Yep" [I say].

Given rubbed the dome of his shaved head, and I saw other differences between the living and this chemical figment. Given-not-Given didn't breathe right. He never breathed at all. He wore a black shirt, and it was a still, mosquito-written pool.

"What if Michael's different?" Misty said.

"He won't be," I said.

Misty threw a wadded-up paper towel she'd been using to clean the table.

"What you looking at?" she said.

"Nothing" [I say].

"Bullshit" [she says].

"Don't nobody sit and stare for that long on something this clean without looking at something." Misty waved her hand at the coke and winked at me. She'd tattooed her boyfriend's initials on her ring finger, and for a second it looked like letters and then bugs and then letters again. Her boyfriend was Black, and this loving across color lines was one of the reasons we became friends so quickly. She often told me that as far as she was concerned, they were already married. Said she needed him because her mother didn't give a shit about her. Misty told me once that she got her period in fifth grade, when she was ten years old, and because she didn't realize what was happening to her, her body betraying her, she walked around half the day with the bloody spot spreading like an oil stain on the back of her pants. Her mother beat her in the parking lot of the school, she was so embarrassed. The principal called the cops. *Just one of the many ways I disappointed her*, Misty said.

"I was feeling it," I say.

"You know how I know you lie?" [Misty says].

"How?"

"You get dead still. People is always moving, all the time, when they speak, when they're quiet, even when they sleep. Looking off, looking at you, smiling, frowning, all of that. When you lie, you get dead still: blank face, arms limp. Like a fucking corpse. I ain't never seen nothing like it."

I shrugged. Given-not-Given shrugs. *She ain't lying*, he mouths.

"You ever see things?" I say. It's out my mouth before I have a chance to think it. But at the moment, she's my best friend. She's my only friend.

"What you mean?" [Misty says].

"When you on?" I waved my hand like she'd waved hers moments before. At the coke, which was now just a little sorry pile of dust on the table. Enough for two or three lines more.

"That's what it is? You seeing shit?" [Misty says].

"Just lines. Like neon lights or something. In the air" [I say].

"Nice try. You tried to twitch your hands and everything. Now what you really seeing?" [Misty says.]

I wanted to punch her in her face.

"I told you" [I say].

"Yeah, you lied again" [she says].

But I knew this was her cottage, and when it all came down to it, I'm Black and she's White, and if someone heard us tussling and decided to call the cops, I'd be the one going to jail. Not her. Best friend and all.

"Given," I said. More like a whisper than anything, and Given leaned forward to hear me. Slid his hand across the table, his big-knuckled, slim-boned hand, toward mine. Like he wanted to support me. Like he could be flesh and blood. Like he could grab my hand and lead me out of there. Like we could go home.

Misty looked like she ate something sour. She leaned forward and sniffed another line.

"I ain't a expert or nothing, but I'm pretty sure you ain't supposed to be seeing nothing on this shit" [she says].

She leaned back in her chair, grabbed her hair a great sheaf, and tossed it over her back. *Bishop loves it*, she'd said of her boyfriend once. *Can't keep his hands out of it*. It was one of the things she did that she was never conscious of, playing with her hair, always unaware of the ease of it. The way it caught all the light. The self-satisfied beauty of it. I hated her hair.

"Acid, yeah," she continued. "Maybe even meth. But this? No."

Given-not-Given frowned, mimicked her girly hair flip, and mouthed: *What the fuck does she know?* His left hand was still on the table. I could not reach out to it, even though everything in me wanted to do so, to feel his skin, his flesh, his dry, hard hands. When we were coming up, I couldn't count how many times he fought for us on the bus, in school, in the neighborhood when kids taunted at me about how Pop looked like a scarecrow, how Mama was a witch. How I looked just like Pop: like a burnt stick, raggedly clothed. My stomach turned like an animal in its burrow again and again, seeking comfort and warmth before sleep. I lit a cigarette.

"No shit," I said [*Sing, Unburied, Sing* 34–37].

Thank you.

Moore: What struck me early on in the reading was that this is set in present time, but it felt like the past. Did you have that feeling as you were writing; they're things like cell phones, like okay, wait, which decade are we in, but there were things like technology, so I knew that we were in present time.

Ward: I feel like one of the ideas that I'm always thinking about and always obsessing over whenever I'm writing, even when I'm writing fiction and when I'm writing creative nonfiction, too, is I'm always thinking about time. And I'm thinking about the past and the present and how, at least the way that I understand it—in the South—that time is not a linear thing, that everything seems to be happening at the same time and that the past bears so heavily on the present. Even though I feel like we live in a culture that chooses not to think about time in that way and that so many people sort of assume that what happened in the past happened in the past and has no bearing on the present. And I just feel like in the South, especially in the South, that that is not the case and that the past lives very closely with us, and so I think that I was trying to depict that in the book and trying to find my way to a better understanding of time in the book because I feel like so much about the characters' pasts, their pasts and Parchman prison, Jim Crow, the history of slavery, so much of that reverberates into the present and lives with the characters in the present. So, yes, I think that perhaps that's the reason why the book has that quality and that the story has that quality, where you're not really sure where you are in time because, you know, my idea was that it's all happening right now.

Moore: And ghosts are literal and figurative in the book: the ghosts of dead relatives, the ghosts of your decisions. And I very much felt the ghost of slavery and Jim Crow throughout, even though no one ever uttered the phrase "Jim Crow."

Ward: Definitely, I didn't think that I was writing a ghost story when I first began writing the rough draft of the novel. I thought, *Oh, this is going to be about a road trip. This family is going to take a road trip and they're going to head north, deeper into Mississippi; they're going to head towards the Delta.* And when people think about Mississippi and think about the heart of Mississippi, they think about the Delta. So I was like, *Okay, they head north into the Delta, and things will be crazy and awful in some ways, and strange, who knows what might happen?* But I just thought it was a road trip, and then when I began researching and reading more about Parchman Prison Farm, which is the Mississippi State Penitentiary, and reading more the history of Mississippi and the history of that place, the history of the Delta, that's when I realized that there would be ghosts in this. And I think that when I read about kids like Richie, when I read that there were actual twelve- and thirteen-year-olds in the 1940s, '50s, who were charged with petty crimes like vagrancy or stealing really small things and then sentenced to Parchman Prison Farm to basically be tortured and to die because that farm is such a brutal system—the inmates were basically slaves.

Moore: I had to stop reading the book and do a quick Google search on Parchman. I was like, does this place exist, is this imaginative of someplace else, and so I went down a little bit of a rabbit hole of the history. Is this a place that you knew those ghosts growing up? How much did you know about Parchman versus how much you had to do research? So Pop, JoJo's grandfather, he spent time in Parchman and then this road trip is Leonie and Jojo, Kayla, and her friend Misty, driving there to get Michael, her boyfriend, their father; he's being released.

Ward: I knew about Parchman when I was growing up; everybody that I knew did. We knew that it was like the big prison in Mississippi, I think, in the same way that a lot of people that grow up in Louisiana and who are Black and poor know about Angola. So we knew about Parchman Prison. I didn't know much about it beyond it was a bad place and you didn't want to end up there. So, when I decided that Michael, the white father in the family, would begin the book in Parchman and that Leonie and Jojo and Kayla and Leonie's friend Misty would go pick him up, I thought, *Okay, I really don't know anything about Parchman beyond this boogeyman that I grew up with*, and so I thought, *Okay I need to research*, and so that's when I began to look for books that were about Parchman, and that's when I learned all of this stuff about Parchman. A lot of it shows up in this book, that there's a character like Richie who is exemplary of one of these little kids that were sent there for stealing food.

Moore: For stealing food for his hungry brothers and sisters. And the Mississippi Freedom Riders were taken to Parchman when they were psychologically tortured. It was told [to staffers] don't hurt them but play mind games with them. I think I read in an interview that you also read *The Half Has Never Been Told* about slavery and the economy. How did that factor into your writing process, your researching process?

Ward: The funny thing is that I actually read *The Half Has Never Been Told* for the next novel that I am in the very beginning stages of working on, so I can't tell you much about it [the upcoming novel], but I keep talking about it [*The Half Has Never Been Told*] to everyone who asks me about what I'm reading because it's an amazing book and because my high school education failed me in some ways because I learned nothing about slavery when I was in school. So I wanted to write this book that's set in New Orleans at the height of the domestic slave trade, and then I realized I've read a couple different books about slave markets, about New Orleans, about Maroons, so escaped slaves who built communities, and then I thought, *Okay I'm ready*, but then I realized I know nothing about slavery. So that's when I started reading that book, and it blew my mind. It's an amazing book. If you haven't read it, you should definitely read it because it's the kind of book that will change the way that you perceive the world, I think.

Moore: Which character came to you first?

Ward: JoJo. When I'm casting about for novel ideas, I tend to think in questions. I know that sounds odd, but whenever an idea comes to me, it's always a question. So for *Salvage the Bones*, the question was, so what would it be like for a teenage girl growing up in a world full of men? That's the question that inspired *Salvage the Bones*. And then with *Sing, Unburied, Sing*, it was like, okay what would it be like for a thirteen-year-old mixed-race boy growing up in the "modern South?" And I do little quotation marks when I say "modern South" because, again, if we talk about the past and the present, if we talk about history, I feel like the South as it is now in 2017, it's a different place from the South that I grew up in the 1980s and in the early nineties in some ways; in other ways, in big ways, it's still the same place. In the big ways, it's still the same place that it was in 1970, in 1960, in 1950 and '40 and '30 and on back. So that's the question that was the spark for the book. And so, his voice, even when I was writing really unsuccessful chapters, which I was, of this novel back in 2009, that I just had to throw away because they were so bad, he was the clearest character for me. His was the voice that I heard when I sat down in front of the computer to write. There's something about him. I feel like he wanted to tell me this story.

Moore: Talk about your decision to write about a mixed-race family.

Ward: You know I think it's like I just said a second ago, like I think that the South of 2017 is very different from the South that I grew up in in the 1980s and the '90s. And I think one of the ways that it's different is that there are more interracial families now, and there's not as much of a social stigma, the kind that there would have been back in the eighties and in the early nineties. But, at the same time, I can see, and this is just from what I've seen in my own community and amongst my own friends, some of them who are in interracial relationships and have mixed-race kids, some of these kids are not accepted by the white side of their family. There was real resistance, you know, on the part of some of the white family members when they brought their Black girlfriends home or vice versa. I've seen some resistance, and so I thought it would be that situation, where this thirteen-year-old kid is trying to figure out who he is in the world and where he fits. And he's trying to figure out how the world will perceive him. But in his own family, there's already the larger, like, spectacles of race and racism and prejudice; they're rearing their heads in very ugly, very personal, very immediate ways, so I thought that would be a situation that's ripe for drama.

Moore: Jojo, you know all thirteen-year-olds are coming of age and figuring out their place, but I never got the sense that he was struggling with any racial identity or figuring out who [he is]. I mean, he calls his father by his first name and also his mother because there isn't the kind of tender parental relationship. And then in scenes with Michael's father, it's those moments where I'm thinking *what decade are we in* because it was such a violent reaction to having Black grandchildren?

Ward: When I think about JoJo's family, in my early drafts of the book, Jojo's mother was white, and his father was Black. And those early chapter drafts didn't work. I think they didn't work because Jojo, as I began to understand him, was firmly rooted in the Black experience. The way that he's oriented in the world, he so closely identifies with Pop that something in me knew, even though I didn't have a clear idea of who Pop was, that an older Black man would be really important to Jojo and would be really important to his understanding of who he is and who he might be and of how he should walk in the world. So, early on, in order to write a successful first chapter, second chapter, and then on into the first rough draft, I had to figure out that the family that was raising him, the family that he was with all the time, that family was Black, and it just, it worked for his mom and for his mother's people to be Black.

Moore: I'm sure it probably annoys you as a writer when people say, well I didn't like that character, as if all characters in books have to be liked, but Leonie, the mother, is pretty unlikable. In some ways, she's trying, but she makes a series of just bad decisions as an individual, but also as a mom, even though I do think that you give her some humanity at the same time. But what was that like writing her?

Ward: I disliked her, too, at first. And I was having a really hard time writing her because I disliked her, because I realized that I tend to love all my characters, and in the beginning, I was not loving her.

Moore: So is this the first character you've ever written who you didn't like?

Ward: Well it took a while for the dislike to turn to something else, to evolve into something else. The reason I disliked her was because she was so awful to her children, in the ways that she mistreats them and abuses them and neglects them, that it was really hard for me to feel sympathy for her. And because I couldn't understand why she was being such an awful person to her children, and specifically to Jojo, I realized that I couldn't continue to write her character without that sense of sympathy. So I had to figure out what was at the root of her behavior, what was making her so awful to her children. I had to figure out her motivation.

So, at that time, I didn't know whether or not Given, the phantom Given, was an actual ghost or whether he was a hallucination. In early drafts, it wasn't even Given that was appearing to her; it was actually a phantom of

Michael, and that really wasn't working because all that shows is that she's wildly in love with this guy and she misses him. But then, once I discovered that it was a phantom of her brother and I wrote more of the book and I thought about who Given was and how he died and who he was to Leonie and the relationship that they had, then I felt like I understood her motivation. Because I understood that she has never really attempted to confront her grief and that she's sort of carrying this pain around with her. And that pain is so great that she can't see past it to be less selfish and to be the kind of mother that she needs to be to her children. So, once I discovered that, then I could feel for her, then I felt some sympathy for her.

I actually felt really bad for her because I feel like, in some ways, she knows that she's failing. And yet, she just can't move beyond herself, and she can't get it together because she's wallowing in this loss and in this grief. And it's not just about the loss of her brother; it's also about the imminent loss of her mother, and it's about the way that she feels like she's lost her father in some ways. At the beginning of the book, she's lost Michael in a way; they've been separated, so she's just all wrapped up and bound by loss, and she can't see beyond that. So, once I understood that and understood the pain at the heart of her, then I loved her.

Moore: I was surprised to see meth in the book.

Ward: The town of Bois Sauvage, which is the town that I write about in all my books, well, my fiction, is modeled in some ways on the small town that I'm from called DeLisle. And for years, when I was growing up, I saw the crack epidemic hit. My town is a small town in rural Mississippi, yet the crack epidemic happened there too; it's different because it happened in rural Mississippi, but during the late 1980s and early '90s, we definitely had a crack epidemic. Many people in my family, many people in my community, struggled with addiction for years. Some of them overcame; a lot of them didn't. A lot of them were still struggling with addiction up until roughly two years ago, and then around two years ago, meth, all of a sudden, was everywhere. I don't know where it came from. I don't know how it happened, but suddenly so many of the people that I know in my community and my family who were struggling with crack addiction had now switched drugs, and they were all now smoking meth and dealing with meth. So, in part, I wanted the book to reflect that.

I remember reading about the meth epidemic five to ten years ago and knowing that it's coming. We're in rural Mississippi, we're slow to get everything, but I knew it was coming. So, to see it coming, to see it replace crack in some ways, and to see how meth as a drug is different and does a number on you psychologically. Now, so many people that I know that are using it are now dealing with that, so I wanted my work to be truthful to what I see the people in my community struggling with. So that's why I wanted to write about it.

Moore: As I was reading, I was thinking the whole book was going to be told from Jojo's perspective, and then you alternate. Why did you decide to have alternative voices narrate?

Ward: A couple different reasons. One, I knew I wanted Jojo to speak and to narrate chapters from the very beginning because I wanted this little thirteen-year-old kid to have voice, to have agency. I wanted him to be able to tell his story. But at the same time, when I was thinking about Leonie, thinking about his mother and thinking about so much of what she struggles with and thinking about how people like her so often are not allowed to tell their stories, I wanted to give her an opportunity to do so. I wanted to give her voice. I wanted to give her agency. I wanted her to be able to communicate to the reader how she understands the world and how she sees the world. So, for that reason, I wanted to give her the opportunity, you know, to narrate certain chapters as well.

In some ways, writers are always growing, we're always maturing, we're always working to better ourselves and to better our work. And in some ways, writing a novel with alternating narrators was my way of challenging myself as a writer. I set the task for myself just to see if I could pull it off because it's difficult to write something like that. You have to think about what does this character know, what do they think they know that they actually are wrong about, when should they tell these things that they think they know, in what order, and how is that going to contrast with what the other characters are saying. So, it can be a tricky thing to do.

Moore: I found myself, once I got into that rhythm, wondering things like why was Jojo so upset at his mother for doing this, and then I'd read her perspective, and it was almost like we, the reader, had to experience what the characters were doing twice.

Ward: Yes, there's a moment in the book when they are on the road and get pulled over by the policemen. In that moment, we're able to see it from Leonie's perspective, and then later, we get to see it from Jojo's perspective, and we get to see how different that experience is for both of them. On one hand, Leonie feels powerless when it's happening, and I think she feels a little guilty because she feels like it's her fault. Then Jojo's experience of that same situation, he doesn't feel any guilt; he feels powerless, too, and there's so much terror and he's angry at his mother for putting him in that situation. So, it was a lovely structure for me to explore because it allowed me to give both characters such depth and understanding. Maybe I'll do it again in the future. Who knows?

Moore: Did that process help you grow to love Leonie?

Ward: I think so. I understand more about my characters as I get deeper and deeper into the novel. I know that some writers will write entire pages of information about each character's background, and I don't do that. So, my understanding of who the characters are at the beginning of a novel is sort of shallow, and as I write, that's how I begin to understand who they are and what they want and how they perceive the world and how they understand themselves. So, my understanding of who the characters are changes as I get deeper into a novel. But the same holds true, also, for the overarching ideas of the novel; my understanding of what the novel is about changes as I get deeper into a novel.

Moore: That sounds so incredibly difficult. I've heard writers say the opposite, that they write these long biographies with so much information that never makes it into the book just so they have this clear vision of who the person is. So, for you not to do that and still be able to write very fleshed-out characters, in the writing process, assuming that you're writing in order, do you go back and revise once you've determined you've taken this journey with this character and you have this full understanding? Does that require any revisions outside of the "writing is rewriting" idea?

Ward: Yes, plenty of revision. I've tried to write from outlines before, but, again, my understanding of who the characters are at the beginning, even if I write an outline, always changes as I am writing the book. The characters begin to surprise me; they do things that I don't expect them to do. The process of writing the book, writing about these characters, writing about the world that they're in, that opens them up, that they're able to assume life and take on a life of their own. Therefore, the things that I thought that I knew about them at the beginning, those things don't always hold true as I write more and more and more, especially after I send my friends drafts of the book and they give me feedback. And then after I've revised a million times, then I send it to my editor, and she gives me feedback as well. Once I do all that, and then I'm going back in and doing even more revision. Some of their feedback is asking me questions about the characters; they're asking me to clarify things, to develop things, so my understanding of who the characters are and what they're capable of and what they will do is always changing.

Moore: Talk some more about your writing process. When things come to you, are you just sitting looking at a blank wall, are you listening to music, are you engaged with the world, or are you more of a writer who's in solitude?

Ward: I am more of a solitary writer. I can only listen to music when I'm thinking about ideas, when I'm casting about for ideas for novel ideas or if I'm thinking about the characters or thinking about the situation. But when I finally sit down to write, I can't listen to music at all because the musicality of the prose is really important to me, the rhythm of the sentences, the rhythm of the lines, the rhythm of the paragraphs, and I can't hear that if music is playing in the background. So, I don't work well in cafés or crowded places. I have to work somewhere that's fairly quiet. I know, for some writers, that noise will become background noise, but for me, it doesn't, unfortunately, so it has to be really quiet. And then I can sort of sink into the world that I'm writing about. And I try to approach writing as part of my routine, so I try to write for at least two hours a day, five days a week.

Moore: Is there a certain time, or does that matter?

Ward: Since I've had kids, that time varies. I'm naturally a night owl. I stay up really late, unfortunately, but now that I have kids—I still stay up— but I'm exhausted, so I can't think and work during that time, and so I try to get up earlier. Fortunately, I don't have kids that like to wake up at 5:30 in the morning. My kids wake up around 8:00 or 8:30, so I can get up earlier than them, and I can work. And then, of course, when they're in preschool, then that's great because on days when I don't have to drive in to Tulane and teach, then I have most of the morning to devote to writing. So, then I can work for more than two hours, which is really nice. I can work for like four.

Moore: If you could read the section from Leonie, that's actually where I felt all that rhythm. I reread that section a few times because it did have a cadence or a musical quality to it.

Ward: The section that Natalie is asking me to read is from one of Leonie's chapters. It's in the middle of the book. Leonie is a teenager; it's a flashback, and she's discovered that she's pregnant. And she's realized that she has to tell her mom, so she works up the courage to talk to her mom to tell her mom that she is pregnant. Her mother has something of a gift. She's a Voodoo or Hoodoo practitioner. She practices herbal medicine. Her gift allows her to understand why people are sick and what she can do to help them. She has a bit of a psychic gift. So, there's a bit in here where one of the characters speaks a little French, and I am going to butcher it, so I'm just warning you in advance, even though I've taken French forever, but I still cannot speak it.

[*Ward reads*] "Here he come. Been singing for weeks."

"Mama," [I said.]

[Mama] stepped down from the pine step stool Pop had built her. He'd carved her name into the top of it; the letters looked like wisps of smoke. *Philomène*. It had been her Mother's Day present years before, when I was so little the only help I could give was to scratch a little star, four lines crossed at the middle, on the side of her name, and Given had carved a rose that looked like a muddy puddle, now worn smooth by Mama's feet.

"I was wondering how long it was going to take you to build up the nerve to tell me," she said, the stool tucked under her arm like she would put it away, but instead of walking to the kitchen, she sat on a sofa and let the step stool hang over her legs across her lap.

"Ma'am?" I asked. Thunder boomed. I felt hot around the neck and armpits, like someone had splashed hot grease across my face and chest. I sat down.

"You're pregnant," Mama said. "I saw two weeks ago."

She reached across the wood in her lap and touched me then, not with the pitiless hand of the lightning, but with her dry, warm hands, soft under the skin she worked hard, just a second of a touch on my shoulder, like she had found a piece of lint there and was brushing it off. I surprised myself and curled in to it, leaning forward, put my head on the wood while her hand rubbed circles on my back. I was crying.

"I'm sorry," I said. The wood hard against my mouth. Unyielding. Wetting with my tears. Mama leaned over me.

"No room for sorries now, baby." She grabbed me by the shoulders, pulled me up to look at my face. "What you want to do?"

"What you mean?" [I said.] The closest abortion clinic was in New Orleans. One of the more well-off girls in my school whose daddy was a lawyer had taken her after she'd gotten pregnant, so I knew it was there, and it was expensive. I thought we had no money for that. I was right. Mama gestured at the hanging plants, the listing jungle above our heads bristling in the cool electric air.

"I could give you something," [she said.] She let the end of the sentence trail off, disappear. She looked at me like I was a smudged book she was having trouble reading and cleared her throat. "It was one of the first things I learned how to do, in my training. It's the one tea I never have enough of." She touched my knee then; she'd found another piece of lint. She leaned back again, and her culottes stretched tight across her knees. Years later, that's where she'd first start feeling the pain from the cancer: in her knees. Then it moved up to her hips, her waist, her spine, to her skull. It was a snake slithering along her bones. Sometimes I think back to that day, to her sitting on the sofa, giving me those little touches, little touches that didn't want to turn me one way or the other, even though she wanted Jojo, I think, because her grief for Given was hungry for life. Sometimes I wonder if the cancer was sitting there with us in that moment, too, if it was another egg, a yellow egg knit of sorrow, bearing the shape of bullet holes, wiggling in the marrow of her bones. That day, she was wearing a blouse she'd sewn herself from a print full of pale yellow flowers. Roses, looked like. "You want this baby, Leonie?"

A whip crack of lightning lit the house, and I jumped as the thunder boomed.

I choked and coughed; Mama patted my back. The humidity made her hair alive around her face, tendrils of it standing up and curling away from her buttery scalp. The lightning cracked again, this time like it was right on top of us, feet away from arcing through the house, and her skin was white as stone and her hair waving, and I thought about the Medusa I'd seen in an old movie when I was younger, monstrous and green-scaled and I thought: *That's not it at all. She was beautiful as Mama. That's how she froze those men, with the shock of seeing something so perfect and fierce in the world.*

"Yeah, Mama," I said. It still twists something in me to think of that: the fact that I hesitated, that I looked at my mama's face in that light and felt myself wrestle with wanting to be a mother, with wanting to bear a baby into the world, to carry it throughout life. The way we were sitting on that sofa, knees tight, backs curved, heads low, made me think of mirrors and of how I'd wanted to be a different kind of woman, how I'd wanted to move somewhere far away, go west to California, probably, with Michael. He talked about moving west and working as a welder all the time. A baby would make that harder. Mama looked at me and she wasn't stone no more: her eyes were crumpled and her mouth crooked, and that told me she knew exactly what I was thinking, and I worried that she could read minds, too, that she would see me shying away from who she was. But then I thought of Michael, of how happy he would be, of how I would have a piece of him with me always, and that unease melted like lard in a cast-iron pot. "I do."

"I wish you would have finished school first," Mama said. Another piece of lint, this time on my hair at the crown of my head. "But this is now, and we do what we do." She smiled then: a thin line, no teeth, and I leaned forward and put my head in her lap again, and she ran her hands up and down my spine, over my shoulder blades, pressed in on the base of my neck. All the while shushing like a stream, like she'd taken all the water pouring on the outside world into her, and she was sending it out in a trickle to soothe me. *Je suis la fille de l'océan, la fille des ondes, la fille de l'écume,* Mama muttered, and I knew. I knew she was calling on Our Lady of Regla. On the Star of the Sea. That she was invoking Yemayá, the goddess of the ocean and salt water, with her shushing and her words, and that she was holding me like the goddess, her arms all the life-giving waters of the world [*Sing, Unburied, Sing* 156–59].

Ghosts of Our Past: An Interview with Jesmyn Ward

Louise McCune / 2017

This interview was originally conducted by Louise McCune and published in the *Los Angeles Review of Books* on October 11, 2017. Reprinted with permission.

When Jojo and his family go to pick up his father Michael from Parchman Prison, they return home with an unlikely additional passenger. Richie—who can be seen only by Jojo and his toddler sister Kayla—is a ghost who has kept residence at Parchman for decades, haunting the site of his untimely death in an attempt to understand it. Richie was only a boy when he was incarcerated for spurious reasons, and he was only a boy when he was killed for trying to escape. *Sing, Unburied, Sing*, a finalist for the 2017 National Book Award, is a novel populated by living characters who contend daily with the consequences of state-sanctioned racial violence. Richie's story intervenes in an otherwise twenty-first-century narrative to indicate that, when it comes to American racism, the past remains very much alive.

In 2011, Jesmyn Ward won acclaim for *Salvage the Bones*, her novel about a family living in the Mississippi Gulf town of Bois Sauvage in the days leading up to Hurricane Katrina. Since then, she has written a memoir, *Men We Reaped*, and edited an anthology about race in America called *The Fire This Time*. With *Sing, Unburied, Sing*, Ward returns to fiction and to Bois Sauvage to tell the story of a family haunted by ghosts.

While *Sing, Unburied, Sing* is a regional story in the sense that, according to Ward, it "could only happen in Mississippi," the book makes a universal appeal to the urgency of retrospectivity in 2017. I spoke with Jesmyn Ward to learn more about the importance of listening to our ghosts.

Louise McCune: In the epigraph to your book, you quote Eudora Welty, saying, "The memory is a living thing—it too is in transit." How might readers understand memory as a "living thing" in *Sing, Unburied, Sing*?

Jesmyn Ward: In *Sing, Unburied, Sing*, memory comes alive and is embodied by the ghosts Given and Richie. They come alive, and they interact with the characters. They interact with their loved ones, and they act on them.

One of the reasons that I love that quote so much—and why I think it is so applicable to the story that I'm telling—is because a question that the book is asking is about how the past bears on the present. For me, the quote about memory being a living thing is another way to say that the past is not the past, and that time isn't linear. That's a theme that I'm wrestling with in the book. These ghosts from the past haunt those in the present because of enslavement, because of Jim Crow, because of the terrible history of Parchman Prison and of places like Parchman Prison. All of that—which hypothetically happened in the past—reverberates into the future and into the present.

McCune: In a review of *Sing, Unburied, Sing* in *The New York Times*, Parul Sehgal pointed out the prevalence of ghosts in literary fiction in the past year or so. She references George Saunders's *Lincoln in the Bardo*, *White Tears* by Hari Kunzru, *Grace* by Natashia Deón, and *The Underground Railroad* by Colson Whitehead. What do you make of the great number of ghosts in fiction this year? Are there any literary ghosts who inspired or instructed you as you wrote your own ghosts into being?

Ward: There actually weren't any literary ghosts that inspired my ghosts. I think that my ghosts came from my nonfiction reading because I was reading a lot about Parchman Prison and Mississippi history in general. I knew nothing about those things, really. I read that there were kids—twelve- and thirteen-year-old Black boys—who were charged with petty crimes like loitering and then sent to Parchman Prison to be enslaved, tortured, and die. When I read that children were sent to prison because they were boys and because they were Black, I knew that I had to have a character like that and that that character had to be a ghost. I wanted that character to be able to interact with characters in the present—Jojo and his family, who I was writing about.

I think that maybe one of the reasons that ghosts are figuring so prominently in literary fiction as of late is that writers are resisting. We're pushing back against this trend that seems to be happening right now, where people in politics are attempting to rewrite history and attempting to undermine our understanding of what came before. That's really horrible. A lot of writers are wrestling with a trend in the larger culture to deny what has happened in the past. Maybe that could explain the appearance of so many ghosts, who are reckoning with the past and bearing witness to the past, in fictional work lately.

McCune: I was struck by something you wrote in the introduction to *The Fire This Time* about how you had initially envisioned that you would categorize the poems and essays into three tidy sections: past, present, and future. You noticed though, when pieces started coming in, they skewed heavily toward the past and the present. Only three explicitly referenced the future. Did that surprise you? How did it feel to make that observation, especially as a writer who is trying to write against the tendency of people in power to rewrite history?

Ward: It did surprise me. It gave me hope to see that so many people were doing that kind of work, to see that so many people were really fighting back against the erasure of facts and knowledge. So on one hand it was heartening, but on the other hand it was disheartening because I think that it's a skill that we need for survival. It's something that engenders hope—we have to be able to imagine our future. It did make me a little sad to see that not many of us were imagining our futures.

McCune: Were there other resonances between *The Fire This Time* and *Sing, Unburied, Sing*? Were you working on those two projects simultaneously?

Ward: I was working on them simultaneously. I referenced Trayvon Martin in my introduction [to *The Fire This Time*]. At the time when I was working on *Sing, Unburied, Sing* and *The Fire This Time*, I was thinking a lot about Trayvon. I was thinking a lot about the seemingly endless list of young Black men who were dying one after another.

I write about characters who are women in the book, and in some respects *Sing, Unburied, Sing* is asking questions about motherhood, about Black motherhood, about womanhood, and about family. But at the same time, I think that the other half of the book is really concerned with Black boyhood and Black manhood. It's about how, across generations, through the decades, and through the centuries, that personhood has been threatened. I was thinking about many of the same things when I was working on both projects.

McCune: You've said in other interviews that Jojo's character was the seed that stirred you to write this book. This book, also, has been called a road novel and bears comparisons to the *Odyssey*. Did you always know that bringing Jojo to the page would mean sending him (and his family) on a journey away from home? Did you always know that it would be a journey to Parchman?

Ward: I did, actually. From the very beginning, I knew that Jojo and his mom would get in the car, and I knew that they were traveling to Parchman Prison. When I began working on the first draft, that's all I saw the novel as. I thought, well, this will be a road trip, this entire novel. I thought it would be a road trip through the modern South, that it would be a little surreal and a bit bizarre. When I was starting out, those were the ideas that I had. As I did more research on Parchman Farm and discovered that kids like Richie existed, my ideas around the story evolved and changed. The story became something else. It became a ghost story, too. That discussion about time and about how the past bears on the present—it became more complicated for me.

McCune: Did Richie come to you with the same clarity that Jojo did?

Ward: Not as immediately, no. He didn't. I had written three or four chapters at the point where I discovered Richie's character. I thought, well, maybe later on in the book I'll have a chapter from his perspective. He can speak; he can tell his story. I didn't do that in the first draft. I completed a first draft, and he wasn't there. I mean, he was there in scene, he was there in action, but everything was filtered through Jojo's or Leonie's point of view. I went through multiple revisions of the book, and when I say multiple revisions I mean like twelve. I got feedback from friends of mine who are writers and went through more revisions. Then I sent it to my editor, and my editor asked if I had thought about writing any of the sections from Richie's perspective. It was only then that I went back and tried to hear him. I think I was afraid to write from his perspective because his perspective required me to build that entire world. I had to build an afterlife. That afterlife had to have some logic; it had to make sense. It had to feel real, and vivid, and believable for the reader. I was afraid to do that because I had never done anything like that before.

McCune: Parchman Prison, in Jojo's grandfather's memory, is guarded by inmates. He says it's a place that'll fool you into thinking it isn't a prison at all because it doesn't have any walls. When Jojo's dad is there many years later, it's low, concrete buildings and barbed-wire fences; he calls it a fortress. In your reading about Parchman, what else has changed from its earlier days until now? What has stayed the same?

Ward: It's not a working plantation anymore. Inmates are no longer guarding other inmates. Back when [Jojo's grandfather] and Richie would have been there, if one of the inmate guards killed another inmate who was trying to escape, they would have been granted their freedom. That system no longer exists. They're no longer whipped. They're no longer tortured. But one thing that hasn't changed between now and then is that the large majority of inmates are still Black men. They still work while they're in prison, and when they get out, they're still disenfranchised. They're not able to vote. Their crime and the time that they spent there follows them. They don't have full rights of citizenship. That part hasn't changed.

McCune: Did you visit the prison as you were writing the book?

Ward: I actually did not visit the prison. I wish that I had the opportunity to, but I didn't. My editor actually visited and took tons of photographs for me. She bought me a book and a collection of CDs that have all of the Parchman Farm songs on them that were recorded in the forties and the fifties. I'm a new mom—I have a daughter who just turned five and an eleven-month-old. Between those two, I couldn't fit a trip to Parchman in.

McCune: You've talked before about this thing you call "narrative ruthlessness"—how, when you were writing *Salvage the Bones*, you resisted against an urge to "spare" the characters you loved so much from the realities of the place you were writing about. Was that something you were thinking about as you wrote *Sing, Unburied, Sing*?

Ward: It was definitely something I thought about when I was writing this book. I was thinking about it with every single character. Say, for instance, with Mam, Jojo's grandmother. She's sick with cancer at the beginning of the book. As soon as I knew she was sick with cancer, I was like, okay. There's a strong possibility that that would lead to death. I knew that even though I would come to love her in the book, that if she had to die, then she'd have to die. I couldn't stand in the way of things that were happening to her.

I definitely felt that way with Leonie, Jojo, and [his sister]. The part of me that loves my characters and wants to protect them just wanted to lift the children out of that situation and take them away from their emotionally abusive, neglectful mother. But I knew that I couldn't do that. They're family, and I knew that they had to struggle through what they were enduring together.

I really felt that way with Richie. Richie is such a heartbreaking character, and that's even more complicated by the fact that I know that kids like him existed. Part of me wanted to save him. I wanted to deliver him, while I was writing, from the life and the death that he had. I also wanted to ease his way in the afterlife. But then there's something dishonest about that, you know what I'm saying? There's something dishonest about being kind to my characters because the world, so often, isn't kind to them. I thought about that with all my characters. It was constantly on my mind. I had to be honest. I had to be ruthless.

McCune: Is there anything that has surprised you about the way that audiences have received and responded to *Sing, Unburied, Sing* so far?

Ward: I'm delighted that people have responded so positively to it, especially because it's a story that could only happen in Mississippi. Readers know that this is a story that could only happen in Mississippi, but at the same time, they're empathizing with the characters. They're identifying a universality in the story. That's been a nice surprise.

Ghosts of History:
An Interview with Jesmyn Ward

Louis Elliot / 2017

This interview, "Ghosts of History: An Interview with Jesmyn Ward" by Louis Elliot, was commissioned by and first published in *BOMB Daily*, November 10, 2017. © Bomb Magazine, New Art Publications, and its contributors. All rights reserved. The *BOMB* Digital Archive can be viewed at www.bombmagazine.org.

Louis Elliot: You've said that your memoir, *Men We Reaped,* was a love letter to your family. Did the characters in *Sing, Unburied, Sing* come out of the ideas you explored there?

Jesmyn Ward: The character that brought me to this book was Jojo. A mixed-race thirteen-year-old boy who lived with his grandparents and had a somewhat absent mother. His father's family doesn't really claim him at all. I wanted to write about him specifically because I felt like so much of what he is struggling with in his life is about trying to understand who he is and who he might grow up to be and what the world thinks of him. Those are very private struggles, yet what he's struggling against and trying to define himself against is so much larger than he is and carries the weight of history behind it. I thought writing about him would be really fruitful for drama. I just thought there was a lot there to unpack when I told his story.

Elliot: One of the beautiful elements of the book is the gap in parenting intelligence between Jojo and his mother Leonie, who's in her late twenties. Jojo is essentially more of a father to his younger sister Kayla than Leonie is a mother. Why create this gap?

Ward: I knew from the beginning that Leonie would be the kind of parent who would be neglectful, who couldn't, for one reason or another, take care of her children. What was harder for me was figuring out exactly why she was such an awful parent, why she doesn't have that kind of parenting intelligence that she should have. My understanding of it was that she has so much unresolved pain from losing her brother and from the various ways she's convinced that she has disappointed her parents that she just can't see past that pain to move beyond herself and focus attention on her children. For Jojo, it seemed a natural thing that if his mother was not caring and providing for him—and he had Pop as a model—he would act in ways that seemed very maternal and nurturing.

Elliot: The central current running throughout the book is the idea that we carry family history inside us like ghosts. Mam tells Leonie, "I think it runs in the blood, like silt in the water . . . rises up over the water in generations." When you first began the book, did you know that family ghosts would play a major role?

Ward: I didn't actually think ghosts would figure importantly in the book. But I knew Leonie would see a phantom of the brother, but only when she was high. I wasn't sure whether or not he was a figment of her imagination. I thought, oh, that's all he's going to be. He's just going to be a figment of her imagination. She's only going to see him when she's high. So he'll be like this manifestation of her brother that is sort of evidence of her overwhelming grief that she hadn't faced.

It was easier to make him an actual ghost once I discovered that Richie was a ghost. One of the books I read in my research was about Parchman Prison, where twelve- and thirteen-year-old Black boys were taken for petty crimes, vagrancy, and stealing—very small things. At Parchman, they were tortured and beaten like slaves. They died like slaves. I was so struck by that, and also horrified that I did not know those things before I read that book. I thought: *I have to write this character.* I wanted to give him agency. I wanted him to be able to interact with the other characters. Because I wanted that to happen, I knew that he had to be a ghost. That's when I realized, okay, so if Richie's a ghost, it makes sense for Given [Leonie's brother] to be as well.

Elliot: Did you have any hesitations about letting the voices of the dead speak so much?

Ward: I did have hesitations about letting them speak. Perhaps not for reasons you think. I had hesitations because I was afraid. I've never written anything where the ghost is telling this story. There's so much world-building I had to do in those sections. I had to invent this supernatural afterlife. And I had to invent a logic for that afterlife. I actually didn't add those sections where Richie speaks until I'd probably done fourteen revisions. Then I got feedback from my editor saying, "Have you ever thought about writing a chapter from Richie's point of view?" Early in the process, I considered doing it, but I didn't, until my editor pushed me in that direction.

Elliot: As Jojo learns about his family's past, he becomes a kind of guide through American history. What does it mean for you as a writer to voice this history?

Ward: I feel really lucky and honored to be given this platform where I'm able to write about things like Parchman Prison, the epidemic of lynching in the American South, and to reach an audience. I feel like some people who read my work are familiar with the institutions and the issues that I'm writing about, but I've found now that a lot of people aren't.

When I started doing interviews and events for *Sing, Unburied, Sing,* I was surprised to see how many people didn't know that Parchman was a real place. They thought it was a figment of my imagination. Everything I bring to the book about Parchman is based on something that actually happened. It feels good to be able to write about these different events and institutions and places, to draw them from history.

Elliot: Jojo's white grandparents live in the Kill at the top of the hill. The animals are out in the open. But in Bois, no one has their animals out in the open. And Leonie knows her white best friend has privileges she does not. How did you get these characters to navigate the differences between these two worlds?

Ward: They don't necessarily articulate it by coming out and talking about white privilege. But in some ways, that's what they are saying. They're reckoning with the fact that the history of slavery in this country, and Jim Crow, and everything that came after, has repercussions. That history necessarily shapes how we move through the world. How someone like Jojo might move through the world. How someone like Leonie might move through the world. Especially in Leonie's point of view. It's something she's very aware of. It's something she's greedy for. She wants the privilege that she sees. It informs her relationship and definitely informs her sense of self and self-worth.

Elliot: These themes are so important to our national consciousness right now. How do they emerge in your work?

Ward: There are always moments when you stumble across a scene that brings everything into sharp relief. Definitely the moment when they're pulled over by cops. As soon as I knew they were hitting the road, I knew they would get pulled over. There's no way that this family can get on the road and avoid the police, considering the car that they drive, the mix of people who are in it.

Elliot: The Black Lives Matter movement became part of the mainstream consciousness after you started writing this book. Around the publication

100 CONVERSATIONS WITH JESMYN WARD

date, we had the white supremacist violence in Charlottesville. Where do you see your work in terms of these conversations?

Ward: I've always wanted to write Black characters who are multidimensional, who are complicated, who are sympathetic, who have soul. Earlier on in my career, when I was in college and I was thinking about writing about the place where I was from, part of what was really motivating me to do that was because I had encountered so many people who thought that the people that I wrote about weren't anything like that. They totally discounted their humanity and complexity. That really made me very angry. In part, I was responding to that when I wrote *Salvage the Bones*, especially because of the national conversation that was happening around Katrina. People were talking about Louisiana, and people from Mississippi, who did not leave, and called them idiots. They couldn't understand why we didn't leave. And they didn't understand why we came back. I was writing against that.

Elliot: Critics mention you alongside Faulkner, and you have a Eudora Welty and Derek Walcott quote at the beginning of the novel. Do you see this book existing within a specific literary heritage, and did you read such books in preparation?

Ward: I definitely see this book as part of a literary heritage. Mississippi has been home to a lot of great writers through the decades. I definitely consider myself one in a long line. I feel like all of those writers—from William Faulkner, to Richard Wright, to Eudora Welty, to Anne Moody, to Margaret Walker—have affected my writing.

Most of the books I read in preparation weren't fiction, actually. I was thinking about some fictional texts when I wrote, perhaps *Beloved*, *As I Lay Dying*, the *Odyssey*. But I didn't read them to prepare. For the first time, I had to research. I was writing about several things I knew nothing about, like Parchman Prison. I was probably in eighth grade the last time I studied Mississippi history. I knew little about Voodoo and Hoodoo and those spiritual traditions. So I had to do a ton of research.

Elliot: This fall you were named a MacArthur Fellow and a finalist for the National Book Award. Do these nominations in any way validate your work in your mind to a wider audience, and suggest its power?

Ward: Yes. When I first started sending out work, I kept encountering the idea that people wouldn't read about the kind of people I was writing about—that this kind of work wouldn't find an audience. People in power probably assumed that because I was writing about poor Black Southerners, no one would want to read about them. It feels good to get this kind of recognition now and to know that many will read about the kind of people I'm talking about and find the stories universal in some way.

This hasn't happened with *Sing, Unburied, Sing* yet. But with *Salvage the Bones*, it's been picked up for Common Reads, and sometimes first-year reads at different colleges. I've visited some places where students are vocal about where there's still pushback. They say that when they first picked up the book, they thought, *Oh, God, I don't want to read this.* What does this have to do with me? Why do I have to read about a pregnant Black girl?

Regardless of the award, though, I still feel like I'm working against that impulse that I keep encountering in people.

Elliot: Do you feel like the spotlight is on you more?

Ward: Yes. I give all the awards to my mom, and she keeps them at her house, because when I'm sitting down to really write, I can't think about nominations, or awards, or recognition. Then I'm too conscious of audience. I'm too aware of what people want. I can't work if I'm so aware of that. It's okay to be conscious of audience in terms of being aware of clarity, of how story builds, and of how it might affect readers. Other than that, it makes me choke to wonder in every scene, "What will people think?"

[National Book Award–winning poet] Nikky Finney was telling me, you have to forget all of that when you sit down and work. Forget all of the attention and forget audience. You have to really embrace the emotion that brought you to it, that brought you to the people you are writing about, to the story you are telling.

Elliot: Is your next novel at all related to this one?

Ward: The next piece is actually set in New Orleans at the height of domestic slave trade, so in the early 1800s. It will be the first time I've written something that takes place completely in the past. It will require me to develop more writerly muscles. This book introduced my audience to the idea that my characters would live in the past, and be informed by the past, and move back and forth between past and present. I think *Sing* will make it easier for readers to accept that transition from me. It's very different from anything that I've even written before.

Elliot: What are the questions you're asking yourself right now in that book?

Ward: I'm asking questions about what it means to endure and to persist, to resist, beyond what you think you can. The institution of slavery was so horrible, so much of what happened to people who were enslaved was unthinkable. And yet, not all of them, but some survived; they lived through it. I'm asking questions about what that means. How does someone live through something like that and retain their humanity and individuality? I'm asking about relationships, especially between parents and children. How do you live through the dissolution, and the violation, of your most fundamental human connections? How do you reconcile yourself to that reality?

It's really hard to sit with that. I'm resisting it. And then I feel guilty for being so reluctant. I think, God, you're so pretentious. You're not living any of this. They actually lived this. They lived this and they suffered through it—and you can't even sit with it and write it. I'm being spared the torment of living through it. So at least, I can witness.

Jesmyn Ward: "So Much of Life Is Pain and Sorrow and Willful Ignorance"

Vanessa Thorpe / 2017

This interview was originally conducted by Vanessa Thorpe and published by *The Guardian* on November 12, 2017. © Guardian News & Media Ltd. 2024.

Jesmyn Ward, forty, who grew up and lives in Mississippi, has been hailed as a tough yet poetic new literary voice. Her novel *Salvage the Bones* and her memoir *Men We Reaped* have both won prizes, while the collection of essays she edited and contributed to, *The Fire This Time*, is a US bestseller and is published in the UK next April. Her latest novel, *Sing, Unburied, Sing*, has been nominated for the National Book Award and the Kirkus Prize. It is told chiefly through the eyes of Leonie, a drug-taking mother, and her watchful teenage son, Jojo, and unsentimentally conveys the pain of bereavement and the risks of life on the edge of survival.

Vanessa Thorpe: There are few physical descriptions of the family home at the center of *Sing, Unburied, Sing*, yet a strong sense of it comes across. Did you draw on sounds and smells of the home you grew up in?

Jesmyn Ward: Place is important to my writing; I believe that if a reader gets a clear picture of the place where a character is from, then they can understand what motivates the character, what limits him or her. I grew up in a lot of different homes when I was younger: my parents rented trailers and small, boxy houses set high on cement block pillars. For three or so years, my family lived in my grandmother's house, which is the house my mom grew up in. There were thirteen of us in a four-bedroom house, and it was one of the happiest times of my life, surrounded by so many people who I loved. There was a wood-burning stove in the living room because the house lacked central heat, and gas-burning heaters installed in the hallway. So I remember the smell of the burning oak and pine most strongly, and the sulfur smell of the gas. And then I remember the food, of course. My grandmother made biscuits almost every morning, and we ate a lot of red beans and rice. We had to eat cheap meals that would feed a lot of people because there were so many of us.

Thorpe: The idea of parallel life forces, spirits and ghosts, play a big part in your new story. What does that mean for you personally? Do you share the beliefs you give to the loving grandmother and grandfather figures, Pop and Mam?

Ward: I don't believe everything Mam or Pop believe. But some of it I want to believe, without reserve, without cynicism. My brother died when he was nineteen, so a part of me indulges and thinks that some part of him that made him uniquely him is out there, on another plane. So inventing the fictional afterlife in *Sing, Unburied, Sing* was a way of making that wish real.

Thorpe: Is it just coincidence that *Lincoln in the Bardo*, the Booker Prize winner that others have linked to your work, also goes into a spirit world to communicate the sorrows of corporeal life?

Ward: Well, we're at a difficult moment in history. Many people in power are attempting to rewrite the past and the present to fit their narrative. Writing about spirits is a way to counteract some of that, because the people of the past are allowed to be present in the moment and tell their own (true) stories, and often, there is a reckoning between the living and the dead. And perhaps both books wrestle with grief; writing about ghosts allows us to puzzle through that heaviness.

Thorpe: Do you welcome being lined up in an emancipatory Black tradition? Or should a writer like you be allowed to speak more individually?

Ward: I celebrate my Blackness. I love the artistic vibrancy of the culture I was born to. I'm proud of the fact that the people of the African diaspora fight to survive, to thrive, all over the world, so of course my work reflects this pride, this investment in telling our stories. And I don't find that problematic. I also work very hard at writing, at developing creatively; I like to think that the work I do means that my books have power and weight and lasting beauty, regardless of my color or the colors of my characters.

Thorpe: Has it become harder for you to write fiction in the current political atmosphere?

Ward: Our current horrors haven't silenced me yet. I don't know if they will. If anything, the current political atmosphere has made me angrier, and that's driven me to my desk, to my computer, to my books. I didn't write for two years after Hurricane Katrina hit, so it will take something like that to silence me again. And even if something like that occurs, I will return. I can't help telling stories.

Thorpe: Were you an optimist or a pessimist as a child? Has that changed?

Ward: I was a pessimist. Nothing has changed. Young people have a right to optimism, and rightly so; human beings have grown and developed and accomplished wonderful feats in the world. But what mires me in pessimism is the fact that so much of life is pain and sorrow and willful ignorance and violence, and pushing back against that tide takes so much effort, so much steady fight. It's tiring.

Thorpe: What are you working on now and where do you work?

Ward: I'm working on a novel set in New Orleans during the height of the domestic slave trade. I write in a room in my house that I've set up as a small library, and my desk faces a window. Outside, I can see a tall cypress tree I planted five years ago and a live oak I planted at the same time that has been super slow to grow.

Thorpe: Finally—a big one—what is the way to combat drug addiction in communities that are hampered by prejudice and poverty?

Ward: Well, you have to go to the root of the problem. When people are struggling with undiagnosed mental illness, they may turn to drugs. When people are hopeless and feel trapped by lack of opportunity, they may turn to drugs. When people don't feel like they are accorded human dignity or freedom, they may turn to drugs. There's a lot to unpack around the drug crisis in America, things like generational poverty and systemic racism and the constant winnowing of the social safety net. All of this is complicated by the fact that a lot of Americans see drug addiction as a moral failure. We have to acknowledge all of that and then put in place policies to counteract those things that drive people to addiction. But I'm no expert.

For Jesmyn Ward, Writing Means Telling the "Truth About the Place that I Live In"

Sam Briger / 2017

This interview by Sam Briger was broadcast on *Fresh Air* with Terry Gross and distributed by NPR on November 28, 2017. *Fresh Air* is a radio program produced by WHYY in Philadelphia. Reprinted with permission of Kyra G. McGrath of WHYY.

Terry Gross: This is *Fresh Air*. I'm Terry Gross. It's been quite a year for author Jesmyn Ward. She received a MacArthur Fellowship, and this month her novel *Sing, Unburied, Sing* won the National Book Award for fiction. Her previous novel, *Salvage the Bones*, also won that award. *Sing, Unburied, Sing* tells the story of Jojo, a mixed-race thirteen-year-old boy. He lives with his Black grandparents. His grandmother is dying from cancer. His drug-addicted mother, Leonie, is unreliable. She's self-medicating her grief from the covered-up murder of her brother when they were in high school. Jojo's white father, who was never much of a presence in Jojo's life, is doing time for drugs at the state penitentiary, the infamous Parchman Farm. Helping bolster Jojo through these trying circumstances is the unfaltering love between him and his grandfather and his toddler sister Kayla.

Ward's characters live in the fictional rural town of Bois Sauvage on the Mississippi Gulf Coast. Ward based it on the town she grew up in and lives in today called DeLisle. Jesmyn Ward has written and edited other books, including the memoir *Men We Reaped*, about five men from her hometown who died young, including her brother, who was killed in a car crash. She spoke with *Fresh Air* producer Sam Briger.

Sam Briger: I'd like to start with a reading, if you could—maybe the beginning of the book. And maybe just set it up for us. Who's speaking here?

Jesmyn Ward: So the narrator here is Jojo. He is a thirteen-year-old mixed-race boy. He's growing up in a small town in the South, in rural Mississippi, called Bois Sauvage. And the novel opens on his thirteenth birthday.

[*Reads*] I like to think I know what death is. I like to think that it's something I could look at straight. When Pop tell me he need my help and I see that black knife slid into the belt of his pants, I follow Pop out the house, try to keep my back straight, my shoulders even as a hanger; that's how Pop walks. I try to look like this is normal and boring so Pop will think I've earned these thirteen years, so Pop will know I'm ready to pull what needs to be pulled, separate innards from muscle, organs from cavities. I want Pop to know I can get bloody. Today's my birthday.

I grab the door so it don't slam, ease it into the jamb. I don't want Mam or Kayla to wake up with none of us in the house. Better for them to sleep. Better for my little sister, Kayla, to sleep because on nights when Leonie's out working, she wake up every hour, sit straight up in the bed, and scream. Better for Grandma Mam to sleep because the chemo done dried her up and hollowed her out the way the sun and the air do water oaks. Pop weaves in and out of the trees, straight and slim and brown as a young pine tree. He spits in the dry red dirt, and the wind makes the trees wave. It's cold. This spring is stubborn; most days, it won't make way for warmth. The chill stays like water in a bad-draining tub. I left my hoodie on the floor in Leonie's room, where I sleep, and my T-shirt is thin, but I don't rub my arms. If I let the cold goad me, I know when I see the goat, I'll flinch or frown when Pop cuts the throat. And Pop, being Pop, will see. [*Sing, Unburied, Sing* 1–2]

Briger: That's Jesmyn Ward reading the beginning of her new novel, *Sing, Unburied, Sing.* Jesmyn, you have three narrators in this new novel. One of them is Jojo, who we just heard from. Can you tell us a little bit more about him? I heard that part of the reason you wanted to write this book was you wanted to tell the story of a biracial boy growing up in Mississippi.

Ward: Yeah. You know, Jojo is the character that came to me first when I was casting about for novel ideas. He popped into my head. And I wondered what it would be like to write about a kid like him, a biracial kid. You know, one parent is Black. The other is white. I knew, because I'm writing about him at this moment in his life when he is attempting to figure out what it means to be a man, what it means to be a Black man in the South, in America—I knew that this would be a moment that had a lot of dramatic potential.

And he's confronting basically the history of the South—right?—you know, of racist violence, of slavery, you know, of Jim Crow. But he's—it's a very personal battle for him because of who his family members are. And I just thought that he, as a character, that—you know, that he would be a very rich character to write about.

Briger: And speaking of his family, his father Michael is white, and he's in prison for drug charges, and his mother Leonie is Black, and she's one of the other narrators of the book. And you've written her into a pretty bad place. I mean, she's addicted to drugs. She's doing meth and cocaine. She's neglectful of her children.

And I don't think you ever spell this out, but I think the reason that she's addicted to drugs is that she's, you know, self-medicating her grief from her brother's murder. He was shot by a white man, and it was covered up as a hunting accident. To make things more complicated for her, the father of her kids is cousin of the person that killed her brother, and his father was an ex-sheriff who helped cover it up. So why did you want to write her into such a hole?

Ward: Bois Sauvage—right, so the fictional town that I write about is actually, I guess, a fictional twin of my hometown, DeLisle, Mississippi. I feel like in every book that I commit to telling the truth about the place that I live in and also about the kind of people who live in my community. There are a lot of people in my community who struggle with addiction. Back in the 1980s and the '90s, it was basically a crack epidemic in my town. But now I'd say in the past five years, that crack epidemic has transformed into a meth epidemic.

And I think that I connected Michael to Leonie's brother's killers because I feel that often racist violence in the South is intimate. You know, it's—it—in some ways, it reminds me of what I know about domestic violence. Like, these crimes seem to be very intimate crimes. They happened between people who know each other, you know, who live around each other, who share community sometimes. And so I think I wanted Leonie's situation to reflect that. But I think you're totally right about the wound that she's carrying with her, the wound of her grief and the loss of her brother. And I think that does motivate a lot of her struggles with addiction.

Briger: You know, you have actual ghosts in your novel. You have two ghosts. There's one who's Richie, who was a thirteen-year-old boy who Jojo's grandfather, Pop, met at Parchman Farm, the Mississippi State Penitentiary, when Pop was pretty much kidnapped and forced to work there. And then there's also Leonie. Whenever she gets high, she sees her brother's ghost, Given. Why did you decide to have actual ghosts haunt the work?

Ward: I knew that Leonie would see a phantom of her brother from the very beginning of the rough draft, right? But I wasn't convinced that he was an actual ghost. I thought, well, maybe he's just a figment of her imagination. Maybe he's just the embodiment of her grief and her guilt that comes alive whenever she uses drugs, whenever she's high. And I thought this until I—you know, I was doing research about Parchman Prison in order to write about it.

And I was reading a book called *Worse Than Slavery* by David Oshinsky. And in that book, I read that there were boys as young as twelve and thirteen, young Black boys, who were charged with small crimes and then sent to Parchman Prison. And, you know, those children were enslaved and suffered and were tortured and sometimes died in Parchman Prison, and their suffering had been erased from history in some ways. And so I was so, like, horrified and also heartbroken when I read that that I thought, okay, I have to write about a kid like this, and this child has to have agency. This child has to have voice. You know, this child has to be able to act in the present moment with Jojo, you know, with Pop, with Kayla. And the only way that I could do that was by making this character a ghost. And so then I understood that I was writing a ghost story too.

Briger: You know, a lot of your book seems to be about the personal traumas the characters are trying to cope with, but there's also trauma on a larger, systemic level. These characters are burdened with a history of oppression that shaped their lives and, you know, limited the choices available to them. And I think that Parchman Farm, the Mississippi State Penitentiary, looms large as sort of a symbol of that in your book. Is that true?

Ward: That's totally true.

Briger: Can you tell us a little bit about it?

Ward: Yeah, I mean, you know, Parchman Prison is the large state—Mississippi State Prison. And when it was established, the people in power sort of changed the laws and criminalized really small offenses or criminalized things that, you know, weren't even really criminal acts, like loitering—right?—vagrancy, right? They also criminalized a lot of, like, petty thievery. And they did all of this in the hopes that they could arrest and send a lot of Black men to Parchman and populate Parchman because basically, they wanted to work them, right?

They wanted free labor, and that's what they did. You know, I mean, Parchman was mostly Black—mostly Black men. They were basically enslaved again, and they worked the fields, right? So Parchman Prison was

110 CONVERSATIONS WITH JESMYN WARD

basically a big plantation in the 1930s, the 1940s. Those inmates were also—so they worked the plantation. They worked Parchman Prison.

But they were also rented out to regional, like, industrial barons. They were rented out to these men who used them to, you know, clear large tracts of land, to lay train tracks, right? So any jobs that, you know, these men wanted them to do, that's what they did. And so, yes, they were re-enslaved. I mean, Richie is based on a real—real children who were charged with petty crimes and then sent to be slaves—right?—and to die in Parchman Prison.

Briger: When you were growing up in Mississippi, did you know of Parchman Farm? Was there the presence in your life?

Ward: It sure was. I mean, I didn't know, you know, specifically, like, what happened. I didn't—I wasn't—I didn't know the history of Parchman Prison. But I knew that it was a bad place that you never wanted to go. But I also knew that the danger of being sent there was, like, ever-present for people like me, for Black people, right? I remember being very, very young. And I wrote about this briefly in *Men We Reaped*. But I remember being seven, eight years old and having nightmares about my uncles and my father being arrested and being sent to Parchman Prison.

Briger: As you said, your novel is based on a fictional town called Bois Sauvage, but it's also based on the town you grew up in and live in now, DeLisle, Mississippi. Can you describe it?

Ward: So DeLisle is situated on the back of the Bay of St. Louis, right? And it's very small. I think—I don't know the exact population count, but it can't be much more than a thousand. You know, maybe it's 1,500. Most of the Black people who live in the town have lived there—you know, their families have lived there for generations. And, you know, this is the case with my family.

It's interesting because it's the kind of place where family and community are sort of the same thing. You know, I'm related to a lot of the Black people who live in the town. Like, if I just count my maternal grandmother's people—so my grandmother's sisters and brothers, and then all their kids, and then their kids and then their kids—there are over two hundred of us.

Briger: Wow.

Ward: That's just a fourth of my—you know, like, of my family tree.

Briger: But you left. You left the town to go to college and grad school, and I think for work too, and, you know, stayed away for a while. And you've said before in earlier interviews how much you dislike the town because of the history of racism, and the state and how it limits the opportunities for

African Americans there, but now you've moved back. How did you come to that decision?

Ward: Well, I did. I returned around six years ago, and I have mixed feelings about it. You know, on one hand, I love my town, you know? And I love the place where I'm from, and I think in part it's because of my family. I think it's because of my community. I think it's because of the beauty of that place. But, you know, it's really frustrating to live in a place where you can see that, you know, the people in power do not care about your community. They don't care about your family. They don't care about people like you. They don't invest in your neighborhoods. They don't invest in your community.

You know, when I think about, like, just living in Mississippi and I feel like my elected representatives never represent my interests, ever, it's very frustrating because I can see what happens when generations of people live in poverty. I can see what happens when generations of people, like, struggle to bear up under the yoke of racism—of systemic racism. I see that when so many of the people in my community are addicted to drugs, you know, when so many of the people in my community never go on to seek education beyond high school—if they graduate from high school—right?—when so many people in my community spend their entire lives without health insurance, without dental insurance, without mental health treatment, when so many people in my community spend their entire lives working dead-end jobs only to, you know, become senior citizens and then survive on grease, basically—and because their family members take care of them.

Like, all of that is very frustrating for me. And because I have two kids now, like, I don't know if I will stay there. I don't know if I want my children, you know, to live there as teenagers. In some ways, I feel like I might be—I don't know, like I might be doing them a disservice.

Briger: Yeah, I was wondering.

Ward: . . . you know, by . . .

Briger: . . . if you were feeling ambivalent.

Ward: . . . by remaining there.

Briger: . . . about raising your kids there.

Ward: Yeah, I definitely am. I mean, I felt that way when I had a daughter, but I especially feel that way now that I have a son.

Briger: Yeah, yeah. Can you describe that a little bit?

Ward: You know, I—you know, my brother died when he was nineteen, right? He didn't even make it to twenty and he was hit by a drunk driver, and then no one was held accountable for his death. And I want my son to live. You know, I want him to live to be an adult. And not only do I want him to live, I want him to thrive, and I don't necessarily know if he will live or thrive, you know, if he spends his teenage years in Mississippi—in rural Mississippi. You know, that—I don't know. You know, part of me is really thinking that it might not be possible.

Briger: You've had some success in life. You've—you were able to—I think you were the first person in your family to go to college. Is that right?

Ward: Yeah, in my immediate family, so . . .

Briger: In your immediate family, right—and then you went to grad school. And you—you know, you've had success as a novelist. And it feels like you have a responsibility—that you feel responsibility to your family in Mississippi. I was wondering if that's also one of the reasons why it's hard for you to leave.

Ward: Definitely, yeah—because I do. I feel a sense of responsibility to them—right?—because I am at this point in my life where I have more resources than they have, so therefore, I feel like I should help. And so, you know, I do what I can. And it does. It does. It makes it harder for me to leave.

Briger: So there's that—the joy of having an extended family close to you, but then there's also responsibilities that come with that.

Ward: Yeah, definitely—plenty of responsibilities.

[*Laughter*]

Briger: Well, Jesmyn Ward, thanks so much for talking with us.

Ward: Thank you.

The Carnegie Shortlist Interviews: Jesmyn Ward

Annie Bostrom / 2017

This interview was originally conducted by Annie Bostrom and published on *Booklist* on December 15, 2017. Used with permission from *Booklist*, a publication of the American Library Association.

Annie Bostrom: *Sing, Unburied, Sing* is narrated by several characters. Jojo, a thirteen-year-old boy who's just beginning to grow out of his softness, inspires such tenderness and awe in readers. What prepared you to write from his perspective, in particular?

Jesmyn Ward: Jojo was the first character who was clear to me. I found his softness and his strength, and the way, as a mixed-race child, he contends with the past and present of the South all at once, immediately compelling. I really fell in love with him, as I do with many of my characters. Perhaps part of what prepared me to write from his perspective was having children, worrying about how they'll grow up here, in the South, with all that history. Jojo's youth, his tenderness, his love for his little sister, combined with the way the world might see him—as a man, as a threat—was something I really needed to write about.

Bostrom: As Leonie and her children head to Parchman Prison, we learn of the horrors this place has already wrought on her family. Do you remember when you first learned about Parchman or knew you would write about it?

Ward: Unlike my last novel, *Sing, Unburied, Sing* required a lot of research. As a child, I knew the prison existed, but I knew nothing about its past. I learned about its history when I first started writing the novel; really, my first encounter with it was in a book called *Worse Than Slavery* (1996), by David M. Oshinsky, which I picked up at Eso Won Books, in Los Angeles. I knew, as soon as I read about the prison, that I had to write about its history. At one time, it was basically a Black prison—98 percent of the inmates were Black—and there were children as young as twelve sent there for petty crimes. Reading that is when Richie, the child who Pop served with in Parchman, became real to me. And that's when I knew that Richie had to speak, and that the novel had to be a ghost story.

Bostrom: Do you, as a writer of both fiction and nonfiction, have a preference for writing one over the other?

Ward: Writing *Men We Reaped* (2013) was incredibly hard, and I don't think I could do something like that again. Editing *The Fire This Time* (2016) was a wholly different experience, emotionally, gathering all those voices to write about race in the US in the wake of so many tragedies; bringing together that diversity of experience and ideas felt really important to me. Generally, though, I find writing fiction to be much easier than writing creative nonfiction because it can be painful to really write into the heart of what I need to say with nonfiction, and I have to work not to be avoidant. Fiction is what feels like home to me.

Jesmyn Ward

Alma Mathijsen / 2018

This interview was originally conducted by Alma Mathijsen and published on Deltaworkers.org in 2018. Reprinted with permission.

"There is beauty to be found in the lives of my characters."

The latest novel from the awarded writer Jesmyn Ward is a sinister road trip through the poor South of the United States. *Sing, Unburied, Sing* is the first of her novels to be translated into Dutch. I met her in a coffee shop close to her favorite bookstore in New Orleans.

Alma Mathijsen: One of your favorite quotes is by William Faulkner: "To understand the world, you must first understand a place like Mississippi." After reading *Sing, Unburied, Sing*, I think I understand life in America's poorest state a little bit better. Is this what you set out to do?

Jesmyn Ward: One of the reasons I appreciate that quote so much is because I'm a Black writer from Mississippi. There are stories there that need to be heard. I want to tell the forgotten stories. That's why I had to write this book.

Mathijsen: You tell the story of Leonie, an addicted Black mother from Mississippi. She has two biracial children: Jojo and Kayla, for whom she doesn't care very well. That's the job of her parents. Leonie, Jojo, Kayla, and Misty (a friend of Leonie) set out on a road trip to pick up the children's white father, Michael, who has been released from Parchman Farm Prison. This goes against the will of the grandparents because the trip takes place during school days. What sparked the idea for this story?

Ward: I wanted to write about a road trip through modern Mississippi, where strange things would happen to a family. Then I started to do research, and soon I read more about Parchman. The story that I initially set out to make wasn't enough. That wasn't where the fire was. It was in Parchman. Black people were detained for the smallest things, like vagrancy,

116 CONVERSATIONS WITH JESMYN WARD

and forced to work. They were enslaved. Amongst these people were also minors, children like Richie. I just had to write about them; I realized the moment I started reading about them.

Mathijsen: Richie is a spirit from the past who was brutally murdered as a child, like many inmates. He's a ghost from Parchman Farm Prison who travels back with the family after they pick up Michael. What was it like to embody him?

Ward: I wanted to give him a voice. I wanted it to be believable. I wanted it to take place in the present. To do all those things, I had to make him into a ghost. I had to construct a world where ghosts exist. As real, as vivid as possible. Never before had I used magical realism in my work. I had to do it. I wanted to show that the past still resonates in the present. That's why he had to be a ghost. Only in the tenth revision, I dared to do it.

Mathijsen: Why then?

Ward: I had to embody a child that really existed, knowing that the child was tortured and died a horrifying death. That had to be done right. Personally, it was hard because of my brother [Ward's brother died at nineteen in a car accident, killed by a white man who was drunk driving. She wrote about it in her memoir *Men We Reaped* (Mathijsen)]. In everything I write, I create a shadow of my brother, to keep him alive in a certain way. If I don't write about him, who will? Richie is the most important character for me. He brings the past and the present together.

Mathijsen: You have revised the novel fifteen times. What changed with every draft?

Ward: First, I write a rough draft. If I discover a flaw four chapters in, I keep writing forward. I don't go back to the beginning. Then I let it sit for two to three weeks. After that period of time, I make a list of improvements. I go over the list one by one. I go back and do a complete revision with just the first point. That's how I work through the list. My fear is that I mess up if I deal with all of them together at once. Only when that's done, I'll ask a group of writer friends to please read it. I'll give them three months. After I have revised their feedback, I'll send it to my editor. I was lucky with *Salvage the Bones*; there were not a lot of notes. It didn't go like that with *Sing*. On almost every page, there was a note. With every book I write, I fear "how do I get all of this in?" I'm in no way a confident person, especially when it comes to my work. I feel inadequate.

Mathijsen: You won the National Book Award twice, for *Salvage the Bones* and *Sing, Unburied, Sing*; last year, you received the MacArthur

Genius Grant. How is it possible that you still feel insecure? And how do you cope with feeling that way?

Ward: It's who I am. I can't change that. I feel so desperate to tell stories. The need to do so is bigger than my insecurity. That wins.

Mathijsen: On the way back from the road trip, the family is being pulled over by the police. Almost everything that can go wrong, goes wrong. How did you set up this chapter?

Ward: During the writing of this novel, almost every month, a Black man was being killed by a policeman. I knew from the beginning that they had to be pulled over. They're poor, they drive a shitty car, the mom is Black. I knew that scene was coming, but still I wasn't emotionally prepared. I don't plot; I'm a pantser. That moment was important; I didn't know what would happen. I wrote blindly. Maybe Jojo would die. I know the characters well; they lead me. I think it's important that I didn't know. I think the reader feels that.

Mathijsen: The contrast between the poetic prose and the harsh environment of the story is very distinctive. Was that a deliberate choice?

Ward: My prose is poetic because of that. I'm not sure if this also counts for the Netherlands, but in the US, there is a trend to write clean, straightforward, without adjectives, no metaphors. That's not what attracted me to literature. Those things made me love reading. I think my work would be very hard to read if the prose was spare. I feel like there has to be some beauty to endure. It also shows that there is beauty to be found in the lives of my characters. Leonie might be a bad mom, but in her heart, she has love for her brother.

Mathijsen: Even though Leonie neglects her children, I did feel sympathy for her. How was that for you?

Ward: In the beginning, I had a hard time writing from her perspective. Jojo came to me first. He demanded that I tell his story. Leonie was difficult. She's awful to the people who love her. Still I can't change her; she is who she is. What if she lost a brother, I thought. Is it possible she's so horrible to everyone because of grief? Then I wrote about how her brother had lived and how he died. Then Leonie made sense. She can't sit with loss. She glances at it but can't sit with it. In order to be healing, you have to learn how to sit with it. Leonie keeps running away from it. Everyone who has lost someone knows it won't go away. You have to accept the pain. You hurt; you cry.

Mathijsen: You say you can't change Leonie even though you are the writer. Could you explain that?

Ward: It's hard actually to explain. A character presents itself. As a writer, I can build on that, but the core will remain the same. That's impossible for me to change.

Mathijsen: Do you know women like Leonie?

Ward: Unfortunately, yes. I come from a really small town in Mississippi where mostly working class or poor people live. It's a very tight community; generations after generations keep living there. A lot of the people have to walk a tightrope. They live from hustle to hustle, being hungry and poor. Lots of them fall prey to addiction. Age[s] range from teens to elderly. Everything comes later to Mississippi. For a long time, it was crack cocaine. Now it's meth and opiates. It's not an easy thing to try to solve. There's so much behind addictions, like poverty, stress of racism, bad education, so many factors. Drugs are a secret relief. That's what it is to Leonie.

Mathijsen: In your acceptance speech for your already second National Book Award, you started with a rejection from a publisher early on in your career: "People will not read your work because these are not universal stories." Thousands of people read your work; it will be translated into many languages. Your stories prove to be very universal. What is it in your stories that make them indeed so very universal?

Ward: The publication of my first novel was a battle. The first reaction often was: why is this relevant? If your characters don't look like the majority, your work is not recognizable. People are looking for similarities. After winning the first National Book Award, people started to see something. What does it mean to be human? What does it mean to maintain relationships? What does it mean to love someone and lose them? Yes, these are stories about Black poor people, and they are just as relevant. They are universal.

Jesmyn Ward on Writing Honest Novels with Good Titles, Inhabiting Ghosts, and Learning to Love Faulkner

Jennifer Acker / 2020

This interview was conducted as part of Amherst College LitFest on February 29, 2020. This edited version was first published in *The Common* on May 21, 2020. Reprinted with permission.

[*Jesmyn Ward reads the opening of* Sing, Unburied, Sing.]

Jennifer Acker: I think what comes through so clearly in that passage are all of the details of that property and all the norms of the community. So I want you to just tell us a little bit more about this place you've created, Bois Sauvage. Tell us what this place is like, and why it's a fictional place, because it is very much inspired by your home.

Jesmyn Ward: When I came up with the idea of creating a fictional town that's based on my hometown, one of the reasons I wanted to do so was because I felt like the place where I'm from is so small that it would be harder to write about if I didn't transform it. Sometimes I feel like the Bois Sauvage that I write about is this idealized version of my hometown, and not my hometown. Even though *Sing, Unburied, Sing* takes place in 2016 to 2017, I feel like Bois Sauvage is the idealized version of DeLisle, my hometown, from maybe in the 1980s when I was a child, when it was even more rural than it is now. Both DeLisle and Bois Sauvage are small rural places where community is very important, where families have been living for generations, because everyone knows everyone, and everyone knows everyone's history. I think part of what I'm trying to communicate or explore in Bois Sauvage is this idea of community and what community looks like in a place like that, and how a community can help its people survive in very specific, particular ways. I think I am also trying to convey the beauty of that area and that region.

Acker: And have you always written about this place while you have been in DeLisle or near it, or have you ever written about it from afar?

Ward: *Sing, Unburied, Sing* is the only book that I've written about Bois Sauvage while living in my hometown on the Mississippi Gulf Coast. When I wrote my first novel, I was living in Michigan; when I wrote my second novel, I was living in California in the Bay Area; when I wrote my memoir, I was living in Oxford, Mississippi—so again, away from home. Most of the books that I've written, I actually wasn't at home. To write about that place while I was living elsewhere in some ways was a relief because I always felt a strong sense of homesickness whenever I was out in the world. And so, to write about this fictionalized version of my hometown allowed me to be there, in a way. I have friends who are writers who said they can't write about the place they're from while they're living there, but I've never had that problem.

Acker: So in the opening passage that you read, Pop is slaughtering a goat, and I was struck by that; at the beginning of *Salvage the Bones*, there's a dog giving birth to puppies. What is it about the characters' relationship to animals that draws you to writing these opening scenes with the animals and people in very close connection?

Ward: You know, *Salvage the Bones*—it took me a long time to find the right beginning for the book, to find the right moment to enter this story. I am normally a very linear writer. I have to write from the beginning all the way to the end. I have some friends who don't; they write around; they write the ending; they write a third of the way through, and then go back towards the end, and my brain just doesn't work that way. It took me a while to find the right spot to enter this story. I don't even know how I found it— suddenly, I was in that shed, I was there with the dog who was giving birth. And it just seemed like the right moment, maybe because I think that the act of giving birth is often hopeful and imbued with a certain sense of promise and potential. This moment with the animals worked so well in *Salvage the Bones*, and so I thought, "Well, maybe I should write about animals in the beginning moment of *Sing, Unburied, Sing*." But, again, it took me a long time to figure exactly when and where that moment would be. Because *Sing, Unburied, Sing* is about death, loss, and the afterlife, maybe it would make sense to begin with this moment of slaughter.

Acker: Speaking about the afterlife in *Sing, Unburied, Sing*, having a ghost as one of your characters was a new thing in that book. I wonder if you could tell us about the process of developing that character and developing the rules surrounding Richie, the ghost.

Ward: So when I began writing *Sing, Unburied, Sing,* I knew that there would be an element of magic there. I knew that I wanted Mam to have these powers, and I wanted Jojo to have certain psychic powers. For a long time, I had wanted to write something that incorporated elements of magic and the supernatural. But I just didn't. I don't know if I was afraid to, or I just felt like, in literary fiction, that was frowned upon, and that's why I didn't do it. But with this book, I just decided to commit to it. But I was not aware of the fact that there would be ghosts. Another thing that I knew from the beginning: the characters were going to take this road trip to Parchman Prison. Originally, I just thought this would be a road trip novel. And then I began researching Parchman Prison because I knew nothing about it. I found out that kids like Richie existed. Richie is this kid who was thirteen years old when he was sent to Parchman Prison for a very minor crime. In the 1940s, when you were sent to Parchman Prison, you were basically re-enslaved. Parchman Prison used to be a working plantation. There, the inmates were guarded by other inmates with guns and overseers on horses. When they broke rules, they were beaten. If they tried to escape and they were killed by a guard (and all the guards were inmates with guns), the inmate, guard with the gun, was given his freedom.

When I found out that children like Richie existed, I was so horrified by that fact. Not only that this was a fact of history but also that I was ignorant of it. I grew up in Mississippi, I took Mississippi history, and yet I never knew that that was the case. I thought it was so awful that kids like Richie existed and that they've been erased from history, silenced, that I thought "I have to write a character like this, I have to write about a child that's been sent to this place." But I wanted that child to have agency and voice, which children like him had been denied in life. And the only way that I could figure out how to do that was by making him a ghost. And that's how I discovered that I was writing a ghost story in addition to a road trip. Then I was scared.

Acker: Ghosts are scary!

Ward: Ghosts are scary, and I had never written anything like that before. I knew then that the afterlife and the world of the afterlife would need texture. There would have to be rules. I had to figure out, okay, who can see Richie, and what are the rules of the afterlife, what is the existence like for him as a ghost, and what can he perceive in the afterlife?

Acker: Do you mind telling us how you came up with the title for this book?

122 CONVERSATIONS WITH JESMYN WARD

Ward: This is always such a hard question for me to answer! I'm really bad at titles. One of the professors I studied with at University of Michigan at Ann Arbor is Peter Ho Davies, and one of the things that Peter taught me was that you should try to have a working title for your novel in progress from the very beginning, and then he told me that as you work your way into the novel, your ideas about what the title will be will change. And it should change because your understanding of who the characters are and what the novel is about and what is at the heart of the novel—that will change as you write your way into the book and as you discover more. And so, I did that. And I can't remember [what the title was]—whatever it was, it was terrible. I did that with *Sing, Unburied, Sing*, but by the time I got to the fifteenth/sixteenth draft, I didn't have a for-sure title. Nothing seemed to fit. I had been generating a list of possible titles as I went along, and so I probably had like thirty titles. I would just try them on, and if it didn't seem right, I would discard them. I really like titles that are very active—that have an active verb. Titles that command. That address the reader in some way. In the book, there is a sort of divine order in the afterlife expressed through music, and I thought, "Maybe I should use the word 'sing' in the title, as a sort of command." But then I thought, okay, I need to be directing this towards someone. And so I thought, I want it to apply to everyone—the living and the dead. What word could I use? Then I came up with "unburied." Then I plugged "Sing, Unburied" into Amazon to try and see if someone already had that title. No one did, and so I thought, okay I can use this, but then there was something about the musicality of the title that wasn't there yet. And I thought, what if I repeat the word "sing"? "Sing, Unburied, Sing." And it seemed to work.

Acker: Moving back in time a little bit to your first novel, *Where the Line Bleeds*, about these two twins, twin brothers. We meet them when they're just graduating from high school, and their primary struggles throughout the course of the book are getting jobs but also dealing with their parents—the mom has been gone a long time but comes back, and the dad is failing to recover from addiction. So they have it hard, these kids. But I've read that you've said that you felt like you were too much in love with your characters and protected them in some ways in the first book. I wonder if you could tell us about that realization about that treatment of characters and how you've tried to adjust that as you wrote your second novel.

Ward: That is something that I realized I did after the book was out in the world. I thought back to when I wrote *Where the Line Bleeds*; it was my first novel, I didn't know what I was doing. I took a couple years off after I graduated undergrad, and I worked. And while I worked, I wrote nothing. When

I went back to school at University of Michigan and was studying to get my MFA, I thought, "Okay, if I don't write a novel here, I will never write a novel," because I am not the kind of writer who can work a forty-hour-week job and also produce novels at the same time. Writing that first novel, I realized that I loved my characters and that they reminded me of people that I grew up with, people in my family, people in my community. And I think that when I was writing that story, the story wanted to go to darker places, that there were harder, darker things that could have happened to those characters, plot-wise, that would arise out of the choices that they've made or didn't make. But because I loved them so much, and because they seemed to be reflections of a lot of people in my family and people I grew up with—the twins especially have characteristics of my brother—I couldn't let the narrative take on a life of its own. I wanted to protect those characters because they reminded me of people that I loved, and so I didn't let the narrative take on a life of its own. I sort of stifled it; I didn't want anything bad to happen to them. And I didn't realize that I did that until a couple years after publication.

After Hurricane Katrina, after I lost a lot of people close to me, I was looking at my family and looking at my community and realizing how difficult life was for so many people whom I loved. If I am going to make the commitment to write about these people, who could be members of my family or members of my community, then I have to be honest about the circumstances of our lives. I can't protect them because nobody protects us, and hard things happen to people I love all the time. So I realized I had to be honest. If I'm gonna take on that responsibility, I have to be honest about the circumstances of our lives.

Acker: Are there any other lessons from the first novel, or even the second novel, or the third novel that you've carried forward?

Ward: I feel like each book that I've written teaches me something. With *Where the Line Bleeds*, I learned about the fact that I have to let the narrative take on a life, and I think that I also learned that I am not comfortable writing from the third-person perspective. With *Salvage the Bones*, I learned that I am comfortable writing from the first-person perspective, and I also learned that I could tell a story that had a very tight structure—*Salvage the Bones* is told over twelve days, and each day is a chapter. In my memoir, I think that I learned that my stories didn't need to have a straightforward, linear structure, and that I could tell a story with a sort of odd, unexpected structure. I could tell a story in a way where it jumps back and forth in time. And then with *Sing, Unburied, Sing*, I think I learned that I could research and then incorporate my research in a way that felt organic to the story—I didn't know

124 CONVERSATIONS WITH JESMYN WARD

that I could do that before I wrote that book—and also that I could tell a story from multiple perspectives because I hadn't done that before either.

Acker: I wonder if you could take us back to the readerly child that you were and say something about what books meant to you as a kid, when you first started thinking about writing, and when you actually did start doing some writing, and what that felt like.

Ward: My family didn't have money for books. So I was a library kid. But the town that I live in is so small that we don't have a local public library, so I depended on my school library— the elementary school library, the middle school library—for my books. I checked all of them out. I remember being in second grade and all the other kids in my class, they hated reading. We had to do these reading comprehension projects—they hated doing them. I just remember one day realizing that everybody else hates reading. But you know what? I love this! I articulated that to myself at a very young age, but I continuously found myself drawn to books where the main character was a girl, some young, scrappy girl. I loved books like *Pippi Longstocking* and *The Secret Garden* and *Roll of Thunder, Hear My Cry* and *The Hero and the Crow* and *Anne of Green Gables*. If a girl was the main character, I was going to read it. Also, if there were witches involved, I was right there. And all the librarians when I was younger, they didn't really give me much direction. So I just perused the shelves and checked things out and just, like, devoured them. And back then, books were magical, and it seemed like there was something magic about what writers did.

But when I was young, I didn't think I was capable of that kind of magic. So when I first started attempting to write, I began with poetry. Poetry seems more manageable, much shorter. So I started writing poetry when I was in sixth grade. I wrote this terrible poem for Arbor Day, but my teachers really liked it, and they asked me to read it. And I got a pretty positive response from everyone. And so, I think that was the first time that I thought, "Maybe I can do this thing." I was a terrible poet for much of my formative years. Then I got to college, and I realized that I was a terrible poet, and I decided to redirect my attention to fiction because I felt like maybe I had a little bit (not a lot) more understanding of what you need in fiction to write a good story than I did in poetry. I had no idea what was going on in poetry.

Acker: What is one thing you would like young people to take away from their reading of *Sing, Unburied, Sing*?

Ward: One idea or one thematic concern that I keep returning to again and again in my work is this question of how do children who have to bear adult burdens survive and how do they hopefully thrive in spite of having to bear those adult burdens? I think that that's one thing I would want teen-age readers to take away from *Sing, Unburied, Sing*—the fact that you can thrive in spite of the fact that you might have to bear adult burdens before you should. There are multiple things that shore you up and help you to survive and thrive in spite of that. You might have a very difficult home life, you might have parents who are failing you in one way or another, and the system might be failing you in some ways. But you can survive and thrive in spite of that.

Acker: What gives you hope as a writer?

Ward: I think a lot about my parents and my grandparents and great grandparents—and I am very aware of how much more difficult their lives were. Because they're Black and because they lived in Mississippi in the 1930s and '40s and '50s and '60s. I think about how they still expressed themselves creatively through art, through gardening, through cooking. How they still did their best to help their children and other people in their families thrive and survive, and it was still important to them to help their community survive and thrive. I think that I would feel as if I were disre-specting them and not honoring their legacy if I did not acknowledge the role that hope played in their lives.

Acker: So, question about Faulkner. Is Faulker, who also wrote about a tiny patch of the US South, a meaningful reference for you?

Ward: Yes. But it wasn't always true. I read Faulkner for the first time when I was in high school. I think I read one of his short stories and I thought, "Why do people love this? I hate this. This is overly complicated; I don't know what's going on." I just didn't get it. I remember specifically thinking that because this kid in my class was like, "Faulkner is my favorite writer." Then we read a short story, and I thought, "God, you're so preten-tious." So I didn't get it when I was in high school. Then I went to college and I read him again, and I still didn't get it. I better understood what was hap-pening, but there was no visceral reaction, no response to his work. Then, I graduated, and I was in my early- to mid-twenties and living in NYC, and I read *The Sound and the Fury*, and I still did not get it.

Acker: But you kept trying!

Ward: I did, I kept trying. I was like, "This is really impressive!" but it just didn't spark a response. I don't know why. Maybe I just wasn't in the right place emotionally and developmentally. I don't know! It wasn't until I went to Michigan. I was twenty-six or twenty-seven. I read *As I Lay Dying*. I remember opening it up and reading the first couple pages. Then I just closed it, and I was like, "Goddamn. This is amazing. Maybe I should just quit, because I can never do that." I recognized everything about that South that he was writing about.

126 CONVERSATIONS WITH JESMYN WARD

And I just had this immediate, very emotional reaction to his work where I felt that deep love and also the hate that I feel for the place that I'm from.

When I was still in school and I did various fellowship programs, sometimes I would get pushback from my peers when they would say, "I don't understand, these people are hardly educated, how are they expressing themselves, why are they using this language, why are they expressing themselves in this way?" My reply was to point at Faulkner and be like, "He did! If he did it, why can't I do it?" I love his work, but I do feel like he fails his characters of color. Because they're not complex people, they don't have rich interior lives. There's a big difference between the lives that they lead and how they are written, while his white characters are fully realized and complicated and complex and they evoke very strong emotional responses in his readers. His characters of color are often flat, and they don't evoke that kind of a response. That's another thing that he taught me.

Acker: I know that you're heavily invested in research now for the novel that you're currently working on. Anything you'd be comfortable sharing about the book that you're working on and how you're digging into that material and how you're building that world?

Ward: It's killing me. I'm at the halfway mark right now. I am writing a novel set in the early to mid-1800s in New Orleans during the height of the domestic slave trade, and it follows an enslaved woman as she is sold south from the Carolinas, marched to New Orleans, and then auctioned off. I knew close to nothing about slavery before I began working on this project. So I've done a lot of research. I am still researching. I've never worked on a project like this; I've never written a book where I needed to research so much. I began reading, and then I discovered that it was good to learn and to attempt to begin to gain my bearings in this world, but it was also an easy way to procrastinate and to push off diving into the work and beginning. After two years, I thought, "You know what? Probably time to write something." And I don't know everything yet, but I'll just research as I go. As I get to a place in the book where I don't know, then I'll try to find that information. But if I continue to research in the hopes that I get to a place where I'm like, "I'm knowledgeable about this," then I'll never start because there is so much information! There is always another book to read, another perspective to find. So that's what I am working on now, I am reading as I go. It is very difficult.

Acker: Well, I think that there are many people in this room that will be cheering you on as you go through the process of writing this next book, and we wish you lots of hope and fun and endurance.

Ward: Thank you.

Two-Time National Book Award–Winning Author Jesmyn Ward on Her Novel *Let Us Descend*

Ayesha Rascoe / 2023

© 2023 National Public Radio Inc. News report that was originally broadcast on NPR's *Weekend Edition Sunday* on October 22, 2023, and is used with the permission of NPR. Any unauthorized duplication is strictly prohibited.

Ayesha Rascoe: In her new novel set before the Civil War, author Jesmyn Ward drops readers into the life of a young, enslaved Black woman named Annis in the American South. We follow Annis through a hellscape as she's separated from her mother, sent to an auction, and sold to another slave owner. But despite her journey through one horror after another, Annis also finds brief moments of tenderness.

Jesmyn Ward: [*Reads*] After the rain passes, the sun dogs us for days. It burns me red. The wind scrapes my face, blowing incessantly for a week. Its rush is strange and loud, and so relentless that I miss the sound of flowing water; we are all startled by the Georgia men telling us to halt in a sudden clearing. There's a green hill, trees all around us in an overturned bowl, a waterfall tossing down into a pool the same deep green as the trees around us. It's so beautiful I feel a turning in my chest, my heart a small bird stirring in its nest. For a moment, I don't feel bound. I forget what holds me. But the ache of me, through wrist and hip and thigh, tunnels me back down into my body, along with this rope. I yank when we stop, pull the wire of it with my arms, just so it can beat back that beauty. I want it to turn my awe to bitter [*Let Us Descend* 59].

Rascoe: Jesmyn Ward is a two-time National Book Award–winning author, and her new novel is titled *Let Us Descend*. Jesmyn Ward, welcome.

Ward: It's good to be here.

Rascoe: So how did you come to understand Annis's life as you wrote her story? Was this something that required a lot of research? What were you tapping into?

Ward: It definitely required a lot of research. I mean, I read for around two and one-half years before I actually began writing her story. So for the first—I don't know—like, four years of me actually, like, working on her story and, like, writing her story, I was having problems. I couldn't write past, like, the first three chapters. It was hard for me to access who she was as a person, and I think that's because I was so hung up on the fact that I was writing about an enslaved person. And I feel like in our imagination, especially Black Americans, I feel like it's very difficult for us to get beyond the fact that enslaved people had little to no physical agency. And I think it makes us just flatten them, right? Like, they're flattened to just be victims often, and even I was struggling with it.

And honestly, it wasn't until I suffered a deep loss. My partner actually died in 2020, and I was dealing with, like, the fresh grief of that and struggling with the fresh grief of that, of his loss. After, you know—I don't know—like, six months of me trying to figure out whether or not I would ever finish *Let Us Descend*, I came back to the book. Like, I figured out that my partner, you know, who I lost, would not want my grief to silence me.

Rascoe: You mentioned your loss. And I am so sorry for your loss and offer my condolences.

Ward: Thank you.

Rascoe: Did you look at the book, *Let Us Descend*—and reading it, it is like going lower and lower, like, descending into something, sinking down into something very dark. Like, did you look at it as a physical representation of grief kind of embodied by the story of Annis?

Ward: I did. I looked at it as a physical representation of grief and also as a descent into a kind of hell, which is why I aligned it with Dante's *Inferno*, right? But at the same time that it was a descent into a kind of hell—you know, the hell of Mississippi and Louisiana and the New Orleans slave markets in the early 1800s—I also feel like it is a descent into an afterlife. In part, the book is about Annis finding her way through her grief to a different life than the one that she thought she might have and the one that she wanted. And in that, I very much identified with Annis, like, with her character because for me—like, that's one of the hardest things about grief—is that this life that you thought you had—once you lose that person, that life, that possible life—it doesn't exist anymore.

Rascoe: For much of the book, Annis is communicating with a spirit that she calls Aza, and it kind of seems to appear to her as a storm or, you know, wind that moves through the trees. That idea of using this sort of spirituality, talking to the ancestors, talking to the land's spirit—why was it important to you to deal with this form of spirituality in this book?

Ward: Because I think one of the ways that Black Americans were able to survive the system of slavery is through an expansive evolving spirituality—right?—the kind of spirituality where they could sort of learn to read the land, where they could learn to use herbs and roots and mushrooms—right?—to heal them—where they just, I think, saw or understood that there was more to this world than their enslavement.

And I wanted that to be present in this novel because I felt like I couldn't write this novel about a person who was enslaved if it was rooted in social realism because I feel like that novel is not reflective of the kind of reality that I've been trying to construct in all my fiction. And it's not true to the way that I think about the world and the way that, you know, the people that I come from down here in Mississippi—that they think about the world, right? I mean, we think the world is suffused with spirit. You know, I thought it important for this tale, you know, this origin story, this woman that appeared to me of Annis—that her reality should reflect that.

Rascoe: In the advance copy of this book, you wrote—and it's, like, on the cover—it seemed like you want to get the message out there that it is difficult to walk south with Annis, but you said, "But I promise that if you come with me, you will rise. It will be worth the work, worth the walking." What do you mean by that phrase, you will rise?

Ward: I recognize that there's a certain resistance to reading books about enslaved people because it is hard to relive trauma, and so I acknowledge that. But I think that this book specifically and this story is also suffused with hope. This book is suffused with resistance because I think that hope is at the heart of resistance. It was very important to me to depict that and, hopefully, in depicting that, to attempt to change people's understanding of what enslaved people live through, you know, and to counter that narrative that they chose to be victims, or they just didn't resist, and they just accepted their fate. No. They fought every step of the way because they believed in the sanctity and the sacred nature of their lives and of their existence. They believed that their lives mattered.

Rascoe: That's Jesmyn Ward. Her new novel is called *Let Us Descend*, and it comes out October 24. Thank you so much for joining us.

Ward: Thank you.

Poured Over: Jesmyn Ward on *Let Us Descend*

Miwa Messer / 2023

This interview was originally conducted by Miwa Messer on *Poured Over Podcast* © 2023 Barnes & Noble on October 24, 2023. This edited transcript is reprinted with the permission of Miwa Messer and Barnes & Noble.

Miwa Messer: I'm Miwa Messer, the producer and host of *Poured Over*, and Jesmyn Ward is absolutely one of my favorite writers working today, twice winner of the National Book Award, a MacArthur Genius Grant recipient. And yes, I'm sorry, MacArthur folks, I know you would prefer we not call them "genius grants." But it's too fun to say. There's a new novel, *Let Us Descend*, and we're not in Bois Sauvage anymore. You've written a historical novel, in a way. Can we talk about the roots of this book?

Jesmyn Ward: So, I stumbled across the idea for this novel around seven years ago. Well, I work and teach at Tulane; I spend a lot of time in the car. And it just so happened that seven years ago, I was on my way to Tulane, and I was listening to NPR, and I heard a show called *Tripod*, [in] which they were celebrating three hundred years of New Orleans history. And I'd heard a couple of episodes before, and they were about different things like bullfighting in New Orleans, or, you know, just random things that happen in New Orleans history that weren't as well-known, right? And so, on the day that I stumbled across this novel idea, I was listening to the show, and that show was specifically about the slave trade in New Orleans. And it was specifically about slave pens and slave pens around the city of New Orleans.

First of all, I didn't know they call them "slave pens." And second of all, I did not know that there were so many of them. Third, of course, you know, because I hadn't taken history since high school, I did not realize that New Orleans was basically the capital of the domestic slave trade once they outlawed the transatlantic trade, right? So, I didn't know any of those things, and so, I was just, you know, I have family in New Orleans; my dad lived there for years, my uncles lived there, I would go to the city all the time when I was a kid. There was nothing that I saw on the landscape of that city that indicated to me that that was the history. And so, that [day], I was listening to the program, and the historian that the journalist was speaking to said that, as of that moment in time, seven years ago, there were only two markers in the city of New Orleans where slave pens had been located or were located. And one of them was in the wrong location. Right? The only one, really, and that was a terrible fact to learn. I immediately teared up.

I admit I was more emotional at the time, because at the time, I was pregnant with my second child, right? But I teared up because I thought all of the people who came who were enslaved and who were sent to that city and came to that city, and suffered in that way, in that particular way, all of that, that suffering and that pain has been erased, right, erased from the landscape, and then also been erased from, like, public consciousness in a way. And so I thought, *What if I write a story specifically about a woman?* She was a woman from the very beginning. *What if I write a story about a woman who is going through that*, right? In my own small way, what if I try to bring it back, bring a person like this and bring this history, this fact back into public consciousness? And so, that's where she was born.

But I didn't actually write anything about Annis– I didn't write a word of *Let Us Descend* for maybe two and a half years after that—because I realized really early on that I didn't know anything, like I knew nothing [about the slave trade], you know. And so, I spent two and a half years reading and still felt like I didn't [know]; of course, I could never know everything, right? But still, I didn't know enough. But I just sort of got to a point after I'd read for so long where I thought, *Okay, if you wait*—I talked to myself, so I was talking to myself; it's okay—*if you wait to begin writing this book until you feel like you know enough, you're never going to begin*, right? Or *if you wait to begin this book until you feel like you know all the facts and you won't get anything wrong, you will never write this book because you can never know all the facts, and you'll probably get something wrong.* And so, I just, I just thought, *Well, I'm gonna—I will start. And if there are things that pop up that I don't know, then I'll just continue to research as I write, but I have to start* because basically, my fear of getting something wrong—because I was writing in a completely different genre, that was—it was—terrifying to me.

Messer: I mean, I understand on the surface that a historical novel is not what you've been doing with the Bois Sauvage novels, you know, *Sing Unburied, Sing, Salvage the Bones*, and *Where the Line Bleeds*; those three novels obviously sit in the same world. And it's present day, and they all share an orbit. But thematically, we're talking about grief and loss and community. And that very thin line between what we consider reality and the supernatural. So, I felt like I was very much in your hands and very much in a novel written by you, even though some of the framework was different. But I see the direct line between the earlier books and this one, certainly, and the women in this, I love them. I love Annis, I love her mama, I love who we come to see as her grandmother, Mama Aza. But you've started with her voice. Annis, you've started with her, you started with her experience. But then there's an extra layer to this as well, which is Dante and the *Inferno*. And there's a very clear connection between the sort of classic world literature which I went back to because of you, and I had not picked up that book in a really long time. And, in fact, I had to buy a new copy, because I didn't want to deal with my original copies. But this connection, right, this canvas, you have this moment, you're in the car, you're listening to NPR, you're doing all the research, but ultimately, it's story that carries you through.

Ward: Right? It is, and I think that was something that I had to muddle my way through, [it] probably took me the first four to five years of writing, which is one reason why this book has taken me a longer amount of time to write than any of the books. Because I think I was so hung up on the fact that it was taking place in the early 1800s. You know, and I was still wrestling with that fear, that it was hard for me to sink into Annis as a character and live in the moment with Annis as a character and hold space for her voice and hear her voice, right? There was my fear around it all being set in the past and getting things wrong. And then also, at first, the fact that she had little to no physical agency as an enslaved person. I was very hung up on that fact; I couldn't move beyond [it], like, it's very hard for me to figure out—how do I write about this person? How do I make her integral to the plot and the plot feel natural to her and who she is, without physical agency, right?

And it took me a good, like I said, like four years at least, of writing, unsuccessful beginning after unsuccessful beginning after unsuccessful beginning, to begin to realize, you know, I had to get chapters in each time, to begin to realize that there are other types of agency that she has: she has emotional agency, she has mental agency, she has imaginative agency, she has a sort of spiritual agency, right? So, she can be bound, you know, and someone else can direct her, right, and make her physically do things that she doesn't want to do. But she has all of these other ways to sort of move through the world and access her own power.

And, you know, I think that's just one of the reasons that it took me, again, so long to get to that is because, unfortunately, the narrative around enslaved people, I feel like, often, I won't use the word "narrative," the public conversation about enslaved people, I feel like that often flattens them.

Messer: Absolutely.

Ward: And maybe the language in slave narratives can be hard to access. So, I feel like it can often be hard for us, as people, you know, who live right now in this moment in time, to immerse ourselves in that experience and see enslaved people as, like, fully fledged, complicated, complex people. And so, I think I had to get over all of that too, at the beginning of that process.

Messer: I think part of it [is], you know, the way we're taught about slavery, certainly in America. I grew up outside of Boston, and the way things get taught or the emphasis that's put on certain moments—they pick their moments when they're teaching, right?—but we're missing so much of the historical record, right? We have names, we have dates, we have physical characteristics. I mean, literally, enslaved people were not allowed—and I use sort of air quotes around them, but—to read or write. And if you could teach yourself or find someone to teach you, that opened up an entire universe, but the idea that you were not—because of who you are, in your circumstances—allowed to learn to read and write, which is a very fundamental human experience. We're missing giant chunks of information. And when we're missing information, people kind of assume that it just didn't exist, right?

And so, part of the joy for me, and I'm using "joy" very specifically, part of the joy for me in reading *Let Us Descend* was watching Annis figure out what mattered to her. And her mother just looms so large in her imagination, and I love her mother's character, but Annis's fighting with Mama Aza. . . . And just saying—well, it's not just immediate, right, it's not immediately—that you have this thing that's bigger than you, and of course, you're just gonna let it dictate what you're doing. And I just, I love those moments, where she's kind of doing this [fighting] now. And it gets us into exactly what you're talking about, that agency, and what she'd do.

Ward: Right, she's coming into her personhood, in a way. I mean, she spent, you know, the time before we entered the novel, and the early parts of the novel—and she's very much, you know, her mother's daughter, you know: her mother has taught her how to navigate this oppressive system. But then, when she no longer has her mother there physically, and she still has her there emotionally, I feel like, you know, in her memory, her mother still looms really large, like in Annis's consciousness. And as she's, like, bringing everything that she has with her, to help her to navigate this world, I think it's to her mother's credit for that.

And [her] approach [to] this spirit, right, I feel like she's very smart about it. And I think that while she's tempted to just, like, it would be easier to just feel that sense of relief at not being alone, and being in the presence of this supernatural being, right, who can definitely do things for you, she doesn't completely capitulate, you know. She doesn't completely sort of put herself in the hands of that spirit, you know. She still thinks critically, and comes to sort of understand that, like you're saying, what she wants is important, how she may one day want to live, that is important. You know, I think she comes to the understanding that she's not without a certain sense of power in the world. And I think, too, like, that's another thing, you know, that I feel like we seldom think about in reference to enslaved people, right? The kinds of powers that they had and the kinds of powers that they exercised, right, even if it's a small thing, like breaking a tool, or bargaining with someone who's trying to buy you, right, and changing the narrative around that. They did what they could.

Messer: I'm also thinking about Annis in terms of not having trust, I mean, why would you? There is somehow an expectation from outside that you would trust the situation you're in, that you keep getting ripped away from your family, you keep getting ripped away from your home, you have no concept of home, because it changes without any input from you. All of these things were—why should you trust anyone around you? I mean, yes, you have peers in a way, and I use that word gently. But at the same time, you don't know them; they don't know you if the ground is always shifting under your feet. So why would you actually trust a supernatural being who comes in and says, well, I can make it all better, just do what I want. Right? Do what I tell you to do. And she's like, she's side-eyeing Aza right now.

Ward: Right? Right. And she's heard that her whole life, I mean, always, right? The people in this world who have power continuously use people like her for whatever they want, to get whatever they want, for profit, for, you know, money, to provide for their families, right, and legacy. So I think, from my understanding of hers, I think that she's like wait, you know; in that respect, you're just like all these [people], you know? You're just like my Sire, you're just like this person, you're just like that person. Because you wield this power, I guess, they're at that time, at least in my understanding of this world, there's still some resistance to adapting, you know, or capitulating to Christianity. Right? So my understanding of her is that that hasn't neces- sarily been drilled into her consciousness, right, in accepting Christianity, to accept, you know, this matrix of power. Right? So, I think for her, there would be more pushback, more resistance. And another thing is, like, it was important for me that not only that would cause her to distrust Aza—these supernatural beings that keep appearing in her world—I thought that it would be interesting if the supernatural world that existed here, if it did have more texture, if it was more complicated, if beings weren't all altruistic and just wanting to bless people just to bless them, right? Like, I don't know, I thought that they would reflect a bit more of the world and the messiness of humanity, I guess.

Messer: And to me, that goes directly to Greek mythology, but also what I know of African mythology, you know, and I wish there were more; certainly, I feel like the Greek myths and the Roman myths were put in front of me very clearly and very cleanly for a very long time. And just like, well, you know, there are other stories, too, but the connection, in this case, and especially that piece, where, you know, Christianity is not the dominant spiritual force in this context; why would it be? We're talking about the 1800s. We haven't—the world isn't the world yet, but we can see the outlines, right? And this idea, too, they're moments where Aza is asking Annis for her gratitude; she's [Aza is] like, you should be grateful to me, I just did this for you. And she's [Annis is] like, actually, that was Mary, or that was Esther, or that was my mother, teaching me something, that everything has its place. But this idea that even in a world that is more familiar than not, power is going to do what power is going to do.

And it's interesting to me that you and Zadie Smith both have written historical novels this year. And it's kind of a first, obviously, and yes, it is a different genre; I do want to recognize that it's a different kind of writing experience. But I love the idea that you found a way through *Let Us Descend* to talk about this moment that we are in and that you never lose sight of it. And I feel like even though I know I'm mentally in the 1800s, I can recognize Annis, I can recognize her mother, I can even recognize Aza.

And when you were saying a second ago that you were sort of struggling with making sure you had space for her voice, I was thinking about something you'd said about the writing of *Sing, Unburied, Sing*, that Leonie gave you a little bit of trouble, that you had a hard time initially with her. And I'm thinking, well, you certainly worked around both of those. I've read the finished books; I know you worked around it. But the idea that these women are who they are, I still see a direct line between Annis and Leonie, who happens to actually be one of my favorite characters in literature; I love her. I mean, I love all the characters in *Sing, Unburied, Sing*, even Michael as much as I can. Like, can we talk about sort of the evolution of the characters and the room that you give them? Because I mean, again, we see characters pop up between all of the three Bois Sauvage novels. I feel like I can see, as a reader, the line between what's happened in *Let Us Descend* and where we get to with your earlier novels.

Ward: You know, I've been learning as I'm going. Right? And I think while my first novel was like, specifically about, you know, two young men with important women around them—their grandma, right, their absent mother, right? I have been thinking about women, and about lineage. And I think that my thinking around that is very specific to me and to where I come from, and to my extended family in DeLisle, Mississippi, in this rural place. Because here, for me, the women are the ones who hold everything together. They're the ones who remember the family history; they're the ones who tell those stories and pass those stories down to their children and their grandchildren and their great grandchildren. They are also the ones who hold the family together in the present, who make holidays happen, who, you know, when the men in their lives sometimes, you know, die or they go away or for whatever reasons, they're not able to be present, the women are the ones who hold the family together.

That is something that I—it's a concern that I've had in all my work. It's something that I've been thinking about from the very first book. And I think that it expresses itself in every book differently . . . until in *Sing, Unburied, Sing*. When I got to *Sing, Unburied, Sing*, here's this character, Leonie, who is at the opposite end of the spectrum, as far as, you know, women are concerned and being a caretaker for a family and a lot of people, right?; she's not doing any of that. And, you know, I've spoken about this before; she was a difficult character to write because I couldn't understand why she wasn't doing any of that. And it was only when I stepped away from the novel, and I just thought about who she was as a person, and I figured out where that behavior was coming from and why she wasn't doing all that. When I figured out what was motivating her, then I could reenter the story. So I've always been sort of thinking about that, right, like, motherhood, caregivers, womanhood, you know, what it means to hold a family together, to hold a community together or not. Right?

And *Let Us Descend* really gave me the opportunity to sort of scramble the circumstances a bit because here in this world, that choice is taken away from the women, right? From Annis's mother, from Annis's grandmother, Mama Aza. In many ways, it's taken away from Annis herself, right, as she's enduring what she endures in the book. And so, one of the questions for me to consider was how would Annis or the women of her line accomplish this in spite of everything that they are made to bear? Like, how do they do that? I discovered a lot of answers along the way. I mean, I think, in part, they were able to do it because they hold onto their stories, because they hold onto their history, because they pass them on, and when they can't pass them on, Annis thinks about them almost obsessively. You know, I think that they're able to do it because they make family wherever they go, you know, with the people that they encounter; they make sort of, you know, bonds with the people that they encounter along the way in order to sort of do their best to survive.

And then I think one thing that's really beautiful to me about Annis, she has a kind of audacity because she dares to dream of one day being able to just do whatever she wants to do, to be able to direct her own day, and to just do whatever it is. And she doesn't have words for it yet. But she wants that; that is freedom for her. And, at that time, that was a big dream. And she follows it. And I love that for her. That's something I haven't spoken about a lot, so sometimes things just occur to me when I'm answering questions, you know. I can't explain that answer more now; I think I need to think on it some more. But I really do feel like that's one of the things that I love most about her, that she dares to dream.

Messer: I think that's really clear, having read the finished book. I love the fact that she's feisty. I love the fact that she really does not want to have it from anyone, that she doesn't feel forced to pull from a tradition simply because it's a tradition. I think what you said is really clear in everything she does. As a reader, for me, I liked the tension between her inability to actually drive things forward because she is enslaved, but she's her own person. And it surprises everyone, including the spirit Aza. I think the only person who might not be surprised is her mom. I think Sasha might be the only person who's like *but of course; she's my child.*

Ward: Because she knows. She knows that she's a fighter, that she loves language, that she's different, that she's all those things that make Annis Annis.

Messer: And the manifestations of grief, when you're pulled from your family, when you're not given a chance to stay put and have a life and grow and all these things. You use ghosts in *Sing, Unburied, Sing*; it was much more sort of clear in *Sing, Unburied, Sing* that it was happening. And here you've taken it to yet another sort of level with the supernatural and bringing in a new chorus of voices. And I think it was Kiese Laymon who has been talking about how you write "hoodoo." And I love that, I love that phrase. And I just, I really do want to sit with that for a second with you.

138 CONVERSATIONS WITH JESMYN WARD

Because it feels like it was in *Salvage the Bones,* too, less so I think with the first novel for me, but I mean, *Salvage the Bones,* obviously, we're coming out of Katrina, and all of that; can we riff on hoodoo for a second? Because I love the idea that this is underlying all of these novels.

Ward: I think we can't explain everything in the world. And I like to think that, especially when I was working on this novel, I don't think that I could have written this novel if there wasn't something more to the world, if there wasn't more besides the physical world, right? Like the fact of the chain, the fact of the whip, the fact of the brand, like those are such hard, brutal facts, that, I think, to write this book without recognition of the spiritual and of living, evolving, messy spirituality—I had to use that in this book—because to write this book without that would just be horror. And then what am I doing? That's not my genre; it's not my mission. It's not what I'm trying to accomplish in my books. And, too, I think that that messy, sort of evolving spiritual element of Black Americans' lives, like, I think that that has allowed us to survive, and not only to survive, but also to thrive through the centuries in this country.

I want to incorporate more of that in my work. And I remember feeling that way when I was writing the rough draft of *Salvage the Bones.* And there's this part in *Salvage the Bones,* which you probably will not remember, which no one will remember, but I think about it often. So there's this part where Esch is at the house, and Skeetah and China are out in the woods somewhere, and Skeetah is training China, he's training the dog. And all of a sudden, you hear this chorus of barks, like one dog starts barking, and then another, and then another, and another. They're all around, right? They're not all gathered by China somewhere out in the woods. It's like they're coming from everywhere, right? And when I was writing that moment, I stopped and I was like, I wonder what's happening, like something weird is happening right now. And I wonder what it is. I wanted to go wherever that barking was; I wanted to figure out which strange, unusual, weird, what sort of felt supernatural thing, was happening at that moment. But I couldn't write it because my story was right here. And so I stayed. But I think that that was the first time that I realized there was more, like something else existed in the world that I was writing about. And a part of me, you know, was very interested in finding out what that other thing was. And it's something that I've always loved in literature, you know, since I was a high schooler and in middle school. I love magic in literature. I took that limit off of myself because I realized, in a way, it was a self-imposed limit. I felt like if I was writing serious literary fiction, there could be no magic.

You know, like, when I think about the people in my family, right, we have all these stories that we tell about my grandmother. My grandmother is older now; she has issues with her memory. That makes it even more important for me to tell the stories that I tell and to acknowledge stuff, like when my grandmother was born, she was one of a set of twins, and she was born with what they call the caul over her face. And so down here, back then, in the late 1930s, early 1940s, it was said that when a child was born with a caul over their face, that meant that they would have a second sort of vision. They would be able to know things, and they would have certain abilities. I grew up with this; it's a fact of my life. Several times in my life where my grandmother has predicted things, said things, had dreams, etc., and we'd just take it as, you know, we're just like, okay, yep, that's facts. But none of that has been reflected in my work.

My great grandmother on my mom's side, my mom's dad's side—it's complicated—she would always tell us a story, when I was a little girl, about her husband dying, and then her husband coming back one night and talking and speaking to her. And I just asked my mom about it like a couple of weeks ago. And my mom was like yeah, supposedly, he came back, and he told her not to remarry, and she never did. And she really, you know, like, that was her experience; it was true to her. Right? She abided by that for the rest of her life. And so when Annis's mother says the world is wet with spirit, like, it's fair sopping with it, I felt that like that is more of a reflection of my understanding of the world, sort of the understanding that people around me have about the world and also, I think, reflects some of that hoodoo, that adaptive, expansive, spiritual understanding that I think Black Americans have developed.

Messer: And then you layer in the *Odyssey*. Right? I know Dante is where we're starting with *Let Us Descend*, but we can't ignore the *Odyssey*. And we can't ignore the magic and the spirituality. You're building on all of these world traditions and layering in Black American experience. Which, I don't want to lose sight of that; that's part of what makes the book so powerful, because it's pulling from every possible source that made you you. And it's partially why I know when I'm reading a book by you, I'm reading a book by you, whether it's *Sing, Unburied, Sing*, which, personal top ten always—you know, sometimes things shift around, no, that never leaves, that's always, it's a book that I hold really, really close. I mean, you can feel the echoes of Faulkner; you're a Mississippi writer, too, so here, Dante, the *Odyssey*, and Greek mythology, and hoodoo, and African mythology as well. But also, we can't really ignore Faulkner. And I heard you have his Nobel speech taped near your desk.

Ward: So I did. I was recently looking through my [memorabilia]. I have so much paperwork, I have photo albums, and I have files where I've secreted stuff and hidden it from myself. So I came across a folder that had everything that I had tacked to the wall above my desk when I was working on *Where the Line Bleeds*. And I was working on *Where the Line Bleeds*, like writing that rough draft, when I was an MFA student at the University of Michigan at Ann Arbor. So here, I'm in my sort of first educational experience where I'm just devoting myself to studying creative writing, studying literature, and then trying to do my best to create some compelling literature. And right now, I don't know how I came across that speech. But I remember coming across it, reading it, and thinking, this is it. Like I can't fully articulate. There were several sentences in that speech where he was saying, you know, like, our duty as writers is to write about the human heart in conflict with itself. And there's something about that sentence and that idea of the essential work that we should be doing that I thought I need to remember this in every moment when I'm writing. So I printed it out, the important parts, I thought, in bold, and I tacked it to the wall above my desk. And I think about that speech that he gives, his Nobel speech, I think about that speech a lot. And I think about his work a lot.

There are so many writers who are important to me. And they taught me how to write, because there are so many things that I find compelling or beautiful or moving about their work. And then I bring it to my own work, and I go, well, how can I do that, but not do that exactly? You know, they're my elders, so they're farther ahead than I, but I feel like I'm always sort of shouting to them or calling to them over a distance. And, I don't know, hoping they hear me in a way, I don't know.

It was important to me in this book, to incorporate other texts, specifically to incorporate Dante's *Inferno*. There was that bit about, you know, Aristotle, like I feel like that desire carried through to the kinds of spirits that Annis encounters on her journey. Because in the same way that it was important for me to incorporate these other elements, because they're all a part of me, you're right; I am having an American experience, I'm telling an American story, right? So why can't I pull in the *Odyssey*? Why can't I pull in Dante's *Inferno*? Why can't I pull in all of these, incorporate all these other cultural touchstones into my work? I also wanted the kind of spirits that Annis met to reflect that, too. Because in the beginning, in the rough draft, I thought maybe I can incorporate some spirits that are regarded in Benin, in that specific kind of voodoo, that African traditional religion that they practice there. I should incorporate them. These are the spirits that she'll encounter in this story, but it didn't work, and then finally, I realized, okay, it's not working because these spirits should be specific to this place, to this moment in time. And so I had to find them; I had to open myself up so that they would appear.

Messer: You set me up to actually toss out something that I was thinking about as I read *Let Us Descend*. And part of that is how ghosts are manifestations of grief and loss. I mean, you talk about this very clearly in *Men We Reaped*, which is the memoir that you wrote, sort of in between *Sing, Unburied, Sing* and *Salvage the Bones*. The idea that ghosts—also like Leonie in *Sing, Unburied, Sing*, ghosts are a piece of her story and a part of Jojo's story—you actually say violence begets remaining—is one of the lines that I think is now officially tattooed on the back of my brain. And violence doesn't necessarily imply death. It can be a violent act to remove someone from their home, it can be a violent act to remove them from their community, but that a piece of you stays behind, and that you haunt whoever is behind, or they haunt you. And so the idea that we're pretending that there's this piece of the world that's exactly what we see in front of us, and you know, walking down the street and all of that, that there isn't some sort of current or echo beneath; it seems like literature is the best place to play with that idea. And you're doing it, and you have been doing it.

I sort of feel like this is going to become more and more of the work. I mean, I realize it took you longer to write *Let Us Descend* than it took the other books, but this feels really right for where you are. But I see it as a launching pad for something else. Like, I have no idea what you're working on. But you're really comfortable in this world, you're really comfortable with the characters, you're really comfortable with the story. And I've read it twice now. Once just because I could and then once when I'm prepping for the show, and it's two different readings, so it's obvious that you're doing that. But yeah, there's something really special about this book, and I can't quite put my finger on it. Like the language is gorgeous, the characters are great. But it's the whole thing. The whole experience, I think, is what makes it really remarkable. As a bookseller, I get to read everything early, which is great. I'm wondering, though, what you are working on next because I may have just put my foot in my mouth . . . .

Ward: Oh no, no, no, no! I want to remember that you said that to me because it will give me confidence moving forward. Because actually, I'm in a weird moment right now where, because of the amount of work that I have to do, you know, before the public event, that I have not been able to work on anything new yet. The next thing that you will see from me is actually a middle grade or YA book. I have a contract to write said middle grade or YA book. I have not written a word yet, but I've been reading a lot, you know, because again, I'm challenging myself as a writer because I've never written anything for that particular audience. So that's what you'll see from me next.

And it, too, I think, will exist in this world where there's always more, you know, than what you see with your five senses. So yeah, so that's the next thing that I'm working on. And then after that, I don't know. There are a couple of different novel ideas that I've sort of been kicking around for, for maybe the past year, year and a half, maybe. I don't know if they'll come to fruition now or, you know, if I'll kick them around for ten more years and then tackle them. But I know that I have to write the middle grade book first. And it's about a girl. There are things that she can do. She can access that world that we normally don't access in our everyday. Now, I don't know exactly what that's going to look like; I'm trying to figure that out. I have lots of notes.

Messer: If anyone can figure it out, it's you. I'm not worried about you figuring out what a world is going to look like for a middle grade or a YA reader. I'm not worried about that. What I am enjoying is the idea, though, of you bouncing back and forth between age groups. I think, you know, when I was coming up, as a young reader, there just wasn't a lot, right? You kind of read everything you could and then suddenly, it was like, well, where's the adult section of the library because I literally have read everything in this room multiple times. Like YA just didn't exist in the way that it does now. All props to M. E. Kerr and Judy Blume, and, you know, those who were doing it, but there just wasn't what we see now. And you know, so we started punching above our weight pretty fast. Not all of it was good.

Ward: Right. Not all of it was good.

Messer: Not all of it was good. But at the same time, you know, to know that we're in a place in books right now where you can be Jesmyn Ward for a shorter set and Jesmyn Ward, you know, for those of us who want all of it. Because, you know, Jojo may not—I love that kid so much. I realize I'm talking about a fictional character like he's real, but I love that kid so much. Jojo might not want to read *Let Us Descend*. Okay. Fair enough. Let's give him something where he sees himself represented, where he sees stories that make sense. I mean, I constantly think about this image of you and your brother driving around, listening to Southern rap and Ghostface Killah. You didn't have this world. And I mean, I have spent many hours in the car with my little brother as well. Not listening to Ghostface Killah. That I'll totally own. But the idea that we can find story in music, that we can find story between the covers of a book, or that we find story in unexpected places and in unexpected ways, I think that's just really important. Really, really important.

You know, and I'm looking at the clock, and I knew this was going to happen, but we ran out of time. I knew this was gonna happen. Jesmyn Ward, thank you so much. Thank you. Thank you for all of the work and joining us on the show. *Let Us Descend* is out now. If for some reason you have not read the Bois Sauvage novels, and that's *Salvage the Bones* and *Where the Line Bleeds* and also, of course, *Sing, Unburied, Sing*, really? There's that. There's also nonfiction, too. There's *Men We Reaped*, which is a powerhouse of a memoir. And I really do recommend that, and also *The Fire This Time*, which is a collection of essays from lots of folks that you know and maybe a couple of you don't, but it's all fantastic. Thank you so much.

Something Beautiful
Out of the Darkness

Regina N. Bradley / 2023

This interview was originally conducted by Regina N. Bradley and published in *Southern Cultures* in the *Gothic South* issue (vol. 29, no. 4: Winter 2023). Reprinted with permission of Emily Wallace, art director and deputy editor of *Southern Cultures*.

When I describe Jesmyn Ward's writing to people, I say, "Her writing leaves me with brittle bones." Originally from the Gulf Coast community of DeLisle, Mississippi, Ward is unapologetically steeped in a Southern Black literary tradition that amplifies the complicated realities of being Black in the South, wrapping her characters in a warmth and honesty that few other writers can match. Among an ever-growing list of accolades, Ward is a MacArthur Fellow and two-time National Book Award winner for her novels *Salvage the Bones* (2011) and *Sing, Unburied, Sing* (2017). Her writing voice is beautifully gentle yet commanding across a variety of genres, including fiction, essays, and a memoir, *Men We Reaped* (2013).

Ahead of the release of her latest novel, *Let Us Descend*, Ward sat down with me to discuss the importance of the Gothic in writing about the Black South, how grief is central to her writing, and why writing helps her confront and understand Mississippi's racially turbulent history.

Regina N. Bradley: This issue deals with the Gothic South. Usually when we think about Gothic in the South, it is white and male. What role do you feel the Gothic plays in how you tell stories about being Black in the South?

Jesmyn Ward: For me, it always goes back to the beginnings for us as Black Southern people. It always goes back to enslavement, and in relation to white Southern writers, for me, that's the dark heart of everything. I think they tend to write around it. I feel like Black writers, specifically Black Southern writers, write more towards it. Maybe because we had less. There was no avoiding it for us. We have always lived with the real ramifications of slavery for hundreds of years. I don't feel like we could write around it. When I think about my own fictional work, there was a hint of the Gothic in *Salvage the Bones*, but I think it became more of a real presence in *Sing, Unburied, Sing*. And then definitely in my most recent work, *Let Us Descend*. Even when I think about *Men We Reaped*, my memoir, it was a presence there too. For me, the Gothic comes out in wrestling with that darkness, wrestling with trauma, wrestling with grief, wrestling with loss, wrestling with this idea that there is more to the world than what we see on the surface. I'm thinking not only about history, but the supernatural, things that you can't explain. That has also been with us since the beginning.

RNB: In your first novel, *Where the Line Bleeds*, you get traces of the Gothic in your dealing with Christophe and his descent into addiction. Then you see it a little bit more in *Salvage the Bones* with Esch and her relationship to China, for example. Then you really just bust the door wide open in *Sing, Unburied, Sing*. I know you did some research for that book because of the way that you described Parchman Farm. The descriptions of it are so vivid and significant. Can you talk about why the Gothic was useful in *Sing, Unburied, Sing*? There's a tangible darkness, a dread that Southern Black folks can't avoid because, on the one hand, white people don't want us to confront the idea of enslavement. They want it to be like, "That happened hundreds of years ago. You don't have to worry about that shit no more." But it hits me every day.

JW: When I was writing *Sing, Unburied, Sing*, it's almost as if that darkness, that Gothic aspect of it, had to be a part of that story. Partly because I was so horrified by the reality of what had occurred that I had to introduce that element into it. I didn't know anything about Parchman at all. I mean, I had some relatives who had been there whom I talked to about it, and they told me their stories about what it was like for them to be incarcerated, but I didn't know anything about the history of the place. I mean, I knew the conditions in the present were terrible, but I didn't really know anything about how that place had come about or what it had looked like in the past.

So I started to read and research. This was before the *Thirteenth* documentary on Netflix came out. I think that documentary exposed a lot of people to the fact that, back in the 1930s and 1940s, kids were sent to Parchman. Twelve- and thirteen-year-old kids charged with stupid things that weren't really crimes, just ridiculous things like loitering, and basically being re-enslaved, because Parchman was a plantation.

146 CONVERSATIONS WITH JESMYN WARD

I grew up in Mississippi and went to school here. I left for college, but for half my life, I attended public school. For most of middle and all of high school, I went to a private school on scholarship that gave me what would be considered a good public school education in another state. There's so much about Mississippi's history, especially when it concerns Black people, that I was not taught, that I did not learn in school. I just remember when I read that young kids were sent to Parchman and some of them died, I was so horrified that I went looking for the information, and looking for it was the only reason that I found it. I was so angry and hurt and aggrieved that they had been erased. All that pain and suffering. Their lives were erased because that fact has been erased.

I believe that erasure is part of the reason that this effort to ban books by Black people, by people of color, by queer people, makes me so angry. Y'all already did it. It's already been done. So much of what we should know about to get a full understanding of American history has been erased and withheld from us. What more can you erase?

I felt so awful for the children like Richie, the character in my book, that his life and the lives of kids like him had been erased from history. I thought, *I want to write him back into the present.* I wanted that child to have the kind of agency that he had been denied in life, to act and have a certain amount of power and freedom in the present moment that he hadn't had in the past. The only way that I could figure out how to do that was by making him a ghost. That's why I introduced that Gothic element into the story, by necessity.

RNB: Your use of the Gothic and haunting allows for stories to be told that otherwise would remain on the margins, be whispers of stories or snatches of history. I also think something representative of your use of the Gothic is the way you describe the landscape, the way you describe nature. It's so intentional. Why pay so much attention to the surroundings of the characters? Your settings become characters themselves.

JW: I think it's something I've intuitively felt my whole life but didn't explicitly think about until I started writing about Hurricane Katrina. I wrote an essay a long time ago about Hurricane Katrina, "We Do Not Swim in Our Cemeteries," that was published in *Oxford American.*

That's one thing about Kiese, too. He grew up with his grandmother. He grew up in this place that's very rooted in extended family and community. We both grew up in these environments—I could cross the street and walk about a hundred yards up and I'm at my great-grandparents' house. A lot of the time I spent with them was sitting on the porch listening to them talk, and they're telling stories. So even though I may not have been educated in school about what it was to be Black in Mississippi in the 1930s, I know it from them. The past doesn't feel very far removed from us. The past feels like the present. When we're writing about what it means to be Black in Mississippi, when we're creating our characters, the past is very present in our work with all its attendant traumas and hardships and joys, all the things that make life worth living here. We are writing from places where people didn't leave. I have relatives who went to Chicago and California, who were part of the Great Migration, but Black Mississippi writers like me and Kiese, we're writing from people who chose not to leave.

RNB: I have another question about legacy. I put you in conversation with writers like Mildred Taylor, Margaret Walker, and Richard Wright. Does it bother you that the first writer people think of when they talk about your writing is William Faulkner? I rant hard about this on Twitter. I'm like, "She's not the heir to Faulkner. She is the first of her name, like *Game of Thrones*." How do you feel about that?

JW: I love that you say that, but right now, it doesn't bother me much. I love Faulkner's prose because of the way he wrote about the landscape of the South, the vivid power of his imagery, and the way he used rhythm in his prose. I just love those aspects of his writing so much. They affect me in the way that good poetry does. In a way, I feel like it scrambles my critical response. And I think that's just because I was a reader before I was a writer. Prose like that, poetry like that, cuts off my critical faculties, and I revert to being in awe. That kind of awe you get when you're just a reader and you're being swept up in something. It doesn't bug me as much as it should. But whenever he writes about Black people, Southern Black people, there's no depth there. And from the Faulkner that I've read, that shallowness, that shallow characterization, bugs the shit out of me.

RNB: Yes! I can see the influences, but the way he handles Black folks, they are just on the side. That's never the case with your writing. We're always front and center.

JW: Right. And it's interesting to me that people can't see that. I read *The Sound and the Fury* years and years and years ago. But I remember in that novel specifically, even when the narrative is closely aligned with the Black characters, even when you're with them in a room and they're talking with no white characters around, they aren't real people. I remember feeling that very strongly in that moment. Yes, they're center stage there; you are right there with them. But they aren't real people. They aren't my grandparents.

RNB: Faulkner's story "A Rose for Emily" is peak Gothic for me, but the one question that I have had about that story since I was nineteen, when I first read it, is about the manservant, Tobe, the Black dude who answers the door. When the townspeople be like, "We're here for Miss Emily," he just walks out and doesn't say anything. I want to know what he was thinking on the way out. All Faulkner says was that he opened the door, he walked out, and he didn't say nothing to nobody. I'm like, this man is waiting to go talk to his people. I need a short story about when he got home. Faulkner could never give me that [*laughs*].

I want to go to your memoir, *Men We Reaped*, which I teach almost every other semester. It is ridiculously good. I think about those moments where you talk about your brother and your friends, how you weren't there in the moments leading up to when they passed, but you describe their deaths. It's almost like an obituary. So I'm wondering: how is that a reflection of the Southern Black Gothic? Because I feel like it was a way for you to gain closure. But also, even with all of their flaws, these men were still loved and cared about. The way you write about them showed that they were loved and cared for and followed in a tradition of Southern Black grieving. What connections are there between grieving and the Gothic in your writing?

JW: I don't know if I can answer that question. One thing that I was doing when I was writing about what it might have been like when each of them died—especially in the chapter with my brother—was that there has to be something more, something more than the terror, something more than the dread, something more than that impending darkness, that impending pain, that transition leading up to each of them dying.

I was trying to expand those moments beyond this narrowed point where their deaths occurred. All the options regarding what could happen sort of narrowed, narrowed, narrowed, narrowed. So at the same time that I was narrowing it down action-wise, I wanted to expand them in terms of the supernatural, as well as the weight of history that also led to this moment. I was trying to depict all of those things as well.

In a way, I think I wanted to do that because I was trying to reckon with the fact of their deaths and reckon with the fact of that traumatic event. But at the same time, I wanted to acknowledge that there's more that exists. Even in that terrible moment, there's more. Without that acknowledgment of more, it's very hard for me to understand and for readers in general. People coming to this moment need to understand how we survived and how we made it through. And how we continue to survive and continue to make it through.

Working on *Let Us Descend* has clarified some things for me, especially around trauma: how Black people reckon with trauma, how we reckon with grief, and how we reckon with loss. What makes it possible for us to continue to not just survive but thrive in spite of it?

I'm glad that I'm here and that I have written that specific book. Because writing that specific book, which is so much about grief and surviving, is also about finding your way through very hard, very traumatic events to this place where you can thrive and retain a sense of self. You can build, find family, and do all these things that may seem impossible even in the face of tremendous pain, tremendous trauma, and tremendous grief. As you know, I've been struggling with a fresh grief for the past three and a half years. I think it has helped clarify—though not fully—some things for me. It made it easier for me to understand how we continue to make a way out of no way and how we continue to wrestle with the darkness at the heart of this country and still make something beautiful out of it.

"Writing is Restorative": A Conversation with Jesmyn Ward

Kemeshia Randle Swanson / 2024

This original interview was conducted by this volume's editor, Kemeshia Randle Swanson, on November 21, 2024, at Pass Christian Books. The full, edited interview is printed here for the first time.

Kemeshia Randle Swanson: So, Jesmyn, thank you so much for being here. We are here, of course, on the Coast, near your hometown, and as a Mississippi native myself, hailing from the Mississippi Delta, what you've once called the Mississippi-est part of Mississippi, I honestly can't say that I've frequented the Coast as much as I feel like I should have. As a local, what would you say are some of the places to go or things visitors should do when visiting your neck of the woods, so to speak?

Jesmyn Ward: I mean, let's see. So, there's a new aquarium on the Mississippi Gulf Coast, so that's really nice. It's in downtown Gulfport. It's right across from the harbor. If there are any people who are with you who like marine animals, or kids with you, that's always a fun place to bring someone, especially because a lot of the exhibits are specifically, I guess, about marine habitats on the Coast in this area. There are a couple of great art museums on the Coast, the Walter Anderson Museum. I think that one's in Ocean Springs. That's a really sort of wonderful museum. And then, for the area around Pass Christian, Bay St. Louis, around this area, I would just say, get in your car and just drive. I mean, as long as you have either an atlas or a map app, you can always figure out where you are when you get lost. But I don't know, I think there's something to be said for just sort of driving around the back roads in this area across the bayou and up a little bit further north towards DeLisle, where I live. Just to get a feel for the landscape, for the beauty that's here, for the attractions that aren't manmade, because it is a really beautiful place. So yeah, that's the other thing that I would say that would be nice to do.

150

Swanson: Get in your car and drive. I like that. I remember reading in your memoir how you felt a little awkward talking to people that you grew up with about the possibility of becoming a well-known author. And here you are now, this literary giant, described by American Booksellers as the new Toni Morrison, putting local experiences and stories out into the universe for the world to hear. And I was just curious about how you and your community are embracing this kind of celebrity or public figure status, and how are you handling actually being compared to Toni Morrison?

Ward: Whenever someone makes that comparison, I feel like I always, I don't know, recoil a little because I grew up reading her work and, I think, idolizing not only the writing that she produced, but also the way that she lived her life. I don't know everything about her, but it seems like she was very invested in community and nurturing other writers around her and sort of nurturing them to bring about great work, in addition to producing her own work. So, I mean, there's no one like her. So, I mean, it is a great compliment, and I recognize it as a great compliment, but I don't know, I feel like she's still on such a pedestal in my head that sometimes, all the time really, it's a little hard for me to accept the compliment.

I feel like the people in my family and people in my community, they're very proud of me and of what I've done and the fact that I'm writing specifically about the place that they are from, too. And I think that a lot of them, they enjoy seeing people like them on the page. And also, I know, for people who are from here but who have moved away, it's a different experience of reading my work for them because it makes them feel like they've come back home. And so, there's a different, I guess, enjoyment or a connection that they get out of reading my work. And then, too, I feel like people don't usually talk about this, but people here are protective of me in a way. And I guess, just because we come from such a small place where everyone knows everyone, and everyone has known everyone for so long, I feel like people are protective, too, at the same time that they're proud.

Swanson: That community definitely is special. And you mentioned kind of recoiling when people make the Toni Morrison comparison. Do you have any particular mentors or people who are helping you on this journey?

Ward: So many of the people in the publishing industry that I've worked with, many of them are older than me. Many of them have been very important to me in helping me navigate this journey and navigate the publishing world because, I mean, when I started out, I knew next to nothing about it. And then when I began, I mean, I started out in the early 2000s, and the landscape for Black literary writers back then was very different, I feel

152 CONVERSATIONS WITH JESMYN WARD

like, than the landscape for Black literary writers now. And so, I think that I needed that help from them. Even more so, in specific terms, I'm talking about my editor, Kathy Belden; I'm talking about my speaking agency that I work with, Lyceum Agency. They've been instrumental in helping me to figure out how to navigate my career, my literary agent, Rob McQuilkin.

As far as writers are concerned, you know I love Kiese Laymon, so whenever I can be out in the world with him and commune with him and connect with him, that's always a good thing because I feel like it makes me feel sort of less alone in this endeavor because I think it's different for writers like me who live much of their lives outside of New York City. You know what I'm saying? Like, it's different. I live in my little hometown where most people who are strangers to me don't know who I am. And that's just a very different existence, I think. And so, I love being in fellowship with him. And Mitchell Jackson, he's very much plugged into the writing scene around New York City, but he's another writer who I am always overjoyed to spend time with because, again, I feel like he always has an interesting perspective on this industry. And I like communing with him.

Just, I think it was last year, there was the Phillis Wheatley [Poetry] Festival, and there I met Patricia Smith, the poet, and also Airea D. Matthews; she's also a poet. And that was very special to me. One, because I love poets, and two, because I think that, again, that's one of the things that I admire the most about the way Toni Morrison lived her life, because she was always in fellowship with other writers. And so, I feel like I've been trying to make more of an effort, because I exist outside of New York City, because, at least on the Mississippi Gulf Coast, I'm not plugged into a local community of artists. So, I've been trying to reach out to other poets, novelists, artists, to try to create more of a sense of artistic community and fellowship. But those are just some of them.

Swanson: I'm glad that you mentioned the Phillis Wheatley Poetry Festival. Actually, I was going to ask a question about that. That's, of course, the first time that we met, but also, we got to hear from awesome speakers, of course, Alice Walker being one of them. And I was just curious, what, of course, you mentioned that you developed community with some of the poets, but what did that experience mean to you?

Ward: I had never experienced anything like that before. And I think that experience of being at that festival with so many amazing Black women who are artists, I think that, in part, is what made me begin to think about what it would mean to sort of have more fellowship with, specifically, Black artists in my life. Because I think it's difficult work that we all engage in. And so, I think that it's worthwhile to be part of a community because in that space, there was so much calm, there was joy, there was deep respect, there was acceptance. There was such a celebration of our genius. I had never been in a physical space where all of that was centered. So, I don't know. I feel like it's difficult for me to talk about and to articulate because it felt almost spiritual. So, it's sort of hard to talk about intellectually because yes, it meant a lot to me mentally, but it really moved me emotionally and spiritually so much, so it's just hard to articulate.

Swanson: No, I definitely get it. I agree. It was very powerful. Of course we talked about doing this difficult work, but we were also able to just fellowship and let our hair down. I told people, "I actually did the Electric Slide with Alice Walker." So, yes, definitely. I agree.

Speaking of the Electric Slide, music, and spirituality, in a 2016 interview with Danille K. Taylor, she actually dubbed you the Literary Voice of the Dirty South. And I know that you all talked a little bit about musical influences, and, of course, in your first few novels, you have epigraphs with hip-hop lyrics. So, I was just curious if your taste for music and hip-hop has changed since you all talked about that. Are there any particular artists that you are interested in or just jam out to or maybe that you think kind of speak a similar message that you try to convey?

Ward: Before I answer that part of the question, I have to include someone else in my answer to your previous question about people who I look to and who I seek fellowship with, because I have to mention this person because I feel like my interactions with her and my friendship with her is really one of the sort of major motivating factors for me to begin to think about how we can help each other in this work, how we can show up for each other in the work we do, Regina Bradley.

I think that she's one of the first... and we sort of came into contact with each other years ago, and we've only been in each other's physical presence a couple of times, but still, the care with which she sort of reaches out to other people. She's very purposeful about pulling people into community, about advocating for other writers, both in the classroom and just out in the world of publishing. She's fantastic. And I apologize for forgetting, for not thinking of her when I answered the first question. But this question that you just asked about music actually made me think of her because a lot of her scholarship is around Southern hip-hop and Black literature.

I mean, I still listen to hip-hop, but I'm sort of sliding into middle age at this point in my life. So, lately I haven't been listening to music as much. When my kids get in the car, I just sort of let them listen to whatever they

154 CONVERSATIONS WITH JESMYN WARD

want to listen to. So, we've been listening to a lot of GloRilla, like a weird mix of GloRilla and Billie Eilish; I don't know what's going on in my car [*laughs*]. But I've been listening to a lot of podcasts, I think, more so. I think maybe because these days, I feel hungry for information in a different way, and I've tried to listen to audiobooks while I'm driving, but for whatever weird reason, I get tired listening to an audio; something that's long-form narrative makes me tired. But as far as podcasts, it's easier for me to listen to them. So. I'm sorry. I feel like that's a disappointing answer, but I still love hip-hop. I still love soul music and R&B; it's just I'm in this weird place in my life where I think I feel like music does help us navigate what we're going through, but I feel like, perhaps, at this point in my life, I feel like I need more information than music in order to navigate the world that we're living in now. So maybe that's it.

Swanson: I completely get that. And when you were describing the person that you forgot, I kind of knew and was hoping that you would mention Regina Bradley. I always think about, of course, people are always comparing you to Faulkner. She's like, no, no, that is wrong. She is *the* Jesmyn Ward. She's not Faulkner's heir.

Perhaps my favorite novel of yours, although I have to say it's becoming more increasingly difficult to choose a favorite, but *Salvage the Bones* has always had a place in my heart. But it has been the subject of book bans and challenges, but people, of course, have defended it as well. And I know that in your conversation with LeVar Burton at the Mississippi Book Festival, you talked a little bit about book bans. I was just wondering if you could share a little bit more about what it means to have your books potentially be banned from schools or libraries?

Ward: So, one of my friends who works in publishing, he's an editor. His name is Yahdon Israel. And so, we went to a random dinner one time, and we were talking about book bans, and he said, think about back in the day when rock 'n' roll came about, and there was this big push, of course, to censor rock 'n' roll, to keep it away from the kids. It was a bad influence, etc., etc. He's like, "And then what happened?" That effort to ban that artistic expression meant that it brought people to it. So, he said that he thinks that is what will ultimately happen with books. And, I hope so; I hope that's the case because there are a lot of people and organizations who do these challenges and who push to ban books.

It makes me very angry and sorrowful because I feel like just because you ban a book, say you ban *Salvage the Bones*, which is about a fifteen-year-old, pregnant girl, that doesn't mean that you're banning the reality. That doesn't mean that there's not some fifteen-year-old pregnant kid in rural New Mexico or in rural Illinois or in rural Alabama or in Florida who is bewildered and trying to figure out how to navigate the world in the position that they're in. And if they had access to a book like *Salvage the Bones*, maybe it could help them sort of figure out how to live through something like that. And so, it makes me very angry because I feel like kids often find their way to the books that they need. They seek out the books that they need, and even if they can't articulate it to themselves, if they read a book, there's something in that book that speaks to them, and that is helping them understand something either about the world or about themselves. And I feel like that kind of work is always a good thing. So, it just makes me really angry, because I feel like the reality of the people that I write about, there are kids all over the United States who are dealing with teen pregnancy or living with abusive caregivers or neglectful caregivers or living with caregivers who are struggling with substance addiction. So, it makes me angry that kids aren't able to find what they need in books in places where books are banned.

Swanson: I've read somewhere someone said that if it's banned, that means it's important, something in it that you need to find. Yes, so definitely, I agree. I actually asked that question because I know that some authors not necessarily are thankful that their books are on the banned book list, but that makes them feel like they're doing what needs to be done, once they have reached that particular point. So, of course people are teaching your novels regardless of if they are challenged or not. I was just curious: Do you actually teach any of your own works in your classes?

Ward: I feel weird about that. No one has ever explicitly said to me, at any of the universities I've taught at, no one's explicitly said you can't teach your own books. But it just feels like, I've never [*pauses*] I take that back. When I was at the University of Michigan, one of my professors did teach from his own book, but the book was nonfiction. So maybe it was more like a craft guide. So, he wasn't teaching from any of his novels. But other than that, I've never had any of my professors teach from their own books. So, it feels like something that I shouldn't do. And then too, I think it might be a little awkward because I feel like it's easier for me to assess other people's work than my own work. It's easier for me to be clear-eyed about what's working and teach craft lessons about what you want to do and what's working well from other people's work, maybe because I think so much of my process feels, at least in the rough draft, and in the first three, four drafts, a lot of that work feels very intuitive. So, I feel like it would be more difficult for me to teach lessons about craft from my own work, because much of the time that I

156 CONVERSATIONS WITH JESMYN WARD

spend creating it, I'm not doing it in an analytical way. I don't do that until I'm writing the ten revisions or whatever after the early drafts.

Swanson: That makes sense. No, I understand that. But is there anything that you would hope that instructors who are perhaps teaching your novels would convey to students? Any particular skills or messages or anything?

Ward: One of the things that I always try to do in all of my work is I try to create complex, complicated characters in the hope that if my characters are complex and complicated enough, they will convince the reader that they're real people, make the reader feel for them and with them. And so, if anyone is teaching my work, I hope that's a component of it because it is something that I try to do in everything that I write. Because I feel like when I was younger and when I started out, when I first committed to writing, one of the reasons that I did was because I thought, *I want to write about the kind of people that I grew up with and the kind of people who are in my neighborhood and the kind of people who are in my community because I want to show the world that we exist and that we're here and that our lives are just as sort of complicated and fraught and lovely as everyone else's.* In part, because I hadn't really encountered much work that was specifically about us in this place. And so, I wanted to do that in my work. So, it's been part of my mission, I feel like, in my writing since the very beginning. So, I hope that I'm doing it well enough so that when people bring my books into the classroom, that's one of the things that they talk about.

Swanson: Definitely so. Mission accomplished. Speaking of characterization and development of your stories, I don't know, I'm just curious: Have you ever thought about, perhaps, any of your novels being adapted to the big screen?

Ward: I would love for that to happen. I have been eagerly waiting for that to happen for a long time, and there are always sort of things cooking behind the scenes. So, three of my books have been optioned for either television or film, but, as of yet, nothing has moved beyond that first step because I guess there are so many steps that come afterwards. So, they have to purchase the rights; it has to move deeper into the development process. So, as [of] right now, none of that has happened, but I'm still hoping that it'll happen one day.

Swanson: We'll go ahead and say coming soon [*both laugh*]. Is there a particular novel that you would like to share with the world first on the big screen?

Ward: I would love to see *Salvage the Bones* on the big screen. I would love to see *Sing, Unburied, Sing* on the big screen. I mean, especially because there's that supernatural element to it. I would love that. I think that would be amazing.

Swanson: I can definitely see more comparisons of Toni Morrison and *Beloved* and all of that in there, but that would be awesome. So yes, again, coming to the big screen. So, I have recently edited a collection of your interviews, *Conversations with Jesmyn Ward*. It will be coming out in [September] 2025, so I'm excited about that. But one of the many ways that I describe you in the book, I say, "Her voice is soft, but her words are firm." And, of course, in reading your works, whether it's novels, your memoir, essays, even your edited collection, of course, I have noticed, clearly in all of your works, you are bold and proud and loving. But I've also noticed that in your interviews, you talk about how sometimes you're a little quiet or shy or less confident. I was just curious: What's the difference between writer Jesmyn and everyday Jesmyn? How do you help others who may also have some insecurities overcome those things so they can share their stories as well?

Ward: I don't know. I think maybe just sort of talking about my own insecurities and because often when I'm talking about my past, when I'm talking about the kind of student that I was, not necessarily in high school because the high school I went to was so small, that it was the kind of place where, it was tiny, I had ten people in my graduating class. So, in a classroom like that, you really can't hide. But when I went to college and then in the years afterwards with graduate school and fellowships, I was very much—and then in my first, I guess, real job that I had, I worked in publishing for two years in New York in my early twenties—I was very quiet, very sort of, I don't know, maybe withdrawn in a way. And I think that part of the reason that I felt that way was because there are a lot of things that are positive about, or that I'm thankful for, about my experience growing up here in Mississippi, specifically on the Gulf Coast. And I wrote about those in *Men We Reaped*. But then, at the same time, there were some things that I lived through that were more difficult and that I think led to me sort of wanting to flee this place when I graduated from high school.

One of the things that I dealt with over and over again was the opinion that some of my classmates and schoolmates in high school had, that the colleges that I was accepted to, the scholarships that I received, they were of the opinion that I didn't deserve any of it and the only reason that I had got any of those things was because I am Black, because of affirmative action. And, so, I think I carried some of that with me. I mean, if you hear something like that over and over and over again as a critique, I think it's very

158 CONVERSATIONS WITH JESMYN WARD

difficult to shrug it off every time. And I think that it sort of introduces this element of self-doubt.

And then, too, I knew that I was from Mississippi, I knew that even though I went to a really good private high school, which it doesn't exist anymore, but it did. And it was a good private school for Mississippi, for the Coast. I knew that going to a university like Stanford, which is where I got my undergraduate degree, my education just didn't compare to my classmates who had gone to these famous boarding schools, elite feeding schools, college prep schools. So, the quality of their education was completely different than mine. And so, I carried all of that into the classroom with me, and I just thought, *I'm not prepared for this because I don't have the academic background that a lot of my peers do.* And so, I carried all of that into the classroom with me, and I would think, and this is very dark, but *I know I'm the least smart person in this classroom. I don't have anything to contribute to this discussion.* And then the anxiety would build and build and build as I'm thinking these negative thoughts. And so, I just wouldn't say anything, and it didn't matter where I sat in the classroom. Sometimes I'd sit in the middle, sometimes I'd sit in the front, but I still just didn't say anything.

So, I don't know. I think that was my experience, and it took many, many years for me to begin to work my way out of it. And really a lot of working my way out of it came about, one when I got the Stegner Fellowship, and again, our classes were so small that it was like I couldn't hide. So, I think that that was part of it. Also, the fact that I got a Stegner Fellowship, so there's such a large pool of applicants. And so, especially in something like that, they're not letting anybody in here just for the fun of it. All the people that they're accepting as Stegner Fellows in this program, everybody deserves to be here. And I would see that in our workshops. I mean, some of the most brilliant writers I've ever studied with, I studied with them in the Stegner Program, so I think that being in that environment began to undo, very slowly, all of that that I had struggled with for so many years.

And then, once I got into the classroom, I think as an instructor, that changed everything for me too, because I was on the other side of the desk, and I was also remembering the kind of student that I was. And so, I'm aware that so many students, they're not just engaging with the work and trying to get a good grade in the class. Right? They're bringing so much with them to the classroom. And so, I just try to be aware of that when I'm in the classroom. And then whenever I get an opportunity like this, I just try to share my story and talk about it, because I think if others are aware that even if I'm in this position that I am right now, once I was a kid like them, I was full of self-doubt and shy, and feeling like I didn't deserve to be in the spaces where I was. And so, I think just knowing that kids like that, that they're not the only people who are struggling in that way, I think that's helpful too, because it can help them to begin to sort of realize that you may feel that way now, but that's not the objective truth. And you can work your way out of it.

Swanson: Definitely. Imposter syndrome is real, but we're so glad that you fought through and believe that you deserve to be here because clearly you do. And we're glad that you're here.

Ward: Thank you.

Swanson: I understand that you write a lot about and advocate a great deal for racial and economic injustice, but of course, a good majority of your characters are female. And I can notice womanism in your works. I was just curious: Do you identify as a feminist?

Ward: I do. I do. And I always have. I mean, I feel like it was a little less apparent in my earlier work, but the family that I come from, I feel like I learned it from, or to think that way, to, I guess, be aware of the power and the strength and the resilience and the beauty of women from an early age, because I was surrounded by them. My mom, she consistently made a way out of no way with four children for years. And then I looked at my maternal and my paternal grandmothers, both of my grandmothers had big families, and they took care of their children. They kept their households together. And then I look, especially at my maternal grandmother and my maternal great-grandparents, my maternal great-grandmothers, and really many of these women, not only were they these forces who were holding their families together, keeping the family history intact, passing it along to people, passing along life skills to their children, raising them up in the world, keeping them safe, but they were also important in the life of the community.

My grandmother, for years, before she got older and she became ill, she was heavily invested in our community. She was always doing acts of service. And so, from a very young age, I feel like I've been surrounded by women who were models for me. And so, I think that as I get older and I'm a mom and I'm part of my community and extended family, maybe I'm thinking more now about the women in my family and in my community and thinking more about them and how important they've been in my life and the lives of so many others. So maybe now that's why these womanist ideas are finding their way more into my work.

Swanson: I know I've read that you are currently working on a YA novel. Will it be set in Mississippi or have similar themes to your other works? Is that something that you could share with us?

Ward: So I don't necessarily know about the themes yet because I'm at the very beginning, and I keep struggling with the beginning in part because I keep writing the beginning over and over again, which I need to just probably jump three chapters in and write my way through and then go back when I'm done, after I reach the end, and then write the beginning. Maybe that would be a better thing to do. But I'm sort of wrestling with it because I'm writing in a completely new genre, which I don't feel very confident in because I've never done [it] before. So, even though I've read lots of YA, I've read lots of middle grade books, and I know what I love about them. I guess I'm sort of struggling to translate what I love about storytelling for young people into my own work. And I've just never done that before. But it will be set in Mississippi. The heroine will be... she's a heroine, right, she'll be a girl. And I don't know; yeah, we'll see [*laughs*].

Swanson: I was worried when you wrote *Let Us Descend* that maybe you were like, *Maybe I've written Mississippi enough and I'll do other settings*, but I'm glad to hear that this will be set in Mississippi. Awesome.

Ward: And then I already have an idea for the adult novel that will come after the YA novel, and that one's also set in Mississippi. So no, I'm returning to Mississippi. *Let Us Descend* was just this brief, I guess, foray out into the outside world. But yeah, no, I'm going back.

Swanson: Do you want to share that idea for the adult novel?

Ward: It's still very rough, and I haven't pinned it down yet, but so for years, okay—this may sound a little strange—so, I love to read books and watch movies, television shows about sort of apocalyptic, end-of-the-world scenarios. And years ago, before I started writing *Sing, Unburied, Sing*, I thought, *Wouldn't it be interesting to write my version of a sort of postapocalyptic novel that was just set in the immediate aftermath of a hurricane, where the world has been just completely unmade, and it's surreal. So, wouldn't it be interesting to write something like that?* Then, after that didn't work out, because that's what *Sing, Unburied, Sing* originally was, right? And then for those specific characters, I kept trying to put Jojo and Pop in that world, and that just wasn't their story. And so, I left that idea alone, and then I found my way to the correct world, the correct story for Pop and for Jojo. But then, I don't know why this came up. So, the last big hurricane before Katrina to ravage the Gulf Coast was Hurricane Camille in 1969. Me and my mom, I've had conversations about that storm with my dad, with my grandparents, with other people, my aunts and uncles. It just comes up a lot because it was such a definitive moment. And so, when I began thinking about 1969, and I thought, what was happening around that time where you have the assassination of MLK, you have the assassinations of other important political figures. You have the civil rights movement like burning through Mississippi, and then you have this hurricane that unmakes the world, I thought it really must have felt, for people who are living through this specifically in Mississippi, like the world was ending. And so, I thought, maybe that's where this next novel should be. So that's the rough idea of it.

Swanson: I'm excited for it already. More of a historical text. I dig it. So, I mentioned that I worked on a collection. I'm also working on another monograph where I analyze your works. But, of course, there are other edited collections of essays and journals and magazines dedicated to your writing. So, someone will one day say, well, not someone, a lot of people will say that they're Jesmyn Ward scholars. How does that make you feel? And then also just a fun thing to think about, of course, in hip-hop, Beyoncé has the Beyhive and Nicki has the Barbs. What might your scholars be called?

Ward: [*Laughs*] I mean, on the one hand, it's flattering, but at the same time, it's strange and it's surreal for, especially as I'm sitting here in this environment, I grew up here. I remember when I was a kid, when people who were from here would let their kids actually swim in the Gulf. We would spend days at the beach swimming in the not-so-great water. So, it's surreal because when I grew up, I mean this was a dream, but it was a distant dream. I mean, no one in my family had even gone to a four-year university. My grandmother stopped out of school in the sixth grade. My mom, she graduated from high school. She went to some junior college, but she wasn't able to finish, right? My dad had dreams of attending art school, but then at the last minute, he had a scholarship and everything, but at the last minute, he decided not to, and that he needed to work to help take care of his family. So that's the kind of background that I come from. So, to have someone say they're Jesmyn Ward scholars and there will be many Jesmyn Ward scholars, it's surreal, and it's amazing. And in a way, because I come from that sort of background, it's also a little hard to believe. But yeah, so I guess it's just, again, it's hard for me to articulate, to give you a good answer to that question because it just makes me feel deeply, and I don't know, I don't know what they would be called. I'd have to think about that, try to come up with a good answer.

Swanson: But no, I completely understand. I mentioned that I'm from the Mississippi Delta. I'm, of course, now trying to make my way and make a name for myself in academia. And my mentor tells me all the time, "Kemeshia, you're too humble. Brag on yourself. Let the people know what you're doing." But like you said, when you come from these very humble

162 CONVERSATIONS WITH JESMYN WARD

beginnings, it's a little difficult to accept that, oh, I do have something to share with the world. But definitely you do, and thank you, again, so much.

So, I mentioned that my favorite novel, perhaps, is *Salvage the Bones*, but Esch is definitely my favorite character, although I love Skeet and Big Henry, and Annis from *Let Us Descend*. But I was really happy when I read *Sing* and I saw Esch and Skeet, although very briefly, in the novel again, but it made me want more of her story. So, I was just curious: Do you think that maybe you might ever revisit her story or any of your characters' stories?

Ward: I don't know. People have asked me that before. And I feel like more readers have asked me that specifically about her and her family than any of my other characters. So, I don't know. I mean, I feel like I can't say that I wouldn't. As of now, I've never returned, not in a real way, not for an extended amount of time to any of the characters that I've written about before. I still love those characters. I still think about them. I still wonder about the kinds of lives that they would lead after I leave them at the end of the book. So that curiosity about them and that love for them, which I feel like, in part, motivated the writing of *Salvage the Bones*, that still exists. So, I could return to them one day, but I realized that I don't have clear ideas about who they are ten years after the book or fifteen years after the end of the book, in part because when I wrote them into the end of *Sing, Unburied, Sing*, I made a mistake, and maybe you've heard this before because I've admitted it a couple of different times.

So, I was writing that scene, and I wrote it, and I was so happy that they showed up at the end of *Sing, Unburied Sing*, Esch and Skeetah. Then I did revision after revision, after revision, after revision. I swear I did probably eight revisions, and then I sent it to my editor. And when I sent it to my editor, my editor was like, hold on [*laughs*]. She said, this book, *Sing, Unburied, Sing*, takes place in— I forget what year it was, 2014, 2015, '16, something like that—she was like *Salvage the Bones* took place in the year that Katrina happened, which is a decade earlier. And she was like, but they're the same age when they're walking, when you see them in *Sing, Unburied, Sing*, they're the same age that they were at the end of *Salvage the Bones*. And so, it made me realize that, in my head, they were stuck, and I didn't even realize it. They were stuck at that moment of time, at the end of the book. And so, I had to go back and revise that section again and sort of push them forward a little bit in time. And I realized that I hadn't thought it through, I hadn't done that in my head. And I guess the reason is because all of my characters, they're just where I leave them at the end of the book. For me, that's where they are in time. I guess, unless I decide to devote a whole project to them, then maybe I can do the work of aging them in my head and moving them forward in my head. But for me, they're stuck.

Swanson: No, I get that. I'm glad to hear that you would be willing to write Esch's story, though, and I know that all of your books are your babies, at least that's what I call them, the one that I have, and moms are not supposed to pick a favorite [*both laugh*], but do you have a favorite or maybe a favorite character from one of your books?

Ward: I don't have a favorite because I love all the characters so much. You know what I'm saying? So, as far as my fiction, all my novels, I don't have a favorite novel. I do feel like, and I said this to someone at a book signing, and it surprised me when I said it because I hadn't really thought about it before, but I do feel like I was born to write *Men We Reaped*. So, I don't think that it's my favorite. I just think it was necessary to tell that story, and it's one of the most important stories that I've ever told. So, I do feel that way about that book, but that makes sense when I think about it, right? I mean, because it's about real-life people who I love and who I felt like were erased. So that's probably why I feel that way.

Swanson: That's understandable. I mentioned that a good majority of your characters are women or girls, but interestingly enough, and I think you've talked about this a little bit before, mothers aren't necessarily painted in the best light in a majority of your works. Is there a particular purpose? Is there a message you're trying to convey?

Ward: I don't know why. . . . So, it's only recently that I've begun to think about that, in part because I've done interviews or I've had conversations with people, and they'll bring that up. And I think when I was younger, that I wasn't writing about the kind of mother that I had or the kind of grandmother, not necessarily grandmother, but the kind of mother that I had. I wasn't giving that kind of mother to my characters. I think, in part probably because it's more interesting to write about a problematic mother, I think, probably in part because they're maybe more difficult for me to understand maybe. And so maybe it's my curiosity and my desire to, because it's so alien to me and to my experience, to understand why a mother wouldn't be a good caregiver. And so, I think that that was part of what was going on in my earlier work.

And I think that that was part of the reason why, especially with my most recent novel, with *Let Us Descend*, that I wanted Annis—who's the young girl, the sort of teenage character—I wanted her to have a sort of strong relationship with her mother. I wanted her mother to really be this sort of nurturing, supportive, protective [mother], as much as she could be. I wanted her to be

164 CONVERSATIONS WITH JESMYN WARD

that kind of mother for that character, in part because I feel like I hadn't had the opportunity to write that kind of mom into my fiction.

Swanson: Speaking of *Let Us Descend*, I know I mentioned earlier that it was somewhat of a departure from your previous novels, but can you clarify one thing for me in my reading? At the end of the novel, does Annis sail to the Mississippi Gulf Coast when she escapes New Orleans?

Ward: [*Nods head in agreement*]

Swanson: Okay, that's what I thought. I just wanted to make sure that I wasn't being too hopeful in saying, oh, no, Mississippi IS here.

Ward: So, geographically, it doesn't make sense, or at least her coming down the river does. But as far as the rest of her voyage, I didn't map it out exactly to sort of know which route, if she went from this lake to this bayou to this. But, imaginatively, in my head, I thought she ends up in Bois Sauvage before it's Bois Sauvage. And so, in a way, I think of the end of *Let Us Descend* as the origin story.

Swanson: It completely made sense to me, so you did a great job. I don't know what the map is supposed to look like, so that wasn't relevant, but I said, I think she's in Mississippi now! So, awesome! What is one word you would use to describe what your writing is for you, and maybe another word for what you hope it would be for others?

Ward: Maybe it's the same word for me and for readers, because the first word that comes to my mind is *restorative*. Writing is restorative for me. It feeds something in me. It nurtures something in me, it releases something in me. It enlarges me as a person, I feel like, and allows me to be more empathetic and hopefully more understanding and more aware of history and the connections between us. So, in all those ways, it is restorative to me. And so, I guess that my hope is that it's restorative for readers too. Maybe not in all of the same ways, but I hope that they do feel restored after spending time with these characters in the worlds that I write about.

Swanson: It definitely has been for me! So, awesome! Do you have any thoughts or concerns about AI and how it might impact the writing and publishing world?

Ward: I sort of do, yes. I mean, I think it was maybe last year, I feel like, when other writers who I am sort of friends with in real life, but also some writers who I only know through social media, but when they began talking about AI and the fact that they'd found their books were being used to educate AI. And so, I guess, AI can sort of generate creative work, which I strongly dislike. Yeah. So, I am worried, [but] I like to think that a computer can't create the works that I create. You know what I'm saying? But I don't know. I also feel like I'm not educated enough about it. I'm not informed enough about it. And I think that perhaps part of the reason that I'm not is because I'm so fearful about it that I'm avoiding it in a way, because the work that we do is deeply personal.

Swanson: Spiritual.

Ward: Yes, spiritual. And so, to think that people would want stories from a computer instead of stories that are born from you and that are personal and spiritual and that you bring your whole heart and soul to, that's devastating. So, I mean, I don't know. It may be a foolish hope. I was having a conversation with someone in the administration at Tulane, and we talked very briefly about AI, and they told me that so far, AI is actually bad at it, that it is just not good at producing creative work yet. So that sort of gives me some hope that, I don't know, maybe it will remain bad at it. I mean, I know when you look at the art that's generated from AI, right, there's like seven fingers, four arms, three arms. So, I don't know. I hope.

Swanson: I'm of the mind that a computer can't recreate your work either, so hopefully...Well, this has been wonderful. I know that, of course, you have other wonderful things to do, but as we wrap up, I'm just curious: Are you celebrating the holidays? Do you cook, you plan to cook anything?

Ward: Oh, yes. Well, I mean, I complain about it because it's work, but I actually like to cook because there's something, I don't know . . . I come from a line of...my grandmother was an amazing cook. My mom's an amazing cook. All the women in my family, my aunts, my great-aunts, the women in my family cook. And so, I do cook, and I enjoy it because I love feeding the people that I love. And then when they actually enjoy it, there's just something so fulfilling about that. So yes, I am going to do a lot of cooking over the next two months, but our holidays are always really busy because I cook at my house, and then I always have to go to my mom's house, and then we go to my partner's mom's house. And there's always a lot of people to visit. So, we're going to do a lot of eating.

Swanson: Any favorite dish?

Ward: Gumbo. I love gumbo. And down here, or at least in my community down here, it's sort of a tradition that you have gumbo around the holidays, whether that's Thanksgiving, or always we would have gumbo at Christmas. And so, I always look forward to my mom's gumbo. I've only recently begun making gumbo, in part because I put off trying for years. I didn't attempt gumbo until probably [*thinks*] 2021 was the first time that I attempted it, in part because it's a complicated dish, and there are tons of steps, and it's an expensive dish. That seafood is expensive. Just the crab alone, like a small container of crab these days, it's going for, it's expensive, $20, $25. So, I didn't want to mess up, fail at the recipe and then waste money, right? Waste all that money. But I don't want to jinx myself. I wish I had some wood that I could knock on, but I sort of have it down now, so I'm going to try to make a batch before Christmas.

Swanson: Awesome. I wish I could experience it, but I'm sure it's going to be awesome like everything else you do. Thank you again so much. Do you have any final words you want to share?

Ward: I don't think so. I'm sorry. Every time someone asks me that question, I always immediately blank. But it's been a real pleasure, and thank you all for coming down here.

Swanson: Thank you for having this conversation. Thank you.

Additional Resources

Select Uncollected Interviews

Edim, Glory. "National Book Award Winner Jesmyn Ward on the Joy of Writing About Black Lives." *POPSUGAR*, 28 Feb. 2018, https://www.popsugar.com/news/Jesmyn-Ward-National-Book-Award-Winner-Interview-44528492.

Felts, Susannah. "Her Postage Stamp of Native Soil." *Chapter 16*, 24 Jan. 2011, https://chapter16.org/her-postage-stamp-of-native-soil/.

Hartnell, Anna. "When Cars Become Churches: Jesmyn Ward's Disenchanted America. An Interview." *Journal of American Studies*, vol. 50, no. 1, 2016, pp. 205–18.

Kellog, Carolyn. "An Interview with National Book Award Winner Jesmyn Ward." *Los Angeles Times*, 19 Apr. 2012, https://www.latimes.com/archives/blogs/jacket-copy/story/2012-04-19/an-interview-with-national-book-award-winner-jesmyn-ward.

Kembrey, Melanie. "Jesmyn Ward Interview: 'My Ghosts Were Once People, and I Cannot Forget That.'" *Sydney Morning Herald*, 16 Oct. 2017, https://www.smh.com.au/entertainment/books/jesmyn-ward-interview-my-ghosts-were-once-people-and-i-cannot-forget-that-20171012-gyzgdr.html.

Murphy, Dwyer. "Jesmyn Ward: Beating the Drum." *Guernica*, 17 Mar. 2014, https://www.guernicamag.com/beating-the-drum/.

Select Essays by Ward

"A Cold Currant." *The New York Times*, 7 Aug. 2013, https://archive.nytimes.com/opinionator.blogs.nytimes.com/2013/08/07/a-cold-current/?searchResultPosition=64.

"How to Survive in Broken Worlds: Jesmyn Ward on Octavia Butler's Empathy and Optimism." Literary Hub, 7 Dec. 2022, https://lithub.com/how-to-survive-in-broken-worlds-jesmyn-ward-on-octavia-butlers-empathy-and-optimism/.

"I Was Wandering. Toni Morrison Found Me." *The New York Times*, 11 Aug. 2019, p. SR3, https://www.nytimes.com/2019/08/09/opinion/sunday/i-was-wandering-toni-morrison-found-me.html?searchResultPosition=23.

168 ADDITIONAL RESOURCES

"Jay Gatsby: A Dreamer Doomed to Be Excluded. The Novelist Jesmyn Ward Explains." *The New York Times*, 22 Apr. 2018, p. BR10, https://www.nytimes.com/2018/04/12/books/review/jesmyn-ward-great-gatsby.html?searchResultPosition=13.

"Magic Mirrors." In *Well-Read Black Girl*, edited by Glory Edim, Ballantine Books, 2018.

"My True South: Why I Decided to Return Home." *TIME*, 26 July 2018, https://time.com/5349517/jesmyn-ward-my-true-south/.

"On Witness and Respair: A Personal Tragedy Followed by Pandemic." *Vanity Fair*, Sept. 2020, https://www.vanityfair.com/culture/2020/08/jesmyn-ward-on-husbands-death-and-grief-during-covid.

"Racism Is 'Built into the Very Bones' of Mississippi." *The Atlantic*, Mar. 2018, https://www.theatlantic.com/magazine/archive/2018/02/jesmyn-ward-mississippi/552500/.

"We Do Not Swim in Our Cemeteries: A Legacy of Not Evacuating." *The Oxford American*, no. 62, Summer 2008, p. 34.

Scholarly Books on Ward's Work

Bone, Martyn. *The Writings of Jesmyn Ward: Matters of Black Southern Life and Death*. University of Iowa Press, 2025.

Harrison, Sheri-Marie, et al., editors. *Jesmyn Ward: New Critical Essays*. Edinburgh University Press, 2023.

Swanson, Kemeshia Randle. *Love and War: Intimacy and Activism in the Works of Jesmyn Ward*. UP of Mississippi, anticipated 2027.

Scholarly Journal Issues on Ward's Work

Bonner, Thomas, Jr., and Robin G. Vander, Eds. *Xavier Review* 38, no. 2 (Fall 2018). Xavier University of Louisiana.

Select Scholarly Articles on Ward's Work

Bares, Annie. "'Each Unbearable Day': Narrative Ruthlessness and Environmental and Reproductive Injustice in Jesmyn Ward's *Salvage the Bones*." *MELUS*, vol. 44, no. 3, 2019, pp. 21–40.

Boisseron, Bénédicte. "Jesmyn Ward's Dog Bite: Mississippi Love and Death Stories." *The Palgrave Handbook of Animals and Literature*, edited by Susan McHugh, Robert McKay, and John Mille, Palgrave Macmillan, Cham, 2021, pp. 513–23.

ADDITIONAL RESOURCES **169**

Bradley, Regina N. "Still Ain't Forgave Myself." *Chronicling "Stankonia": The Rise of the Hip-Hop South*. U of North Carolina P, 2021.

Brown, Holly Cade. "Figuring Giorgio Agamben's 'Bare Life' in the Post-Katrina Works of Jesmyn Ward and Kara Walker." *Journal of American Studies*, vol. 51, no. 1, 2017, pp.1–19.

Chase, Greg. "Of Trips Taken and Time Served: How Ward's *Sing, Unburied, Sing* Grapples with Faulkner's Ghosts." *African American Review*, vol. 53, no. 3, 2020, pp. 201–16.

Chevalier, Victoria A. "The Multiplicity of This World: Troubling Origins in Jesmyn Ward's *Sing, Unburied, Sing*." *The Palgrave Handbook of Magical Realism in the Twenty-First Century*, edited by Richard Perez and Victoria A. Chevalier, Palgrave Macmillan, 2020.

Chevalier, Victoria A. "'The Negro Speaks of Rivers' in Jesmyn Ward's *Sing, Unburied, Sing*." *Langston Hughes Review*, vol. 27, no. 2, 2021, pp. 164–87.

Choiński, Michał. "Coming Back Home to Oppressive Mississippi: A Figurative Study of Jesmyn Ward's *Men We Reaped*." *Polish Journal for American Studies*, vol. 15, 2021, pp. 161–77, 205.

Clark, Christopher W. "What Comes to the Surface: Storms, Bodies, and Community in Jesmyn Ward's *Salvage the Bones*." *Mississippi Quarterly*, vol. 68, nos. 3–4, 2015, pp. 341–58.

Crawford, Cameron W. "'Where Everything Else Is Starving, Fighting, Struggling': Food and the Politics of Hurricane Katrina in Jesmyn Ward's *Salvage the Bones*." *Southern Quarterly*, vol. 56, no. 1, 2018, pp. 73–84.

Cunningham, William. "Silent Spaces in Jesmyn Ward and Natasha Trethewey." *CLA Journal*, vol. 63, no. 1, 2020, pp. 50–67.

Cucarella-Ramon, Vicent. "Reading Toni Morrison's *Beloved* in Jesmyn Ward's *Salvage the Bones* and *Sing, Unburied, Sing*." *Feminismo/s (Universidad de Alicante)*, no. 40, 2022, p. 79.

Davis-McElligatt, Joanna. "'And Now She Sings It': Conjure as Abolitionist Alternative in Jesmyn Ward's *Sing, Unburied, Sing*." *Mississippi Quarterly*, vol. 74, no. 1, 2021, pp. 103–23.

Dib, Nicole. "Haunted Roadscapes in Jesmyn Ward's *Sing, Unburied, Sing*." *MELUS*, vol. 45, no. 2, 2020, pp. 134–53.

Ewing, Rachel. "Mapping the Lost Home: Psalm 137 and Jesmyn Ward's *Sing, Unburied, Sing*." *The Mississippi Quarterly*, vol. 75, no. 2, 2022, pp. 143–60.

Foltz, Mary Catherine. "Salvaging the Bones Means Fighting for Reproductive Justice: Jesmyn Ward's Literary Representations of the Trauma Produced by Attacks on Reproductive Rights, Comprehensive Sex Education, and Access to Maternal Health Care." *Trauma and Motherhood in Contemporary Literature and Culture*, edited by Laura Lazzari and Nathalie Ségera, Palgrave Macmillan, Cham, 2021, pp. 31–57.

Granda, Paula. "They Endured: Precarity, Vulnerability, and Resistance in the Works of Jesmyn Ward." *Unhappy Beginnings: Narratives of Precarity, Failure, and Resistance*

170 ADDITIONAL RESOURCES

in North American Texts, edited by Isabel González-Díaz and Fabián Orán-Llarena, Routledge, 2023.

Hartmann, Alexandra. "Precarity, Mourning, and Notes of Consolation in Jesmyn Ward's *Sing, Unburied, Sing." The Black Humanist Tradition in Anti-Racist Literature.* Palgrave Macmillan, Cham, 2023, pp. 159–94.

Henry, Alvin. "Jesmyn Ward's Post-Katrina Black Feminism: Memory and Myth Through Salvaging." *English Language Notes,* vol. 57, no. 2, 2019, pp. 71–85.

Jacobson, Kristin J. "Pregnant Possibilities in Recent Climate Fiction by Ward, Lepucki, Lee, and Erdrich." *MELUS,* vol. 47, no. 4, Winter 2022, pp. 148–71.

Keeble, Arin. "Intertextuality, Domesticity and the Spaces of Disaster in *Salvage the Bones* and *Zeitoun." Narratives of Hurricane Katrina in Context: Literature, Film, and Television.* Palgrave Pivot, Cham, 2019, pp. 31–63.

Keeble, Arin. "Siblings, Kinship and Allegory in Jesmyn Ward's Fiction and Nonfiction." *Critique: Studies in Contemporary Fiction,* vol. 61, no. 1, 2020, pp. 40–51.

Khedhir, Yesmina. "Ghosts Tell Stories: Cultural Haunting in Jesmyn Ward's *Sing, Unburied, Sing." British and American Studies (B.A.S.),* vol. 26, no. 26, 2020, pp. 17–23.

Krieg, C. Parker. "Teaching Jesmyn Ward and William T. Vollmann in Finland: Genres of Environmental Justice." *Contemporary American Fiction in the European Classroom,* edited by Laurence W. Mazzeno and Sue Norton, Palgrave Macmillan, Cham, 2022, pp. 237–50.

Lado-Pazos, Vanesa. "Haunting Back: A Study of Spectrality in Jesmyn Ward's *Sing, Unburied, Sing." Southern Quarterly,* vol. 58, no. 3, 2021, pp. 113–30.

Lloyd, Christopher. "Creaturely, Throwaway Life After Katrina: *Salvage the Bones* and *Beasts of the Southern Wild." South: A Scholarly Journal,* vol. 48, no. 2, 2016, pp. 246–64.

Lloyd, Christopher. "Everything Deserve to Live": *Salvage the Bones,* Hurricane Katrina, and Animals. *Corporeal Legacies in the US South.* Palgrave Macmillan, Cham, 2018.

Manzella, Abigail G. H. "Afterword: The Mobility Poor of Hurricane Katrina: Salvaging the Family and Ward's *Salvage the Bones." Migrating Fictions: Gender, Race, and Citizenship in U.S. Internal Displacements,* Ohio State University Press, 2018, pp. 188–98.

Marotte, Mary Ruth. "Pregnancies, Storms, and Legacies of Loss in Jesmyn Ward's *Salvage the Bones." Ten Years after Katrina: Critical Perspectives of the Storm's Effect on American Culture and Identity,* Lexington Books (Rowman and Littlefield Press), December 2014.

Matthews, John T. "Heirs-at-Large: Precarity and Salvage in the Post-Plantation Souths of Faulkner and Jesmyn Ward." *Faulkner Journal,* vol. 32, no. 1, 2018, pp. 33–50.

McCormick, Stacie. "We Are Here: Jesmyn Ward's Black Feminist Poethics of Place in *Men We Reaped." a/b: Auto/Biography Studies,* vol. 38, no. 2, 2023, pp. 543–58.

ADDITIONAL RESOURCES **171**

McKesson, Kelly. "The Subsident Gulf: Refiguring Climate Change in Jesmyn Ward's Bois Sauvage." *American Literature*, vol. 93, no. 3, 1 Sept. 2021, pp. 473–96.

Mellis, James. "Continuing Conjure: African-Based Spiritual Traditions in Colson Whitehead's *The Underground Railroad* and Jesmyn Ward's *Sing, Unburied, Sing.*" *Religions*, vol. 10, no. 7, 2019, pp. 403–.

Moynihan, Sinéad. "From Disposability to Recycling: William Faulkner and the New Politics of Rewriting in Jesmyn Ward's *Salvage the Bones.*" *Studies in the Novel*, vol. 47, no. 4, 2015, pp. 550–67.

Nance, Kevin. "Where the Writing Will Take Her: The Responsibility that Jesmyn Ward Feels Toward the Southern Town Where She Was Born Shapes Not Only Her New Memoir, *Men We Reaped*, but Also Where and How She Lives Her Life." *Poets & Writers Magazine*, vol. 41, no. 5, Sept.–Oct. 2013.

Railsback, Brian. "A Twenty-First-Century *Grapes of Wrath*: Jesmyn Ward's *Salvage the Bones.*" *Steinbeck Review*, vol. 13, no. 2, 2016, pp. 179–95.

Santana, Elana Margot. "Bodies Tell Stories: Race, Animality, and Climate Change in Jesmyn Ward's *Salvage the Bones.*" In Borkfelt, S., Stephan, M. (eds.), *Literary Animal Studies and the Climate Crisis*. Palgrave Studies in Animals and Literature. Palgrave Macmillan, Cham, 2022, pp. 107–30.

Stevens, Benjamin Eldon. "Medea in Jesmyn Ward's *Salvage the Bones.*" *International Journal of the Classical Tradition*, vol. 25, no. 2, 2018, pp. 158–77. *JSTOR*, https:// www.jstor.org/stable/48698420. Accessed 26 Jan. 2024.

Swanson, Kemeshia Randle. "A Southern Song for My People: Seeing Self in the Works of Jesmyn Ward." *Callaloo*, vol. 42, no. 3, 2024, pp. 256–60.

Swartzfager, Megan A. "'Ain't No More Stories for You Here': Vengeful Hauntings and Traumatized Community in Jesmyn Ward's *Sing, Unburied, Sing.*" *Mississippi Quarterly*, vol. 73, no. 3, 2020, pp. 313–34.

Tribbett, Marcus C. "'Pulling all the Weight of History Behind Him. . . . Like a Cotton Sack Full of Lead': Locating Jesmyn Ward's *Sing, Unburied, Sing* in the Blues Novel Tradition." *Journal of Ethnic American Literature*, no. 9, 2019, pp. 23–43, 121.

Tsing, Anna. "Improbable Metaphor: Jesmyn Ward and the Asymmetries of the Anthropocene." *Transscalar Critique: Climate, Blackness, Crisis*. Edinburgh University Press, 2023, pp. 140–72.

Wei, Huiying. "*Sing, Unburied, Sing*: The Dual Lack and Pursuit of Love and Identity Among Black People." *International Journal of Linguistics, Literature and Translation*, vol. 5, no. 11, 2022, pp. 87–95.

Wendland-Liu, Joel. "'*We Are Here*': Race, Gender, and Spaces of "Common Ground" in the Works of John Edgar Wideman, bell hooks, and Jesmyn Ward, *MELUS*, vol. 46, no. 3, Fall 2021, pp. 188–209.

Index

activism, xviii–xix, 48, 153; mobilizing, 45; reckoning, xix, 21, 24, 30, 48, 92, 99, 104, 148–49; writing as political, 9, 23–24, 40, 43–44, 53, 57, 64, 92–93, 99, 104, 131, 159
anger, xiv, 7, 12, 30–31, 45, 100, 104, 146, 154–55; infuriation, xii, 8; rage, xi–xii, xiv, xvi, xviii
Angola (Louisiana State Penitentiary), 81
Artificial Intelligence (AI), 164–65
awards: American Library Association Alex Award, xxv; Black Caucus of the American Library Association (BCALA), xxv; Heartland Prize for Nonfiction, xxv, 46; Library of Congress Prize, xiii, xxvi; McArthur Fellowship, xiii, xxvi, 100, 106, 116, 130, 144; Mississippi Institute of Arts and Letters Award for Fiction, xxvi; National Book Award, xiii, xv, xviii, xxi, xxvi, 10, 12–13, 22–23, 28–29, 39, 46, 50–51, 66, 73–74, 91, 100–101, 103, 106, 116, 118, 127, 130, 144; Stegner Fellowship, xxv, 46, 158; Strauss Living Award, xiii, xxv; Virginia Commonwealth University Cabell First Novelist Award, 46

Baldwin, James, xi–xii, xviii, 42; *The Fire Next Time*, 42
Black Lives Matter, xvi, xxvi, 41, 55, 99, 129
Bland, Sandra, 42

Bois Sauvage, xi, xx, 4, 27, 57–58, 84, 91, 106, 108, 110, 119, 130–31, 136, 143, 164
book bans, 146, 154–55
Bradley, Regina N., xi, xvi, 144–49, 153–54
Brown, Mike, 40
Burton, LeVar, 154

civil rights movement, 161; MLK assassination, 161
Civil War, 24, 127; Confederate monuments, 53
classical archetypes, 25; Lady Macbeth, 64; Medea, 8, 14–15, 64; Medusa, 89; Odysseus, 25
coronavirus pandemic, xvi, xxvi

Dante's *Inferno*, 128, 132, 139–40
Dedeaux, Joshua (brother), xiv–xvi, xxv, 9, 13, 18, 19, 21, 23–25, 28–30, 33–34, 36, 40, 54, 104, 106, 111, 116, 123, 142, 148
disenfranchisement, 95

empathy, xiii, xiv, xvii, xxii, 13, 41, 96, 156, 164

Faulkner, William, xii, 7, 47, 60–61, 100, 115, 119, 125–26, 139, 140, 147–48, 154; *As I Lay Dying*, xii, 7, 100, 125; "A Rose for Emily," 148; *The Sound and the Fury*, 125, 147
Finney, Nikky, 35, 68, 101
Fire This Time, The, xviii, xxv, 43, 47–50, 52, 71–72, 91, 93, 103, 114, 143

173

174 INDEX

Game of Thrones, 147
Gay, Roxane, xiv, 35–38
Grant, Oscar, 40
Great Migration, 147
grief, xiv–xviii, 30, 31, 35, 37, 61, 63, 84,
    89, 98, 104, 106, 108–9, 117, 128,
    132, 137, 141, 144–45, 148–49

Half Has Never Been Told, The, 81
Handmaid's Tale, The, 40
hurricanes, 38, 50, 51, 54, 160–61;
    Camille, 28, 160; Harvey, 51, 54;
    Katrina, xiv–xv, 7–10, 12, 14–17,
    23–24, 28, 33–34, 36, 46, 50, 54,
    91, 100, 105, 123, 138, 146, 160, 162
Hurston, Zora Neale, xii, xiv, 47; *Their*
    Eyes Were Watching God, 47

intertextuality, 140

Jackson, Mitchell, 152
Jim Crow, 80, 92, 99, 107

Laymon, Kiese, xii, xiv, 39–41, 42, 137,
    146–47, 152
Let Us Descend, xiv, xvi–xvii, xxi, xxvi,
    127–31, 133, 135–36, 139, 141–43,
    145, 149, 160, 162–63, 164; concept
    of, 130–31

McCullers, Carson, 61
magic(al realism), xx–xxi, 50, 52, 75, 116,
    121, 124, 138–39
Martin, Trayvon, 40, 43, 93
Men We Reaped, xix–xx, xxv, 19, 22–26,
    28, 32, 35–37, 39, 46, 50, 52, 55, 91,
    97, 106, 110, 114, 116, 141, 143–45,
    148, 157, 163; structure of, 24, 37;
    title of, 23
mental illness, 37, 105, 111; depression,
    30, 32, 37
Miller, Brandon (partner), xvi, xxvi, 128

Mississippi, xii, xiv, xviii, 3, 15–16, 18, 20,
    28, 33, 39, 41, 47, 50, 57–58, 80, 84,
    92, 96, 100, 110–12, 115, 118, 121,
    125, 128–29, 139, 144, 146–47, 150,
    158, 160–61, 164; Bay St. Louis, 150;
    Biloxi, 46; DeLisle, xi, xv, xxv, 4–6,
    17, 19, 28–30, 34, 50, 84, 106, 108,
    110, 119, 136, 144, 150; Delta, 80,
    150, 161; Gulf Coast, 33, 46–47, 54,
    58–59, 75, 106, 144, 150, 152, 157,
    160; Gulfport, 30, 150; as home,
    33, 45, 100; Jackson, 15; love/hate
    relationship, xi, xviii, 41, 111, 126,
    157; Pass Christian, xv, 17, 150
Mississippi Freedom Riders, 81
Moody, Anne, 100
Morrison, Toni, 29, 64, 151–52, 157;
    Beloved, 29, 64, 100, 157
motherhood, 8, 14–15, 52–53, 61–63, 69,
    83–84, 88–89, 93, 97, 136, 163; *16*
    and Pregnant, 8; *Teen Mom*, 8
music, xviii, xix, 3, 17–18, 25–26, 29, 36,
    48–49, 87, 122, 142, 153, 155, 161;
    blues, xix, 7, 48–49; Ghostface
    Killah, 142; hip-hop, xviii, xix,
    3–4, 7, 48–49, 153; Jackson 5, 30;
    Pastor Troy, 3–5; Prince, xviii;
    rap, 18, 25, 142

Navigate Your Stars, xiii, xxvi

Odyssey, 93, 100, 139–40
"On Witness and Respair," xvi, xxvi
Orwell, George, 23
Oshinsky, David, 109, 113; *Worse Than*
    Slavery, 109, 113

Parchman (Mississippi State
    Penitentiary), xx, 53, 57–58, 63,
    80–81, 91, 92–94, 98–100, 106,
    108–10, 115, 120–21, 145
Patcher, Ann, 53

INDEX **175**

Petrarch, 63
Phillis Wheatley Poetry Festival, 152
poverty porn, 12
pregnancy, 11, 15, 37, 62, 87–88, 101,
131, 154–55; abortion, 15, 88;
birth control, 15

religion, 140; Bible, 3–4, 7, 64;
Christianity, 134–35; God, 3–4,
30, 34; Voodoo (Hoodoo), 57, 59,
64, 87–88, 90, 100, 137–40
representation, xxii, 47
Reynolds, Jason, 68
Rice, Tamir, 71

Salvage the Bones, xiii–xvi, xix–xx, xxv,
4, 9–10, 12–14, 17–18, 22–26,
32–33, 35, 39, 46, 50–51, 54, 62, 64,
71, 82, 91, 94, 100–101, 103, 106,
116, 120, 123, 131, 138, 141, 144–45,
154–56, 162; title of, 8
Sing, Unburied, Sing, xiii, xv, xvii, xx,
xxvi, 50–55, 57–59, 61, 63, 66,
69–70, 73–79, 82, 91, 93, 97, 99,
101, 103–4, 106–7, 113, 115–16,
119–25, 131, 135–37, 139, 141,
144–45, 156, 160, 162; title of, 122
slavery, xviii, xxi, 24, 55, 64, 80–81, 92,
98–99, 101, 105, 107, 109–10, 116,
121, 126–34, 137, 144–45
Smith, Zadie, 135
social media, xii, xviii, 43, 48, 164;
Instagram, xviii; Facebook, 62;
Twitter, xviii, 42–43, 45, 66, 74, 147
Southern Gothic, 144–46, 148

Taylor, Mildred, 147; *Roll of Thunder,
Hear My Cry*, 124
terroir, 58
Thirteenth (documentary), 145
Trethewey, Natasha, 5
Tubman, Harriet, 23

Vick, Michael, 9

Walcott, Derek, 100
Walker, Alice, xiv, 47, 152–53; *The Color
Purple*, 47
Walker, Margaret, xiv, 47, 100, 147
Welty, Eudora, 91, 100
Where the Line Bleeds, xix–xx, xxv, 4,
18, 39, 46, 122–23, 131, 140, 145
white privilege, 99
Whitehead, Colson, 92; *The
Underground Railroad*, 92
Wright, Richard, 100, 147
writing, 31–36, 38, 45, 47, 54, 60, 63, 69,
79, 85, 94–95, 100–105, 114, 123,
132, 138, 140, 142, 147–48, 151, 156,
162–63, 164; character development, 32, 52, 54, 59, 61–62, 69,
70, 85–86, 95, 116, 118, 136, 147,
156; figurative language, xvii, 7,
41, 60–61; mission, 156; narrative
ruthlessness, 95, 123; process, xv,
xvii, xx, 17, 18, 21, 23, 26, 30, 48,
51, 52, 55, 58, 67, 68, 69, 70, 81, 82,
83, 85, 86, 87, 93, 94, 98, 116–17,
120, 122, 128, 131–32, 140, 155,
160; poet(ry), 29, 44–45, 57, 60,
117, 124, 147, 152; revision, xv, 17,
36, 39, 55, 59, 67, 69, 86, 94, 98,
116, 162

About the Editor

Photo courtesy of the author

Kemeshia Randle Swanson is a college professor currently serving a joint appointment in English and African American Studies at Mississippi State University. She previously dedicated ten years of service to the Department of English at Garner-Webb University in Boiling Springs, North Carolina. Her work focuses on twentieth- and twenty-first-century African American literature, Southern literature, gender and sexualities studies, and hip-hop and popular culture. She has published in edited collections such as *Words, Beats, and Life: The Global Journal of Hip-Hop Culture*; *Like One of the Family: Domestic Workers, Race, and In/Visibility in "The Help"*; and *Street Lit: Representing the Urban Landscape*. She is the author of the award-winning *Maverick Feminist: To Be Female and Black in a Country Founded upon Violence and Respectability*, published by University Press of Mississippi.